EDWARD EVERETT

The Intellectual in the Turmoil of Politics

Paul A. Varg

Selinsgrove: Susquehanna University Press
London and Toronto: Associated University Presses

© 1992 by Associated University Presses, Inc.

All rights reserved. Authorization to photocopy items for internal or personal use, or the internal or personal use of specific clients, is granted by the copyright owner, provided that a base fee of $10.00, plus eight cents per page, per copy is paid directly to the Copyright Clearance Center, 27 Congress Street, Salem, Massachusetts 01970. [0-945636-25-3/92 $10.00 + 8¢ pp, pc.]

Associated University Presses
440 Forsgate Drive
Cranbury, NJ 08512

Associated University Presses
25 Sicilian Avenue
London WC1A 2QH, England

Associated University Presses
P.O. Box 39, Clarkson Pstl. Stn.
Mississauga, Ontario,
L5J 3X9 Canada

The paper used in this publication meets the requirements
of the American National Standard for Permanence of Paper
for Printed Library Materials Z39.48-1984.

Library of Congress Cataloging-in-Publication Data

Varg, Paul A.
    Edward Everett : the intellectual in the turmoil of politics /
Paul A. Varg.
       p. cm.
    Includes bibliographical references and index.
    ISBN 0-945636-25-3 (alk. paper)
    1. Everett, Edward, 1794–1865. 2. Legislators—United States—
Biography. 3. United States. Congress—Biography. 4. Governors—
Massachusetts—Biography. 5. United States—Politics and
government—1783–1865. 6. Massachusetts—Politics and
government—1775–1865. I. Title.
E340.E8V37   1992
328.73′092—dc20
[B]   91-50191
                                                                         CIP

PRINTED IN THE UNITED STATES OF AMERICA

To Cozette, again

Contents

Preface	9
Acknowledgments	11
1. Early Years	15
2. Everett's Role in Politics	35
3. Governor of Massachusetts	66
4. Everett's Debut in Diplomacy	87
5. Harvard Presidency	127
6. Voice of Moderation amid Reckless Adventurism	140
7. To the Point of No Return: The Kansas-Nebraska Act	154
8. Everett the Orator	173
9. Everett Confronts the New Age	181
10. Role of the Orator in the Civil War	196
Notes	219
Bibliography	244
Index	249

Preface

Everett, in his day, gained an image as a man of learning, skilled in oratory, and judicious. In politics he was the conservative Nationalist. Above all other leaders of the Nationalist persuasion Everett held that the preservation and growth of the Union was of the greatest importance. It should be strengthened so that it could fulfill its mission of creating an orderly society because government alone could bring together the talents of people, preserve internal peace, create a community of well-being, and provide for security. Government ranked higher than individual talents, great inventors, and the wonders of art and science. It alone could provide for the order, security, and benign environment that permitted human talents to flourish.

In the case of the American republic the fragile Union must be strengthened if the nation was to realize its potential. This stood out above all other worthy goals. Everett was to adhere to this view. Nationalism was grounded in his admiration for the Adams family, Thomas Jefferson, and James Madison. Their political goals transcended local prejudices, sectional differences, and personal ambitions. They were dedicated to the interests of the republic, which they saw as the hope of all humankind to achieve representative government. Everett saw them as his models. He was an intimate friend of John Quincy Adams and carried on a friendly correspondence with both Jefferson and Madison, seeking their views on political questions.

His nationalism had a second source, his experiences as a student in Germany immediately after the Napoleonic Wars. He came home from Europe very impressed by the great universities, the rich libraries, and the fine museums. This awakened a thirst to alert Americans to their deficiencies. In Europe, in the wake of destruction and loss of life, he saw the follies of the French Revolution and how high aspirations ended in a return to rule by Louis XVIII and the aristocracy. He attended a German university and traveled widely in the small German states. The Congress of Vienna was in session and determined to restore the old regimes, and there the representatives of the major powers decided the fate of the small and helpless German states. Nationalism was suppressed. Everett sharply criticized the decisions.

England had been saved from revolution, he believed, because of the check-and-balance system and rule by King, Lords, and Commons. Unchecked monarchical rule was obviously an evil, but as he read Edmund Burke's *Reflections on the French Revolution* and discussed what had occurred—the uprising of the mobs, the triumph of passions over reason, and the madness of the scenes— Everett could only conclude that stable governments, checked by laws embodied in a constitution, laws made by people, and an independent judiciary and representative assemblies were the most important institutions in society.

On his return to the United States he saw a fragile Union that needed strengthening. Here in the new world was endless territory, untouched mineral resources, rivers for transportation, a favorable climate, and free labor. The potential for greatness thrilled him and his many orations rang with optimism. Much remained to be done. Success would depend on a strong government pursuing a sound financial course that would attract capital for this underdeveloped nation.

Everett's nationalism was deeply rooted and shaped by an age that was about to come to a close. A new type of leadership emerged. Party rivalry and sectionalism, new problems in the emerging urban society, the coming of immigrants with different cultural backgrounds, and a revolution in transportation created great social change.

Acknowledgments

I am deeply indebted to the many scholars whose articles and monographs have enriched our understanding of the turbulent politics of the decades preceding the Civil War. Their contributions made it possible to place Edward Everett in the broad political context and to understand this enigmatic intellectual and his struggle to maintain his own independence when under pressure.

I am also indebted to the Massachusetts Historical Society for preserving the vast collection of Everett papers and for making them available on microfilm. Fortunately for the author the Michigan State University Library purchased the microfilm edition.

I wish to thank the Susquehanna University Press for its generous cooperation. The readers for that press made many useful suggestions.

Two of my colleagues at Michigan State have been helpful. David Mead, a highly skilled editor, offered useful suggestions as to literary style. Fred Williams, an authority on the coming of the Civil War, read with care the final two chapters.

In the years of research and writing my supportive wife saved me from being discouraged. To her I owe a very special thanks.

EDWARD EVERETT

1
Early Years

In the spring of 1793, George Washington began his second term as president of the United States. The years since the British surrender in the War for Independence had been filled with struggle and uncertainty. The highly decentralized government under the Articles of Confederation left the republic unable to cope with the British monopoly of transatlantic trade and the continued occupation by the British of territory in the Northwest that lay within the boundaries of the United States. The newly opened territory south of the Ohio River offered no access to either world markets or to the markets on the East Coast because Spain controlled the lower regions of the Mississippi River, the thoroughfare provided by nature. In the nation's capital two factions struggled for control, each with different blueprints for the republic's future. Nevertheless there was a spirit of optimism in the land, an awareness that whatever the trials of the moment, the republic had a great future.

The celebration of Washington's second inaguration had scarcely come to a close when Edward Everett was born in Dorchester, Massachusetts, on 11 April 1794.

Everett's father had enrolled at Harvard at the age of twenty, supported himself by helping with custodial work during the summers, and for a few years served as minister in Boston, until ill health forced him to resign. He then moved to a small farm in Dorchester with his wife and four children. Poverty did not stand in the way of his taking an interest in politics. He admired George Washington and later supported John Adams. Amid the modesty of his circumstances he was respected in the community as a man of good sense and some learning. Thanks to this, in 1799 he was appointed judge of the Court of Common Pleas even though he had no legal training. He served without salary, and his income of a few hundred dollars a year came from court fees. In 1802 he was nominated for Congress. Before the election he died.

Although Edward was only eight years of age at the time of his father's death he had vivid memories of a father who devoted time to his children, who won their affection by attention, and who instilled good behavior, not by reprimands but by loving care. The few books they owned included two children's books, including *Mother Goose,* and the plays of Shakespeare and the writings of Lord Kames. The children thumbed through these weightier volumes, and Everett at an early age developed a love of *Hamlet.* By the time of the father's death two more children were born, and a third was born seven months after his father's death.

Everett's mother, the daughter of Alexander Hill, was born in Philadelphia where her father was a merchant. Both her parents died at an early age, and she and her sister were brought to Boston to live with their grandfather, a prosperous merchant. At the outbreak of the Revolution the grandfather had no sympathy with the rebels, and he shared these feelings with his neighbor, Pastor Dr. John Eliot. Both remained in Boston during the British siege feeling secure. The lifting of the siege, it seemed to them, left them hostages of a hostile population. Fearing retribution the grandfather and his family in great haste boarded a ship bound for Halifax. The voyage to the refuge for loyalists was interrupted by the seasickness of the girls, and it was judged best to put into the harbor at Marblehead. Sober second thought now took over, and the family returned to Boston where the grandfather merchant adjusted to the new environment and became even more prosperous. This happy outcome, with wealth stored for the next of kin, gave Everett's stricken family hope that they would be saved from penury by inheritance, but Everett's father died before the grandfather. Not until later did Mrs. Everett inherit some fifty thousand dollars. It was then that the newly enriched widow moved to Boston.

Of the five children who survived infancy, Alexander enrolled in school, and he taught Greek at Philips Exeter Academy. Young Everett entered public school at the age of five. After one year he was transferred to the private reading school of Master Little, whose six-foot four-inch height belied his name. At the end of the first year, he later recalled, he could parse almost any sentence in the *American Preceptor.* When the family moved to Boston in 1803, he was sent to Ezekiel Webster's privtae school where he first met Daniel Webster who substituted when his brother was ill. Two years later he attended the Boston Latin School, where he was unhappy with the poor instruction, and after pleading with his mother to send him to Exeter he transferred there. Here he studied Latin and Greek.

By this time he earned a reputation as a brilliant student, and he was admitted to Harvard at the age of thirteen. He was, as he said, too young to be tempted by the worldly pleasures of his classmates. Most students found Locke difficult, but Everett found "that the shortest process was to learn the text by heart nearly *verbatim*." As he later recalled he had a memory that recoiled from nothing. His interests were clearly literary, and in his third year he and seven or eight other students established a literary magazine. In 1811 he graduated first in his class.[1]

He was spared the cold and rigid teachings of his Puritan forefathers, and he was charmed by the gentleness and learning of his minister, the Reverend Joseph Stevens Buckminster, with whom he met privately once a week. During his travels in Europe, Buckminster became acquainted with the new biblical criticism that centered in the University of Göttingen, and he brought home three thousand books. His gentle eloquence in the pulpit became a legend. The dangerous evils of the day, said Buckminster, were the love of money and frivolous distinctions, the pursuit of vicious pleasures, and the tyranny of fashion. To correct these faults Buckminster recommended a love of literature and intellectual pursuits. To be sure, he said, a passion for knowledge was no proof of a principle of virtue, but "it is often a security against the vices and temptations of the world."[2]

Two other inquiring minds in the vicinity of Boston also encouraged Everett, Moses Stuart of Andover Seminary and the Reverend William Bentley of Salam. Both men possessed collections of books on the new studies of antiquities. Stuart was an adherent of orthodoxy, but Bentley ignored current fashions of both Federalist politics and church orthodoxy. Bentley assembled a rich library, and mastered the major European languages plus Arabic and Greek. Everett was not only an eager student who readily devoured the prosaic college studies of the day, he possessed an inquiring mind and sought out sources of learning.

His reading of Lord Byron's *Childe Harold* in 1812 opened to him a new and exciting vista. The beauty of Byron's lines has hardly ever, if ever, been surpassed, and Everett, like many others, had his attention turned toward ancient Greece. Everett seized on the lines: "Who now shall lead thy scatter'd children forth, and long bondage uncreate?" Byron's attention was focused on the importance of humans, the people who so often throughout history had wandered off into foolishness, superstition, and cruelty. He awakened in Everett an enthusiasm for ancient Greek and search for a freer life.

After his graduation from Harvard, Buckminster encouraged Everett to enroll in the Divinity School. The still teenage boy now made a decision he was to regret. The Divinity School was a school in name only, and Everett occasionally met with professors but devoted most of his time to reading at random. After completing his preparation for the ministry he was invited to the most prominent pulpit in Boston, the Brattle Street Church. It was a flattering offer that was difficult to resist. He was to be paid twenty-five dollars per week and be supplied with fire wood. This modest salary appeared less important than the distinction it would give him. He quickly earned a reputation for pulpit oratory. Ralph Waldo Emerson, before entering the church each Sunday, peered through the window to make sure Everett was preaching.[3] Departing from the tradition of the day that called for exegesis of biblical texts, Everett delivered carefully prepared essays phrased in elegant language. A conservative churchman commented that Everett's sermons contained "more of the flowers of rhetoric than of the fruits of the gospel." He exhorted his congregation to see what was to be valued was not the fleeting and outdated opinions of their forefathers, but their questioning attitude. He asked, "Why should we forget that dissent, improvement, and the reformation are part of our patrimony? All is subject to correction and improvement."[4]

Young though he was, however, he harbored private thought about the confinement of a clergyman whose intellectual life must be in tune with the fashions of the day. For a Boston clergyman he decided on a dangerous venture, a trip to Washington and Virginia where he could make the acquaintance of Thomas Jefferson. When he asked for leave, he said nothing about his interest in meeting Jefferson. Once in Washington he received a letter from a friend reporting that the congregation had learned that he planned to call on Jefferson, and they were upset. Everett did not seek out the former president, but he vowed that the day would come when he would be his own man.[5] He did call on President James Madison, received an invitation to come to dinner, and with it commenced a friendly and lifelong association. The intervention of his parishioners in his plans confirmed his opinion that a career in the ministry was equivalent to surrendering one's intellectual freedom.

An offer from Harvard at the close of the first year in the pulpit enabled him to escape. He resigned with such promptness and without the slightest apology or explanation that the church membership was offended. In his newfound freedom, with the grant money for studies in Europe to prepare himself for a professorship of Greek at Harvard, he set out for Göttingen.

Escaping from the ministry delighted him. He confided to his brother, Alexander, now American chargé at the Hague, that "had they done the thing in style, they would have probably fixed me there for life, for a minister does not easily get to believe too much . . . it is really hard for a man who preached twice a week and is hemmed in by all the prejudices and prepossessions of the business of *espirit de corp,* the unwillingness to owe that you are wrong and forty other obstacles to truth, to study the subject of religion fairly."⁶ When Alexander suggested that Edward's experience in the pulpit would be a great asset in the future, Edward said it was quite the contrary. The pulpit inculcated the bad habits of selecting three points for emphasis and filling in with pleasant similes. Conversely, he confessed that he did not know that he ought "to regret the time I have spent in studying divinity, because it probably made me feel easy in scruples, which had I known no more of the subject than those who pursue another profession generally know, would have troubled me much. But I tremble to think how near I had come to giving credit to the poorest of all systemizing, systematic theology, of which the very terms now are loathsome to me."⁷

Disillusion with the ministry did not add up to a rejection of Christianity, but Everett did break with traditional teaching. He freely shared with Alexander his most private thoughts. "With all this," he told him, "I feel a strong attachment to the act of preaching; and sometimes think something might be done to separate public worship to God and the public teaching of duty, from all connection with arbitrary facts, supposed to have happened in distant nations and ages; and of which he generaly believes most, who knows least."⁸

Public announcement of such an unorthodox idea would, as Everett well knew, have made him an outcast in his own country. He concluded that he was not the man who could assume such a daring role and withstand the gales that would blow about him. He would be content "with hammering upon Greek, and leave the world to fight out the cause of religion, as piously as they have fought it out hitherto."⁹ It was the first indication that he would retreat when the gales would blow. The gales did blow in the future, and Everett did retreat. He was not a crusader and had no wish to be.

He advised Alexander to follow the same course, as Alexander informed him of plans to return to the United States and that he was ready to do battle against the reigning political orthodoxy, "I doubt," he advised Alexander, "your inclination to enter heartily into the caucus and electioneering service, the only one almost, in the power of a young man to make himself active in, and if ever you were so much inclined, the preponderance of the federal party in Boston is likely, for some time at least, to be so great, as to make it very unpleasant and not very successful."¹⁰

His choice of the University of Göttingen was a foregone conclusion. It was there that the critical studies of the Bible had been centered. The university was now past its heyday, but it was still the home of several of the most famous scholars—Carl Offried Muller and F. G. Welcker, both classical scholars; Christian Gauss, the great mathematician; John Gottfried Eichhorn, the earliest authority on scientific biblical criticism; and Johann Friedrich Blumenbach, professor of natural history, known for his studies of the natural history of the human species and often called the father of anthropology.

Everett shifted his focus from biblical studies to the broader field of antiquities. He shared the general belief that these studies would furnish models for the highest form of living. Friedrich Wolf, who had reached his peak before Everett's arrival, was the leading proponent of what the Germans called "bildung." The great historian, Barthold Georg Niebuhr, said of Wolf: he has shown the way to the higher life that is only attainable through classical antiquity. The professors at Göttingen were tireless in their research, and students were no less so; they won the admiration of Everett and George Ticknor who had accompanied Everett to Göttingen. Such a community of scholars was not yet dreamed of at home. While the university was in session, Everett labored long hours, allowing himself only six hours of sleep and a walk each day.

Not all learning occurred in the classroom. Everett had a genius for finding prominent literary personages and scholars everywhere he went. He had the ability to engage complete strangers in conversation and to elicit from them their personal views. During the months he lingered in England on his way to Göttingen, he visited at length with Lord Byron, Sir Walter Scott, and numerous others. At Göttingen he associated with the professors, and they expressed opinions that enlarged Everett's views. Part of his genius was in being a good and disarming listener. He was caught by surprise when Lord Byron—this before Napoleon's defeat—stated that he would be reluctant to see his countrymen defeated but would rejoice in the effect such an event would have on the state of domestic politics. To this he added that he hoped he would live to see Lord Castleteagh's head carried on a pike under his window.[11] His host in Liverpool also brought the young Federalist from Boston up short when he was loud in his denunciations of the English government and complimented American policy. In his private conversations with the professors at Göttingen he likewise heard opinions that were new to him. In a conversation with Professor Blumenbach, the professor related how the famous Moravian, Count Zinzendorf, started a mission in Labrador. The mission did not survive, but the missionaries translated Calvin and parts of the Bible into the local Indian language. Everett expressed dismay: "From the Bible just those things were selected, which one wishes were not there—Samson and the jaw bone, Jonah in the whale's belly, and Daniel in the lion's den."[12]

Early Years

There were the trips to Dresden, Paris, and the Hague. The eight-week tour of Germany served to familiarize him with the latest findings of ancient Roman manuscripts. He learned that Barthold Georg Niebuhr, historian and philologist, had discovered two previously unknown manuscripts containing fragments of Roman law. At Weimar he met Johann Wolfgang Goethe, now sixty-nine years old. Both he and his fellow American, Ticknor, were overwhelmed by the libraries and museums in Dresden. He spent the summer of 1818 at the conclusion of his studies in Paris.

Above all else in his European experience it was his exposure to philological studies that excited him most. The open and free intellectual atmosphere in Europe carried him off to dreams of a new day. After attending lectures of Boetiger in Dresden he wrote: "I have yet met with nothing abroad that gave me a deeper impression of the rich resources of European instruction than the lectures I heard from its learned and most able scholar, in the splendid halls of the Japanese palace, surrounded by the monuments themselves of ancient art."[13] At Göttingen he "sat at the feet of Professor Dissen, one of the most promising scholars in Germany, a pupil of Heyne, but a thinker for himself."[14] He also studied with F. G. Welcker, one of the most distinguished scholars in the field. Everett and Welcker became close friends. It was probably from Welcker that he learned much about German domestic politics. Welcker had served as a tutor in the home of William V. Humboldt in Rome and admired Humboldt who was the Prussian minister in Rome. This association led Everett to publish two articles in the *North American Review* on his return to the United States. Everett stressed the importance of the professional schools in German universities. He considered philology so important that he equated it with studies in law and other professional fields.[15] He was thrilled by a new course on the Justinian code. Philology now opened the door to analyze manuscripts and to determine what had been written when, how many generations had contributed to the record, and which documents were forgeries. It was a science that enabled scholars to recover the teachings of the ancients and to discover the free human spirit that had distinguished the Greeks whose open-mindedness and intellectual curiosity was a way of life that would serve contemporary people and enable them to reach their full potential.

Everett regretted that Americans had not yet become aware of the intellectual riches of Germany. "Oh, that my dear stupid native land would awaken from her unblessed Cartaginian torpor, and send out her sons in errands like this." The few who had come were ill prepared and stayed too short a time, then return—when our pilgrimage is over—to our wallowing in the academic mire. "Why even the Modern Greek, sighing as they are under the Turkish plague," he feared, might put us to shame. While pursuing further studies in Paris, he found that there were ten or twelve Greeks studying, and there were at least two in each of the German universities.[16]

He remained enchanted with Eichhorn who now read his old notes in his lectures, but the work that Eichhorn had done in his studies of the prophets of the Old Testament fascinated him. "Thus," he wrote, "on the book of Isaiah, he finds a chronology of over 200 years." Everett thought that Eichhorn had done the most toward the foundation of the New School in Germany.[17]

Everett was amused at the stir Eichhorn's studies would create at home. "England and America are safe enough from the influences—good or bad—of this work and others of the same stamp, by their being locked up in the German language; a few will read them but not enough to affect and no attempt to publish a translation," he thought, "would succeed."[18]

He spent the summer and fall in Paris. He attended what he termed an excellent course of lectures in King's Library on studies of antiquities. He also worked on transcribing a collection of inscriptions. He was doing this at the request of Professor Bouhk of Berlin.

At the conclusion of his stay in Paris, he toured England where he sought out people of interest. In London he met William von Humboldt, the Prussian Minister, a distinguished scholar in linguistics and a statesman who contributed in a major way to the establishment of the educational system in Germany. He also made the acquaintance of William Wilberforce, famous as the promoter of foreign missions and for his crusade against slavery. He heard Wilberforce speak; he said of this diminutive and unprepossessing figure: His fluency-happy use of metaphors—affectionate and cordial manner of allusions to the persons and topics in questions—made him one of the happiest speakers he had ever heard. Mr. Wilberforce, he noted in his journal, "has the consolation of having done more good than any man living." He questioned however, the promotion of foreign missions and termed them the vainest of vanities. "I would," he wrote, "as soon try to send up a man in a balloon to the sun with a great prism in his hand to turn all light into a rainbow, as to send out an ignorant, obstinate sprig of divinity to convert a foreign nation; and as for the Bible it is the last book that ought to be used, as an instrument of improving Barbarian natives."[19]

There followed the grand tour through Switzerland, Italy, and

Early Years

Greece to Constantinople. What he might do on his return to the United States was uncertain.

Before leaving Paris he wrote in reply to Robert Walsh, a kindred soul of Philadelphia, who had spent three years in Europe, who now proposed that they join hands in editing a periodical. The proposal appealed to him, and he explained that he did not look down on periodical literature. It was, he wrote to Walsh, the only literature that our country could bear. "Our literature," he wrote, "is like our physical climate. We cannot produce neither good grapes nor good books. Works for the day spring up like wheat, in the short summer of popularity; and he that trusts for patronage beyond this season is nipped by the frost." He explained the difficulty. "We are fierce champions at the North, and our religious quarrels interesting the community one way and our political the other, there is little left behind but one little chequer spot of men who think alike on both points, and ever make it a rule to read nothing not written by a man who swears with us on both points."[20]

Walsh had complimented Harvared University. To this Everett responded: ". . . she is really a high minded literary mother, and does everything for her children which the state of society will admit. If the fierceness of party zeal in Politics and Religion should ever abate in the community, and especially the real nature of education should begin to be understood, something may be done."[21]

* * * * *

In 1822, Everett married Charlotte Brooks, daughter of P. C. Brooks, reputed to be the richest man in Massachusetts. Brooks had embarked on a career in marine insurance in 1789, and he was so successful that in 1803 he retired. His wife, Nancy Gorham, came from a prominent Boston family. She bore him seven daughters and one son. Brooks soon tired of retirement, and he started the New England Marine Insurance Company. He retired again after a few years, but kept turning over his money in loans and mortgages.

How Everett met Charlotte and how long he courted her before marriage we do not know, but that the marriage was happy is certain. Throughout the years when Everett was away for periods of time there was an almost daily exchange of affectionate letters. Adding to the happiness of the young couple was the warm relationship between Everett and his father-in-law. Brooks invariably addressed him as "My son," took great pride in Everett, and was generous in assisting him. He granted Everett two thousand dolars a year, and assisted him in buying a home. Had Everett not had

Brooks's financial support he could not have afforded a political career, for the salary of a member of Congress fell well short of covering the expenses of residing in Washington for several months each year. Wealth gave Everett freedom from financial worries and enabled him to be independent. In the absence of financial worries, Everett, as we shall see, was free to resign from positions when he suffered from pressure or the position was not to his liking.

The family of Brooks was remarkable. Two of Charlotte's sisters married men of great reputation: Nathanial Langdon Frothingham and Charles Francis Adams, son of John Quincy. As Henry Adams, who knew them all as a boy, said: "One might have sought long in much larger and older societies for three brothers-in-law more distinguished and more scholarly than Edward Everett, Dr. Frothingham, and Mr. Adams. One might have sought equally long for brothers-in-law more unlike."[22] Charles Francis Adams's brilliant career as minister in England during the Civil War left him a prominent place in the country's history. Nathanial Langdon Frothingham was a distinguished preacher but also a scholar in his own right who was well known for his translations of classical and German poetry. He and Everett shared similar views. It was Frothingham's church that Everett attended.

* * * * *

The Everett who returned from Europe viewed his role as the promoter of a culturally richer America, one where neither political nor religious controversy blinded the citizenry to the humanistic values and a richer cultural life in which people spread their wings and took off for fulfillment in a life unbounded by the confining barriers imposed by concentration of material success or absorption in theological questions. The years in Europe expanded his vision, enriched his own life with a knowledge of antiquities, and endowed him with respect for the inquiring mind that rebelled against popular prejudices and materialistic measures of success. His religious feelings were no longer tied to the deductions based on the authority of ancient writings; religion was a matter of ethics and feelings toward fellow people and the creator. His politics were no longer based on the narrow and self-serving sectional interest propounded by the Federalists. He saw the United States as one entity and the Union as the political organization that could accommodate conflicting interest, avoid the warfare that despoiled Europe, and demonstrate that representative government could meet the challenges, the dangers, and the changing interests that were inevitable in the historical process. His patriotism was not of the flamboyant variety; it was rooted in the feeling that the Union was the promoter of stability, and the organ that overrode the outburst of passions and resulted in scenes such as the French Revolution and the sufferings accompanying the Napoleonic Wars. He had become an admirer of Edmund Burke. With that conviction went the faith in the conciliation of diverse interest. Everett was never a crusader either by temperament or intellectual conviction.

The United States was on the point of entering a new era at the time of his return. The republic of the future was foreshadowed in the developments underway in Boston. The wealth that had been acquired in commerce and shipping was giving way to the new textile mill in Waltham. The manufacture of textiles was not new in New England, but the enterprises had been small and had experienced more downs than ups. The Boston Manufacturing Company was a large enterprise in which the stockholders combined to supply the capital. An accumulation of four hundred thousand dollars enabled the associates to build a large mill on the banks of the Charles River in Waltham. The plans and the machinery were copies of what the owners had inspected in England. Along with these imports came the conviction that the depressing conditions of factory workers and industrial centers in England should be avoided. There was a lively element of the philanthropic spirit present. This was the beginning of an industry that would line the rivers of New England, where water power was available, with long red factory buildings and row houses for employees.[23]

On his return from Europe, Boston was still dominated economically by shipping and commerce that had brought wealth to the city, but the mushrooming growth of the new textile industry that resulted in a transition in Massachusetts politics brought about the rapid growth of Boston into a great urban center, promoted the influx of thousands of Irish immigrants, and made Massachusetts a center of Whig politics. It was amid these scenes of change that Edward Everett gained importance as a public figure.

He aspired to promote cultural development in the United States and to advance a community in which men reached out for lives that extended beyond both materialistic strivings and orthodox religion with its adherence to doctrines based on arbitrary facts derived from past ages. He was not enthusiastic about the prospect of teaching at Harvard. His experience as a student at Harvard caused him to dismiss them as immature and lacking in serious interests.[24] Success had come easily, and he envisioned a large role for himself. Once again fortune was on his side. Edward Channing, editor of the *North American Review,* received an appointment at Harvard as professor of rhetoric. In 1820, Everett took his place as editor. It was a position that opened the way to contributing to a new public interest in literature and the fine arts. What he had learned in Europe, the enthusiasm he had experienced as a student of antiquities, and his broad knowledge of literature assured that the *North American Review* was in capable hands.

The journal now bore the imprint of Everett in every issue. Everett approved of rapid economic growth, but he asked if Americans were to be satisifed with a reputation for only industry, for frugality, for sharp bargaining. The country, he never tired of saying, must remedy the poverty that prevailed in the arts and education. The arts, literature, and theater, and exploration of the new learning that had enriched life in the German states were vital to American society.

"There is nothing, perhaps, to which our country is so plainly deficient, as the means of pursuing the study of the subject, which is treated in this memoir; we might perhaps say, in general, as in the state of the fine arts," he wrote in a review of a book on the history of Grecian art.[25] "Museum collections of the great masters," he wrote, "are unknown among us; and of course the acquisition of liberal ideas awakened by their inspection and study, forms no part of a finished education in this country." A reading of the classics, said Everett, "inspired a spirit favorable to free institutions, for the ancients accorded no status to hereditary monarchs and vigorously asserted their independence."[26]

The *North American Review* presented the ideas and thinking that were later to find expression in the Transcendantalist movement. Everett, at this stage, was still the enthusiastic man of free spirits. He gave expression to this mode of thought in the lectures he delivered in Cambridge on antiquities. Ralph Waldo Emerson was as enthusiastic as he had been years before when he attended the Brattle Street Church and heard Everett's sermons. In letters to his friend, John Boynton Hill, he wrote, "I am so much enamored as ever, with the incomparable manner of my old idol, though much of his matter is easily acquired from common books. We think strong good sense to be his most distinguishing feature; he never commits himself or makes a mistake."[27] Two months later Emerson wrote to his friend again praising both Everett's articles in the *North American Review* and his "noble course of lectures." His only desire, he wrote, was to hear more.[28]

He wrote two essays on the tariff question. In 1821, his free-trade views were still in accord with Boston's great interest in commerce and shipping. He opposed protective tariffs because they would bring about drastic changes in the economy, ruin foreign trade, and enrich manufacturers at the expense of their fellow citizens. He dismissed the argument that many manufacturers had failed because of foreign competition; they had failed because of their own mistakes.[29] In a second article he maintained that the protectionists could not refute free-trade arguments.[30]

The *North American Review* became the first and the leading literary journal of the day. Subscriptions increased to three thousand, and it had readers in the South and West. It offered new horizons that were refreshing. In this respect it was a precursor of Emerson and the Transcendentalist movement. A highly respected scholar, Harry Hayden Clark, a historian of American literature, concluded that Emerson "could have found practically all of his early transcendental and romantic ideas in the pages of the *Review*."[31] Emerson, however, was to become an advocate of the philosophical ideas of Immanuel Kant and Coleridge. During Everett's student days at Göttingen, Kant was dismissed as of no account, and Everett had accepted that view.

In the course of his life Everett wrote 118 pieces for the *Review*, 61 while he was editor in the years 1820 to 1824. In those years he took a stand in favor of internal improvements and exhibited a national spirit in defending the republic against the derogatory accounts of British travelers. To Everett, the future of the republic appeared bright.

* * * * *

Everett passed readily from the days when he had occupied a pulpit to the day when he became nationally known for his oratory. It was his success on the lecture platform that brought him a national reputation. In later years he was to refer to his popular lecture as ephermeral, and so they appear today long years after the days when rhetoric was fashionable.

His Phi Beta Kappa address at Harvard in August 1824 centered on "the circumstances favorable to the progress of literature in America." He acknowleged the speculative nature of his subject, the difficulty of identifying with certainty which physical or political facts explained which historical consequences, but having admitted that he set forth to explain why the future appeared bright.

> We then dwell, not on a distant, uncertain, perhaps fabulous past, but on the impending future, teeming with individual and public fortune; a future, toward which we are daily and rapidly moving forward, and with which we stand in the dearest connection that can bind the generations of men together; a future, which our own characters, actions, and principles may influence for good or evil, for lasting glory or shame.[32]

He spoke of the unique political order in which "all the great organic functions of the body politic are subjected, directly or indirectly ... to free popular choice." Here was a system that awakened the intellectual energy of a very large portion of the population and created a climate favorable to education. Too much energy had been siphoned off by politics, but this evil was not inherent in the system and had only happened because of the necessity of building an administration in a new state. We are now, he said, approaching the stage when we are producing a large amount of cultivated talent not needed by the state and this was only the beginning. In a free society a respectability attached itself to the production of literary works, whereas in the absolute monarchies of Europe, society accorded the greatest distinction to men engaged in government and in war.[33]

The political and social organization of the United States was also favorable to the culture of the mind, he said, because it opened the gates to talent wherever it existed. The American social order did "not consign the greater part of the society to torpidity and mortification." Openness of opportunity stimulated men and this, in turn, would affect the literature. The American situation furnished strong stimulants to action in a vast and highly prosperous country. Because it was all so new Everett found it "impossible to foresee what garments our native muses weave for themselves."

He cited Greece, where the same spirit of freedom had produced noble and elegant arts. The arts, to be sure, had prospered in other societies but not because of the patronage; some of the greatest artists and writers lived in poverty. European governments were too often not friendly to intellectual progress, and they frequently repressed creative genius.[34]

In America, moreover, a common language over a vast area with a large population widened the circle of readers. In contrast, the different languages of the numerous European countries made the literature of one country inaccessible to most people in other countries including the neighboring ones.

These considerations, elucidated in detail, furnished the backdrop for Everett's pièce de résistance—a panoramic view of America's great future. "Let me not be told that this is a chimerical imagination of a future indefinitely removed; let me not hear repeated the poor jest of an anticipation of 'two thousand years.'—a vision that requires for fulfillment a length of ages beyond the grasp of any reasonable computation." The country, he said, is growing with a rapidity hitherto without example in the world.[35] His Phi Beta Kappa audience readily believed that the country had become prosperous in an amazingly short time. The evidence of it was all about them.

Arts, letters, agriculture, "all the great national interests, all the

Early Years

sources of national wealth," he asserted, "are growing in a ratio still more rapid." Our people, he said, are being drawn out "and tempted on by an horizon constantly receding before them." Enraptured by what was occurring, Everett observed, "The wilderness, which one year is impassible, is traversed, the next, by the caravans of industrious emigrants, carrying with them the language, the institutions, and the arts of civilized life."

Moved by the bright hues of the future he had portrayed, Everett declared:

> This, then, is the theatre on which the intellect of America is to appear, and such the motives of its exertion; such the mass to be influenced by its energies; such the glory to crown its success. If I err in this happy vision of my country's fortunes, I thank Heaven for an error so animating.[36]

Then, turning to Lafayette, the French hero in the American Revolution, who was present, he closed with a grand peroration:

> Welcome! thrice welcome to our shores! and withersoever your course shall take you, throughout the limits of this continent, the ear that hears you shall bless you, the eye that sees you shall give witness to you, and every tongue exclaim, with heartfelt joy, Welcome! welcome, La Fayette.[37]

Everett's address won applause. Henry Ware, Jr., a Unitarian minister, wrote to his mother, "Everett's address was very fine. The concluding address to Lafayette was one of the most affecting and overpowering efforts of eloquence I ever witnessed; it shook the whole audience, and bathed every face in tears. When he sat down, it was followed with nine cheers in an interminable clapping."[38] Thomas Jefferson, after reading the speech, wrote to Everett: "I have yet to thank you for your Phi Beta Kappa oration delivered in presence of La Fayette. It is all excellent, much of it sublimely so, well worthy of its author and his subjects, of whom we may truly say, as was said of Germanicus 'fortitur famä sui.' "[39]

Four months later Everett delivered an oration at Plymouth at a celebration of the anniversary of the landing of the first settlers, an occasion that provided him with the opportunity to glorify the character of the founding fathers and the British heritage. The isolation, the rocky soil, and the severe climate of New England, he asserted, proved to be fortuitous blessings, for the distance was too great and the environment too poor and forbidding to invite intrusion. Plymouth did not attract adventurers in search of gold or subtropical plantations producing a quick profit. Only people with high motives and willingness to endure hardship setted there.

The colony was likewise fortunate in its English heritage. Everett cited England's great power and riches, and the vast empire maintained "at the price of guilt and blood." But, he said, her real greatness lay in the fact that above all other countries England was "the cradle and refuge of free principles." British political ideals provided the framework for the United States to develop a government committed to civil liberties. Out of that framework had come the vast and prosperous republic even now only on the threshold of a great future.

Everett extolled the past, but it was the future that pressed on him as the major concern. He called on the present generation to make the experiment in self-government and liberty a success. Much remained to be done.

At Concord, on 19 April 1825, at the fiftieth anniversary of the battle fought at the historic bridge, he told his vast audience that it was wonderful to win the war and create a representative government, but duty required that more be done. No pains should be spared to remove "the sad inequalities of condition; to place the advantages of a good education within the reach of every individual; and to add the blessings of social refinement, high civilization, and moral and religious culture."[40]

* * * * *

Everett's position at Harvard did not accord with what he hoped to be doing. He complained to Joseph Story, the future professor of law, that he had no opportunity to lecture "on the higher parts of ancient literature" and that his many duties were "not respectable enough in the estimation they bring with them, and lead one too much into contact with some little men and many little things."[41] Teaching elementary Greek grammar offered no more than dull routine. In expectation of being part of a larger world he had taken up residence in Boston only to be told by the overseers that he must live in Cambridge.

The revolution in Greece against Turkish rule immediately enlisted Everett's support. During his studies he had met young Greeks who came to Germany and France to study antiquities. Everett took lessons from one of these students in modern Greek. Their presence gave him hope that Greece would once again recover the spirit that enriched ancient society. In 1823 he published an eloquent plea for support of the Greek cause. The new state, should the revolution be successful, would point the way to a new era when the spirit of freedom would have greater play. We cannot but think, he wrote, "that a more general opinion never existed in the civilized world, than the Greeks ought to be aided in this conflict." This was not a contest between two barbarous nations, but a struggle between Turkish cruelty and a Christian people of education and enterprise. This was a war between the crescent and the cross.[42]

Everett saw in the Greek cause an opportunity for the United States to demonstrate that it could rise above petty self-interests. Duty called because an enlightened and liberty-loving people were calling for assistance. The people of Europe had contributed generously as individuals, but the nations of Europe dared not, as governments, render aid because each would distrust the other of having ulterior motives. The American government, said Everett, would come with clean hands and be free of suspicion. To help people struggling for liberty was, he said, our destiny. "Wherever the chosen race, the sons of liberty, shall worship freedom, they will turn their face to us. We should have one of our naval ships in the Mediterranean call at a Greek port and we should send a minister or a commissioner."[43]

The American public, wrote Everett, would respond with enthusiasm to such a move. Congress had heartily endorsed recognition of the new republics in South America even though in that instance the measure was dubious. There need be no reservations in the case of Greece. The United States has no treaties with Turkey imposing a restraint on us. And we seek no gain. In that youthful idealism, one that was to enter into American foreign relations many times in the future, Everett appealed to the American people:

> We feel more of the scruples, which perplex the cabinets of Europe. We see nothing but an enterprising, intelligent, Christian population struggling against a ghastly despotism, that has so long oppressed and wasted the land; and if an animating word of ours could cheer them in the hard conflict, we should feel that not to speak it, were to partake the guilt of their oppressors.[44]

Daniel Webster read the article and found it admirable. "I feel a great inclination to say or do something in their behalf early in the session."[45] Webster had become disillusioned with the trivial interests that entangled Boston politics in constant dispute. Some months before he had confided to a friend that he never felt more "down sick on all subjects connected with the public." He was disgusted with "this miserable, dirty squabble of local politics." Massachusetts was buried in local concerns. "There is a Federal interest, a Democratic interest, a Bankrupt interest, an Orthodox interest, and a Middling interest, but I see no national interest, nor any national feeling in the whole matter."[46] Everett's article pointed to a higher cause and one that might help Webster recover from that stamp that was still upon him as a former Federalist who had opposed the War of 1812.

Before President James Monroe's message to Congress Webster learned that it would contain strong expressions of sympathy for the Greeks. He confided this information to Everett, and he added that Everett's name had been mentioned to the president "as the fittest person for such a service."[47] Webster assured Everett that he would do his utmost on his behalf. He thanked Everett for the information he had furnished and looked forward to an early copy of the article on which Everett was working. Webster felt certain that Congress would pass a resolution and appropriate a fund for sending an agency to Greece. If the measures were adopted, Webster informed him, "I verily believe you may have the appointment if you wish it."[48] This, of course, was exactly what Everett greatly hoped to have. Everett had already written to Secretary of State John Quincy Adams requesting the appointment.[49] Everett's plea was rooted in self-interest. Since his days in Europe he saw an appointment in Europe as enabling him to continue his studies. This was the way the famous Niebuhr was enabled to continue his career of research and writing.

The bright promise of a career in the foreign service was doomed to be extinguished. While Webster and Everett carried on their correspondence, John Quincy Adams was working on those parts of President Monroe's message that dealt with foreign affairs. The president favored sending a commissioner to Greece, but Adams persuaded him to omit it. What emerged was to become known as the Monroe Doctrine, setting forth three principles that would embody American foreign policy. Adams feared nothing more than the American propensity to take up good causes overseas that would lead to involvement in the entanglements in Europe. For the past several years Henry Clay had crusaded for early recognition of the new republics in South America. Until Spain had agreed to the Transcontinental Treaty, negotiated by John Quincy Adams and Luis de Oñis, this would have been hazardous move, and Adams had firmly opposed it. Now there was a crusade in favor of Greece. Adams asked if we were ready to make war on the Turks. In assisting with the drafting of the president's message, he grasped at the opportunity to lay down a basic principle of policy that the United States would not intervene in the internal affairs of Europe. To this he added that the United States would view as unfriendly European intervention in the new world and the principle that the Western Hemisphere was no longer open for colonization.

On 19 January Webster presented his resolution in favor of sending an agency to Greece. Borrowing from his correspondence with Everett he maintained that he saw no reason to believe that we did not have a greater interest in Greece than we did in the more remote republics of South America.[50] The speech was received with enthusiasm, and Webster believed that if his resolution should come to a vote it would be approved.[51] His old friend Jeremiah Mason of Portsmouth, New Hampshire, reported that the speech had been received with universal praise, and that it had identified Webster with human causes.[52] This greatly pleased Webster who found that this was indeed true.

Then came a letter from Joel Poinsett who had at first been enthusiastic about the proposal but admitted that on reflection he had some second thoughts. More disturbing was Poinsett's report that President Monroe opposed it because such a proposal should originate with the executive.[53] On 20 January, the day after Webster's speech, Poinsett spoke in opposition to Webster's proposal. It was well understood that his views were those of the administration, and, indeed, Adams had spoken to Poinsett and advised him that passage of the resolution would wreck the ongoing efforts of the administration to negotiate a commercial treaty with Turkey. Adams had also added that Everett was too partisan to be a satisfactory envoy.[54] On 15 February Webster informed Jeremiah Mason that the most formidable obstacle to it was the opposition of John Quincy Adams. As Webster saw it the resolution should have been passed, and it would have added to the glory of the republic to have been the first power to have courageously stepped forth to aid the struggling Greeks.

With his dreams of going to Greece at a close, his attention shortly turned to another possibility, an opportunity to go to Congress as the representatives of the Middlesex district. Observing the convention that a candidate should be sought out by the people before making his ambitions public, Everett was properly coy. That Everett and Webster had discussed the possibility of Everett becoming a candidate during Everett's visit to Washington the previous winter appears a near certainty. Everett received information that the present incumbent had decided not to be a candidate by midsummer. On 5 August, Webster wrote to him that he had suggested Everett's name.[55] That same month Everett delivered his famous Phi Beta Kappa address in Cambridge, and Webster was there to hear him. He informed Everett shortly that he had taken the opportunity to sound out some of the political leaders as to how they viewed Everett as a candidate.[56] As a man had already been nominated by the party caucus there might be some difficulty, but

Everett's address had added to his luster and to his following among young people. A group of young men took up his cause, held a volunteer convention on 14 October, nominated Everett, and three weeks later Everett was elected by a margin of 1,529 to 603.

President Kirkland at Harvard had assured him that he could continue to teach at times when he was not in Congress, but after the election he was promptly notified that he was dismissed. The corporation based its decision on a rule adopted fifty years earlier. The rule had not been previously applied, and Everett attributed the summary dismissal to his having been party to a recent faculty protest. He accepted the decision in good grace and returned the money Harvard had advanced to him for his studies in Europe. The return of the money signified a final break with the world of scholarship. He was never to consider returning to the classroom. His career had taken a turn of lasting importance.

The decision to enter politics sidetracked the promising young scholar and placed him in a public position not wholly suited to his talents nor to his temperament. He must now become entwined in the coil of the pressures of his constituents, his obligations to his party, serve the special interest of his district in which were located a large part of the growing textile industry, set aside his plans for writing and research, and devote his great skill in writing to reports for the numerous committees on which he served. He must likewise endure the party strife and the politically inspired attacks of the opposition. It is doubtful that the candidate for political office appreciated the trials of politics. He might well have asked himself what do I do now. Whatever attention he may have paid to these questions, Everett felt that it was his duty to serve the public. The Union was as yet a fragile institution buffeting the storms of state rights and sectionalism. It was a young republic still in the making for which Everett entertained great hopes. Membership in Congress carried with it social standing.

Actually, at the moment Everett had few options. He would have much preferred a post in the foreign service, but that was not yet his to have. He was devoted to Harvard, but that institution with its bright future had yet to become a university in the Göttingen sense, or a community of scholars and students eagerly pursing their research and studies. He entertained no hope of bringing his studies of antiquities to fruition in a career of scholarship. That field had been preempted by the geniuses in Germany, and the materials for research for that field were not available in the United States.[57] Everett, in politics, was to undergo changes; the promising scholar deviated from his first love, and the deviation changed Everett.

2
Everett's Role in Politics

Everett completed his stint as editor of the *North American Review* in 1824, and he found his teaching at Harvard less than a challenge. During his stay in Europe, he had commented that politics was about the only field open to a young man in the United States. The professions of law, the ministry, and medicine were not attractive to him. He was already too old to enter the professions, unless it be the ministry for which he had a strong distaste.

As editor he became interested in public questions, and, although he had not been a participant in politics, he had developed strong views as to the future of the republic. He was, above all, committed to an increasing role of the central government and the welding of the fragile Union into a major agency for the promotion of both economic and cultural growth. Only if the central government overarched the localism and sectionalism that prevailed could the United States achieve standing as a truly national state and put aside the anachronistic debilitation that had been at the core of American politics. He shunned the sectionalism of the New England Federalists as much as he looked on all sectionalism as an anchor holding back the ship of state.

He firmly believed that the future of the republic was tied to economic development. The government must become a promoter of industry, transportation, and trade. These would bring with them a strong Union, and foster growth enabling the republic to stand on its own and not be a shadow of Great Britain. These views were identical with those of John Quincy Adams, and when Adams became secretary of state, Everett thought it marked the beginning of a new day in which the central government would assume its proper role. This outlook was also central in the politics of Daniel Webster, the man who had shed his former sectional federalism, and who despised the divisiveness and absorption of politics in petty local issues.

Everett's career as editor and professor left him free to contemplate the future, and his oratory brimmed over with faith the republic would achieve economic growth and with that would come a richer cultural life. His studies in Europe emancipated him from parochialism and from the narrow federalism that dominated Boston. He had already adopted the nationalism of John Quincy Adams and had developed an admiration for Thomas Jefferson and James Madison, both of whom were able to transcend local loyalties and focus their attention on the interests of the nation as a whole.

The republic he envisaged, a representative government where the people ruled, owed much to its British heritage. At the heart of that heritage were the political ideals of the Glorious Revolution, and government by the King, Lords, and Commons. Everett was already an admirer of Edmund Burke who had written with such force on the follies of the French Revolution and who had instilled in his readers the political principle that successful governments were the creation of past experience and not of blueprints that bypassed the lessons of the past. From his studies of antiquities Everett had developed an admiration for free men who held their heads high and insisted on thinking for themselves. Reason and not passions opened the way to advancement for society. Given this basic tenet of his intellectual convictions it followed that Everett was firmly committed to the check-and-balance system in which the executive, the legislature, and the judicial system stood in the way of disorders of unruly passions and demagogues.

Everett's was not a narrow nationalism that exalted a mythical state. It was deeply entrenched political philosophy that saw the central government as the agency that would assure law and order, and enable the republic to put the many contemporary advances in science, technology, and learning to use in creating a model republic. It was as yet a fragile institution much in need of greater strength if it were not to remain a loose federation in which truly national interests were or could be overpowered.

* * * * *

The ideals and political philosophy held by Everett, born in another age, were to be tested in a rapidly growing society, characterized by rapid change; a new kind of politics emerged in party warfare, and intense and ambitious sectionalism. Conflicts of interests characterized the period. The centrifugal forces at work ran counter to Everett's postulates. The dynamism of the new drives exceeded his expectations and made it difficult for him to accept.

For the first time political parties rose to power and became the major agents of decision making. Parties became the focus of individual loyalties, and individual political careers became subordinate to party considerations. Members of Congress only gained influence and only achieved success when they had the support of their party. The man entering politics owed his success to a party, and along with that he took on the obligations to promote the party, to be guided by party interests, and party welfare curbed his individual judgments and his ambitions. In turn, came party warfare. The greatest issues before the nation became subordinate to the promotion of the party. Organization was the name of the game. Outside of the party the man was a maverick who endangered his future. The rise of political parties was not to the liking of either Daniel Webster or Everett, but theirs was not freedom to decide.[1] Not until 1832 did Everett conclude that a two-party system was emerging. He thought it probably inevitable, but he disliked it. Rival parties would, he held, submerge intelligent and wise statesmanship in a rivalry that would place electioneering above responsibility. In this too, he shared the views of John Quincy Adams and Daniel Webster. Adams, in 1829, refused to use patronage to strengthen his campaign for a second term, and he proudly asserted that the presidency was not a position that men sought, but one in which the nation sought the best man. He did not wholly abide by this stand, but he did not campaign for office. Daniel Webster, a most ambitious man and anxious to erase from the record his opposition to the War of 1812, preferred that committees, enabled to debate merits of a question, should be free of party dictates. All three leaders were to confront the changing forces that gradually gave rise to the Democratic and Whig parties.

* * * * *

The rise of industry and the factory system alongside the continued expansion of shipping and commerce gave rise to new interests, new opportunities, and resentments. The changes that occurred in Massachusetts did not suddenly erode the culture in which deference to leadership, both political and economic, influenced political alignments, but deference increasingly gave way to bold assertions by groups moving upward to participation. It was an upwardly mobile society. It was also a society that recognized people of talent, whether it be talents in the way of business or literary and cultural fields. Edward Everett came from the most humble of births. He was a self-made man, who by dint of his ministry, scholarship, and reputation for learning won recognition as a leader.

Boston's newfound wealth was concentrated in a few families. In the state as a whole it appears that the top 1 percent may have owned half the total wealth by 1850. Around this top 1 percent was a cluster of the rising elite who stood apart from the general population and were the leaders of community life. The historian of Boston politics, Frederic Cople Jaher, has written that the city was the citadel of Brahminism. They ruled city affairs, and they pursued an enlightened public policy that led to marked improvements, including street cleaning, removal of refuse, paved streets, a public water supply, the building of schools, the creation of the Public Garden, the establishment of the first state hospital for the mentally ill, the first reform school, and the establishment of a party system.[2]

Everett lived in the center of this new elite class, and was prominent as a leader in the Atheneum, secretary of the American Academy of Arts and Sciences, active in the Massachusetts Historical Society and the American Antiquarian Society, and when the time arrived to build a public library, Everett and his close friend, George Ticknor, took the lead.

Everett throughout his ten years in Congress, stood firmly for the Whig program, and he was from his first days in Congress a leader among the National Republicans who, in 1834, quite fittingly called themselves Whigs as it became clear that there was no hope of working in cooperation with the Jacksonians. His political program would strengthen the federal government. It was also that of Boston's business interests: promotion of the economy, rapid development of internal improvements, a sound financial system headed by the National Bank, bankruptcy laws, and a protective tariff.

Everett's politics challenged powerful sectional interests. Differences had their source in the broad division of those who were concerned with matters on the periphery and those who focused their attention on the center, development of a national government that would implement a program shifting power from the local units of government to the national government.[3] To the people employed in agriculture and residing far from the centers of trade and finance, Washington was far away, and national questions encountered apathy.

Everett welcomed the coming of the new age, but he could not share in the feelings of those who feared the passing of the old, and worried about the economic dislocations and the ups and downs of the business world that sometimes left them facing panic; he could not share the feelings of Southerners who feared northern dominance; and he could not feel the hardships of factory workers or miners. In this respect Everett never fully understood the new age.

The political eruptions he deplored were the by-product of the very economic developments that he most admired.

This left him in the position of seeking to defend what he valued most in the existing political order and deploring the new developments that came into conflict with his admiration for the Constitution, the check-and-balance system, and the arrival at decisions amid calmness, free of passions, and the answers to problems based on reason. He was not unjustified in his fears of how the new order of sectionalism and overheated politics would destroy the Union. The political atmosphere that became ever more intense did not permit wholly rational or a calm search for solutions to the pressing and difficult questions. Democracy in that atmosphere might well fail. Everett could deplore the fevers that prevailed, but neither he nor other statesmen could withstand the dictates of the new order.

* * * * *

Everett, during his early years in Congress, asserted that the two parties stood at opposite poles, and indicted the Democrats for being the enemies of order and for demagaguery. His was a highly partisan and prejudiced view. Historians have long since dismissed this overly simple analysis. They have come to varying conclusions. Some have stressed that the party was the party of frontiersmen. At the other end of the spectrum Arthur Schlessinger placed the emphasis on the working class in the cities. Another historian, Joseph Dorfman, sees Jacksonians as spokesmen for the middle class, devoted to the principles of laissez faire and opposing high tariffs, corporations, and monopolies. There is evidence to support each of these conflicting interpretations.

The two parties did not represent two diametrically opposed developments. Both parties were dependent for success at the polls on support from all sections, and they tailored their programs accordingly. Democrats and Whigs were approximately equally strong in each of the sections. It was this hard fact that caused both parties to steer away from the troublesome slavery question. Only after the Mexican War did the parties become increasingly sectional parties.

Jacksonian Democrats and Whigs included more than one shade of opinion. Glyndon G. Van Deusen, in his article "Some Aspects of Whig Thought and Theory in the Jackson Period" found the Whigs more optimistic about the economic developments underway, placed great importance on finance and sound currency, and saw corporations as highly useful in a country suffering a scarcity of capital. Whigs were more consistently in favor of expanding the responsibilities of the central government. Having set forth these as attributes of the Whigs, Van Deusen then warns: "It would be a mistake, however, to conclude that the Whig and Democratic parties of the Jackson period were at opposite poles of political or even economic thought."[4] Class lines were definitely blurred, there were Democrats who supported the protective tariff, the National Bank, and both parties supported universal suffrage. There were shades of differnces between the two parties, but as Robert Rantoul, prominent Democrat in Massachusetts, wrote: "We cannot help admitting the obvious truth, that our party contests have not the intrinsic importance, with which lively fancies of the heated partisans often invest them."[5] Contrary to Everett's occasional rhetoric the Democratic party was essentially middle class. Setting aside campaign propaganda, an analysis of Everett and Rantoul shows they were in close agreement.

It is a striking fact that during ten years in Congress the intellectual Everett was a zealous partisan and accepted the current line of hard line Whigs in Boston. He belonged to an earlier era. His was a world of fixed and final truth associated with calm reason and the suppression of passions.

As a new member of the House of Representatives, Everett assumed that it was a wise course to maintain a low profile until he established himself. Not until April 1826, did he make a major speech. The frustrated supporters of Andrew Jackson for president charged that Jackson had been duly elected in 1824, and they were now intent on defeating John Quincy Adams in the next election. With this as his aim, George McDuffie of South Carolina proposed an amendment to the Constitution to correct the alleged error of delivering all the electoral votes of a state to the candidate for president who had the most votes in the state. This, he said, was the equivalent of depriving the minority of a voice. McDuffie proposed that the election should be based on districts within a state.[6]

McDuffie's purpose was to call the attention of voters to the miscarriage of justice in the previous election, and this, Everett, the close friend of Adams, could not let pass. He took his stand on the Constitution; to alter the Constitution, he feared, was to set the republic adrift. It would destroy the framework laid down by the founding fathers. The Constitution, he contended, was a contract between different interests, reached after great difficulty. The established system of choosing the president had served the country well; every man who had occupied the chair served the whole of the people.

Everett's Role in Politics

Everett then turned around, however, and committed a blunder that was to haunt him. He assured the South that in the event of a servile insurrection he would don a soldier's uniform and knapsack to suppress a revolt. This was the same Everett, who on his trip to Virginia in 1814, after a firsthand view of slavery, wrote, "The commerce between master and slave is a perpetual exercise of the most boisterous passions—the most unremitting despotism on one part, and the most degrading on the other."[7]

Everett, who in a few short years before hoped that Christianity could be separated from basing its teaching on "facts" derived from past ages and commit itself to truly ethical teachings, now retreated and cited the fact that the Bible did not condemn slavery. Immediately under attack he pleaded, unconvincingly, that he had been misunderstood. Back in Boston, the Jacksonian newspaper, *The Statesman,* called his views revolting.[8] Webster, privately, called Everett's views a heresy. P. C. Brooks, his father-in-law, put it mildly; he wrote that some of their friends were critical. Brooks, who spoke for a past generation, thought that many Southerners must consider slavery an evil and should be "allowed by us all to be the best judges of what shall be done." Everett, himself, was troubled.[9] Slavery, he granted, was an evil, but after much thought, he feared that it could only be rooted out at great cost.

* * * * *

Well before the election took place in 1828, Everett gave way to panic fearing that Adams would be defeated. Although Jackson gave no hint of what course he would pursue if elected, Everett was certain that he would promote government economy and that he would limit the role of government. Given the positions already taken by supporters of Jackson, Everett had reason to fear. The fact that Jackson was a military hero alarmed him. It was likely, Everett believed, that Jackson would prove to be a demagogue.

With the victory of Jackson in 1828, the politics of the country did change. The new alignments no longer centered around the rivalry of New England and Virginia. The new West and a new South altered the balance. New issues replaced those of the past. The rise of manufacturing in New England, New York, and Pennsylvania catapulted the tariff question to the fore. The opening of new areas in the Mississippi Valley gave a new importance to the land policy of the national government. The rise of the cotton kingdom assured resistance to protectionism. In the new configuration the major issues would be the Indian policy, the National Bank, land policy, the tariff, and internal improvements.

Jacksons's election also brought about a new style of politics. The new president, in contrast to his predecessors, saw himself as the spokesman for all of the people and the members of Congress as the representatives of only their particular constituencies. His political consultants placed a high premium on electioneering, and skillfully rallied support for the admistration. Jackson, once sure of his position, did not hesitate to override both Congress and the Supreme Court. Jackson was the hero of the people. He shared with many the uneasiness over the changes taking place. There was fear that in this new era of powerful corporations, that these corporations received charters from state legislatures that deprived people of their rights.

A prominent Jacksonian in Boston, Nathanial Greene, editor of *The Statesman,* at a Jackson celebration, expressed sentiments that would be heard often in the years ahead. He told his audiences that Jacksonians "refused to bend in adulation of principles that are disapproved, and [leaders] whose conduct we could not justify." This section of the country, said Greene, was strongly devoted to Adams from local, personal, and party considerations, and Jacksonians were surrounded "by a proud, vindictive persecuting aristrocracy."[10]

Jackson's role was to serve as the spokesman for those who protested against the changes taking place. To them the enterprise of the few appeared to be at the cost of the many. Power, it appeared, was slipping out of the hands of the people. Jacksonian populism was an uprising of popular feelings.

* * * * *

The removal of Indians from their lands became national policy as soon as the republic gained its independence. Possession by the Indians stood in the way of frontiersmen satisfying their land hunger. From their viewpoint Indian occupancy did not confer ownership, and they should be removed from the path of western settlement. The presence of a few white missionaries among the Indians appeared to threaten permanent possession by the Indians. Moravian missionaries working among the Indians who had fled from the Wyoming Valley in New York to Ohio established the village of Gnadenhutton. In 1782 frontiersmen attacked the village and killed the Indians who had become Christians. This was the first ugly chapter in a tragic story.

Beginning with the Washington administration the national government made treaties with the Indian chiefs, paid low prices for their lands, and Indians had to move. These negotiations included bribes plus plying them with liquor, thereby facilitating negotiations. Time and again the treaties were renegotiated to accommodate the next wave of settlers.

By 1815, the Cherokees and the Creeks in Georgia found themselves on the agenda of the removal program. American troops arrived during the War of 1812, and among them was Andrew Jackson. About one thousand Cherokees fled to Florida and joined the Seminoles. Jackson negotiated a treaty that transferred about half of Alabama and a wide strip north of Florida to the national government.

In the years preceding and later a remarkable development occurred among the Cherokees. Missionaries of the American Board of Commissioners arrived and a few half-breeds who had married Indian women introduced the ways of the white man. A Cherokee leader developed a script and taught Indians how to write and read. The net result of this development was the emergence of an Indian community able to govern itself. There emerged a group of Indian leaders capable of making an eloquent defense of their interests who made their way to Washington. The secretary of war denied them a hearing, but they faired better in discussions with members of Congress.

It was in 1823 that Edward Everett, friendly to the New England missionaries in Georgia, wrote an article for the *North American Review* praising the missionaries because they did not aim at conversion of the Indians to Christianity. To do so, he wrote, would have been to begin at the wrong end. It was right that they concentrated on teaching the Indians farming. Their activities would prepare the Indians to defend themselves against the inroads of the frontiersmen. To save the Indian it was necessary to permit him to adhere to his traditional way of life. If the Indian should be forced to adopt the white man's culture, the Indian would then become no more than a man with copper-colored skin, and he would no longer be an Indian."[11]

In 1825, the Treaty of Indians Springs ceded all of the Creek lands and provided that the Indians must move by 1 September 1826. Suspicious as to how Indian approval of the treaty had been adopted, President John Quincy Adams ordered an investigation and discovered barefaced bribery. The scandalous treaty was withdrawn, and new negotiations began.[12]

By 1827, a showdown approached between the state of Georgia and the Cherokees. The Cherokees drafted a constitution establishing a state government and declared themsevles a sovereign state. The Georgia legislature appealed to Congress to remove the Indians and enacted a law declaring that the Indians were subject to the laws of the state of Georgia, denying them the right to appear in court or to resort to state courts in appeals for justice.

The election of Jackson reversed the policy of John Quincy Adams. Jackson was convinced that the Indians and the frontiersmen could never live in peace as long as they lived side by side. If the Indian was to preserve his traditional ways he must be removed to the territories west of the Mississippi River. This view was shared by secretary of war, Lewis Cass, and Indian affairs were in the sphere dominated by the Department of War.[13] Cass dismissed the gains made by the Cherokees as of no consequence. Given its ties to the western areas of the country and its reliance on frontier support, the Jacksonian party had political considerations that played some part. Jackson, in his message to Congress in 1829, recommended the removal of the Indians.

In 1830, after heated and prolonged debates, Congress debated the Removal Bill. Critics sought to postpone action maintaining that the area to which they were to be moved was unknown and should be investigated to determine if they met the Indian's needs. An amendment providing for a delay was only defeated after the Speaker of the House, Andrew Stevenson of Virginia, voted against it. New Englanders led the fight against the act, and they had strong support from Senator Theodore Frelinghursen of New Jersey and Joseph Hemphill of Pennsylvania.

The debate over removal of the Indians occurred against a backdrop of intense debates over land policy and internal improvements. In late January one of the most famous debates in American history occurred concerning the nature of the Union. In a masterful speech, Daniel Webster defined unionism. He appealed to the sometimes latent feelings of unionism and, as the editors of the papers of Webster have said, out of the second of his speeches emerged a nation "transcending any federation of local sovereignties and standing as a potential equal in the nineteenth century world of national states."[14] Webster embodied in rhetoric Everett's dream for the republic.

Georgia's bold assumption that she should exercise jurisdiction over the Indian territory raised the question of states' rights, alongside the issue of human and moral considerations. In the debates over the amendment that would have delayed action and would have permitted the Indians to remain on their ancestral lands until they chose to move, Everett spoke of the severe difficulties the Indians would face. In the West, he said, the thousands of Indian families would find themselves surrounded by warlike tribes, and they would be compelled once again to move farther west. The result, said Everett, was a constant uprooting and degradation of the Indians into a state of perpetual warfare. The Indians, he declared, were human beings and not barbarians. To push them out of their homes, ten or fifteen thousand of them, and send them into a wilderness was worse than any act in all the annals of history. In a final peroration he summed up what was now being done: "The evil, sir, is enormous: the violence is extreme; the breach of public faith deplorable, the inevitable suffering incalculable."[15] Toward the close of the debate McDuffie of South Carolina warned that Georgia "has assumed an attitude from which she will not shrink; and if we refuse to exercise the power which we constitutionally assume on this question, the guilt of blood may rest upon us." Congress passed the Removal Bill.

After the passage of the act Everett wrote on the tragic history of the Cherokees and the triumph of injustice. Self-interest had always been able to engage advocates to enlarge, fortify, and defend the pretensions of the whites. The Indians, conversely, had no logicians to expose the sophistry of those who make the worse appear the better. Orators they had whose eloquence temporarily set at naught the greedy speculator and the intriguing agent, but the schemes were always renewed and repeated until they were successful. The eloquence, by which they were resisted, was evanescent; however, the motives by which they were prompted never ceased to operate.[16]

Everett was asked what right the Indians had to the whole continent. He answered that they had the real right—the right of occupancy. That right did not rest on legal papers. "The formality of deeds, and convenants, and guarantees, has respect to the evidence of title, and not to the substance of it."[17]

Well before the Georgie law was to be tested by the Supreme Court, Everett contended that the Indian question was and alway had been considered a national interest that must be under the jurisdiction of the national government. From the very beginning of the national government during the administration of Washington this had been acknowledged. He recited the early history beginning with Georgia's appeal to Congress under the Articles of Confederation.

"In point of fact," Everett wrote, "the several states had never exercised any right of legislation over Indians within fixed limits, upon their original territory."[18] Relations with the Indians were subject to treaties, and treaties were the supreme law of the land. He took issue with his friend, Timothy Flint, a former missionary to the Mississippi Valley and editor of the *Western Monthly Review*. The advocates of Indian removal argued that the Indian question was an open one. It was not. We are bound by a hundred treaties, he wrote, and those treaties are as binding as the Constitution.[19] Everett held that the Indian treaties, like other treaties, could not be set aside by one of the parties. If the terms of the treaty were burdensome, then relief must be sought by negotiation.

The Removal Act of 1830 did not set a date for the removal. It sought to encourage the Indians moving promptly by providing for a payment of $5 million for their lands, for a few tools and provisions on the trek, and promised them protection once they arrived. The absence of a stipulation of a date for removal had no real significance for Georgia claimed jurisdiction, and the experience of the Indians at the hands of Georgia's state government sufficed to promote removal. Many lingered until 1838, but most moved not long after the new law was passed.

The Cherokees and their supporters challenged the constitutionality of the laws of Georgia restraining their freedom. Former Attorney General Wirt represented the Indians. The United States Supreme Court, with Chief Justice Marshall presiding, dismissed the case on the ground that the Cherokees were not a foreign nation within the meaning of the Constitution. He observed that if the courts "were permitted to indulge their sympathies, a case better calculated to excite them could scarcely be imagined; but apparently much against their inclination the court was obliged to hold against the right of the Indians to maintain the action against the State of Georgia."[20] While this case was before the court, an Indian in Georgia sentenced to hanging, petitioned the court for a writ of error, and this was granted by the court. When the governor of Georgia conveyed this to the state legislature, that body declared that the Supreme Court had no jurisdiction over a subject of the state of Georgia. The Indian was promptly hanged.[21]

Marshall's decision did include a ruling that the Indians constituted "a distinct political society . . . capable of managing its own affairs and governing themselves." In another notable case, *Worcester vs Georgia,* Marshall appeared to give cause for cheer. Marshall held:

> The Cherokee Nation, then, is a distinct community, occupying its own territory, with boundaries accurately described, and which the citizens of Georgia have no right to enter, but with the assent of the Cherokees themselvse, or in conformity with treaties and with the acts of Congress. The whole intercourse between the United States and this nation

is, by our constitution and laws, vested in the government of the United States.[22]

President Jackson, who held himself an equal of the Supreme Court, stated that he was not bound by the court's decision. Georgia continued to apply its law to the Indians, making life in Georgia intolerable.

Time and again the Indians appealed to Everett for assistance. He advised them to move because even if Congress and the president should intervene on their behalf, and there was no hope of that, and "still more even if the state of Georgia would repeal her oppressive laws, it would be impossible for the Cherokees to live in peace." They would be harassed by the lawless frontier population to a degree that would make their situation very uncomfortable.[23]

By 1838, after constant harassment, sixteen thousand Cherokees migrated to Oklahoma. Fifteen hundred died along the way. It appeared that General Gaines had been right in 1825 when he had warned the Indians: "I tell those Indians the white people will cheat them out of their lands, get all their money, and then kick them to Hell."[24]

* * * * *

Within a year of the first inauguration of Andrew Jackson, the opposition led by Henry Clay and Daniel Webster was an impotent minority. A new party to embrace their views had not yet come into being, and the future of these dissidents appeard gloomy. Jackson's popularity was greater than ever; even when people might disagree with a particular measure of Jackson, he still remained their hero. As Webster put it, politics was in a state of chaos. This was exactly what Everett had concluded.

Jackson's program appeared wholly negative to Everett. Jackson stood in the way of economic development, was obsessed with reducing the national debts, blocked the desperately needed internal improvements, opposed strengthening the navy on no better grounds than that the navy bred aristocratic ways, opposed the restoration of dry docks on economic grounds, favored a low tariff, and was critical of the Bank of the United States. Jackson appeared to be the champion of retrogression. Everett, full of dismay, wrote to his older brother that Jackson "has raised up the most miserable dregs of the community" and receives "the support of an overwhelming majority of the rest of the Union . . . to trample what is decent among us with the dust."[25]

To the populace this was not retrogression but efforts to restore the good old days in a time of rapid change. Jackson's success owed much to popular myths of a past that had never been, but also to new expectations and resentments inherent in a period of rapid change.

Everett could not take offense to Jackson as a person. As a guest at the White House he found Jackson cordial, articulate, and well mannered. When Jackson's trip to New England was being arranged, Everett served as chairman of the committee of arrangements and invited the president to be a guest in his home.

Jackson's politics were abhorrent to Everett, however, and he refused to look beyond the political principles he cherished as eternal truths. In a speech in New York in the autumn of 1831, Everett not only held that the protective tariff was constitutional, but that it was the duty of the national government to foster economic growth.[26] There were also pressing immediate needs that were being neglected. The army must be strengthened if it were to meet the expectations of the South for protection. Industry must be fostered as the founding fathers had contended. Fortifications stood in need of being rebuilt. More dry docks were needed, and some way must be found to put an end to the distracting and dangerous controversy over the tariff.[27]

The government had no reason to be overly concerned about the debt as it had a surplus every year. Given this situation, Everett told his friend, C. A. Davis, that the price of public land ought to be reduced. "I w'd give them away to *bona fide* settlers." If there were concerns about going that far he would lower the price from a dollar and a quarter an acre to fifty cents, and give away land that was unsold after ten years.[28] At this point he was out of step with many New Englanders who were protesting that the West was draining New England of labor.

The question of the tariff disturbed him greatly. A way must be found to bridge the differences between the North and the South, however. He believed that George McDuffie of South Carolina was wrong in holding that tariff duties on British manufacturers must result in fewer exports of cotton to England. Everett hoped that men of goodwill and reason, regardless of party, could find a solution. He testified that he respected McDuffie's talents and probity. He gave further evidence of his faith in proposing to Samuel D. Ingham of Pennsylvania, who had split with Jackson over the Eaton affair, that he would protect the industry of the country most needing it, but duties could be reduced on all other imports. He asked Ingham: "How would it do to raise a committee of twenty-four members, one from each state and by this representation of all the interests of the country to put this distracting and dangerous controversy to rest."[29]

Everett soon lost hope for a negotiated settlement of the tariff question. In 1831 he began to concentrate on the next presidential election and how to get rid of Jackson. Obsessed with this problem he briefly entertained the delusion that Jackson could be impeached, and in a letter to Henry Clay he outlined what he chose to label as Jackson's violations of the Constitution.[30]

Clay professed that there was no doubt of the president's liability to Everett's charges, "But at present . . . from the composition of the Senate, there is not the least prospect of such a prosecution being effectual." To this Clay added: "To attempt it, therefore, you would not be able to carry with you the judgment or the feeling of the public. Indeed there would be danger of exciting the sympathies of the people in behalf of a person whom they have not yet altogether ceased to idolize."[31]

Clay's response made it clear that Everett's proposal could not be carried forth, but Everett did not wholly drop the desperation move. Testimony by some of Jackson's late supporters, if continued, would, Everett thought, drive the Whigs toward impeaching Jackson. In late summer of 1831 there was still hope that Jackson's treatment of Calhoun would so weaken the Jacksonians that they could be defeated. Everett had corresponded with Duff Green, friend of Calhoun, who declared that the president simply could not be rechosen.

The National Republicans were losing any hope of success. As a mere faction without a name and without a committee they were outsiders. No one knew this better than Daniel Webster who, in 1830, wrote to Clay: "Parties must, now, necessarily be sorted out, anew; and the great ground of differences will be the tariff and internal improvements."[32]

* * * * *

By 1832, a new movement, Anti-Masonry, upset the scene. It began after the alleged murder of William Morgan of Batavia, New York, because he had revealed secrets of the order. Failure to solve the crime was attributed to the Masons because they refused to cooperate with the authorities. Historians once dismissed Anti-Masonry as a mere crackpot movement, but it promptly became something more, an effort to create a party more responsive to the people. As the movement grew it won adherents among the middle class, people who were on the upward grade in the mobile society.

Anti-Masonry gained strength among the orthodox Congregationalists who resented the Unitarians because of their success in taking over many of their churches in Massachusetts, their control of Harvard, and their latitudinarian teachings. Orthodox clergy complained because the Unitarians held that differences in doctrine did not matter. Aside from the religious orthodox there was resentment against what appeared to be a closed society. Republican principles implied a faith in openness of decision making. Secrecy ran counter to faith in government by the people.

Everett feared that the rise of the Anti-Mason party would diminish the strength of the National Republicans in the next election. Clay had foreseen the difficulty. The National Republicans nominated Henry Clay who was a Mason, and this would be exploited by the new party. In his letter to Clay on 5 August 1831, he assured Clay, "I have paid great attention to what you say on the subject of Antimasonry." Everett reported that in Massachusetts some of the Masonic lodges were on the point of dissolving. He had written an article for a Boston newspaper recommending that the lodges dissolve. They, he confessed, "have taken it in dudgeon." If the lodge in Lexington should do so and with the support of Clay, this would probably remove the difficulty. If Clay would write a letter to John Quincy Adams stating that he wished to see lodges dissolved, Everett thought that this would cause Adams to give Clay his support.[33]

The Anti-Masonic party nominated William Wirt, a Virginia lawyer who was not a Mason, who had served as attorney general under President John Quincy Adams. The division between the Anti-Masons and the National Republicans appeared to assure another Jackson victory, and to Everett that was tantamount to a threat to the public safety. He wrote to Duff Green of South Carolina: "I am of opinion with you that the great object which all honest men ought now to have at heart as the first thing to be done is to rescue the country from the fangs of Jacksonism and this can only be done by the united efforts of all opposed to it." In the closing weeks of the campaign the Antimasons appeared to be gaining ground everywhere.[34]

On 27 October, Edward conferred with his brother Alexander, and they agreed that Henry Clay, the candidate of the National Republicans, should withdraw from the race. Two days later they conferred with General Henry A. S. Dearborn, a leading National Republican. The meeting erupted into a sharp clash of views. Dearborn wrote to Clay the same day, informing Clay that he had told the Everetts that Clay would win and that to desert him now was unforgivable. Clay had spent his whole life for the best interests of the country. To desert him now would be "dishonest, dishonorable & disgraceful." The next day he wrote to Clay again telling him not to withdraw, and added that he should not be deceived by friendly advice.[35]

The Everetts rejected Dearborn's advice and wrote to Clay. They were certain that Clay could not win. Wirt was likely to receive more votes than Clay. The only way to have National Republican electors cast their votes for Wirt was for Clay to withdraw.[36]

Abbott Lawrence entered the fray with a letter to Clay telling about a conversation with Dearborn who informed him of the plan of the Everetts. Lawrence opposed Clay's withdrawal and expressed the opinion that the Everetts were influenced by John Quincy Adams who, said Lawrence, opposed Clay.[37]

Clay, of course, rejected the advice of the Everetts, but the incident created sharp dissent within the ranks of the Republicans in Massachusetts. When the election was over and Clay had lost by an overwhelming margin of 219 to 49, Everett, in an impromptu speech at a political meeting in Charleston, attributed the loss to the division among the anti-Jacksonians. His comments on that occasion were to lead to an unhappy and temporary coalition with the Anti-Masons. The Masons in Massachusetts never forgave him. Three years later many of them deserted him in the election for governor, and they made difficulties for him while he was governor.

* * * * *

The election year, 1832, brought the difference between the Jacksonians and the National Republicans into sharp focus. The bank question, internal improvements, and the tariff questions occupied Congress in a prolonged session that lasted until July. The tariff question had the highest priority. In March, Everett called a meeting of the Massachusetts delegation to consider the tariff. He and Clay both favored a reduction of duties on imported consumer products that were not in competition with home production. They stood by protection for the new industries. A new bill was eventually drafted incorporating this feature, one that would significantly lower the revenues from import duties on noncompetitive imports but adhere to protection for industry. The bill passed both houses of Congress. McDuffie's vehement attack on it signaled trouble. The bill played directly into the hands of the nullifactionists in South Carolina. "Your duties have been reduced on goods used by the rich," McDuffie charged, "and have been raised on goods of necessity marketed in the South." He estimated that the burden on the South had been increased by $1,406,080.[38] The test of nullification was close at hand.

The immediate question was the tariff but more was involved. In September, as developments were moving toward the nullification crisis, John C. Calhoun wrote:

> I consider the Tariff, but as the occasion, rather than the real cause of the present unhappy state of things. The truth can no longer be disguised, that the particular domestock [sic] institutions of the Southern States, and the consequent direction which that and her soil and climate have given to her industry, has placed them in regard to taxation and appropriation in opposite relation to the majority of the Union; against the danger of which, if there be no protective power in the researched rights of the States, they must in the end be forced to rebel or submit to have their domestick [sic] institutions exhausted by Colonization and other schemes, and themselves and their children reduced to wretchedness.[39]

Calhoun was not alone in seeing the crisis as involving the whole spectrum of southern institutions. A reading of the debates in Congress shows that slavery was on the minds of the participants from South Carolina, and, thanks to the studies of William Freehling, we can place the crisis in this broader perspective.

Everett's program faced a challenge. There was, George McDuffie declared, an interested majority "which feels power and forges right." That majority, he charged, steadily aimed at an imperial ban on rivals. They had set out to annihilate foreign commerce, and had already brought about a revolutionary change in the nation's economy by replacing foreign trade with manufacturing. This demonstrated the tremendous power of the majority and left people of the South no choice but to rise in defense of their liberties.[40] McDuffie reflected the more general fear that had contributed to Jackson's victory in 1828. A national government that was increasing in strength, a national bank that wielded great power, the chartering of innumerable corporations, and the rise of a class of wealth brought about the turbulent politics of the era.[41] Everett and his fellow National Republicans now faced a crisis that defied their concept of government.

In October a convention called by the legislature in South Carolina declared the tariff laws null and void, and forbade the collection of duties within the state. Jackson met the challenge with a combination of firmness, careful preparation for hostilities should they occur, and a conviction that tariff duties should be lowered. On

20 December, he issued a proclamation declaring nullification incompatible with the existence of the Union. He appealed to nationalism in some of the same language Daniel Webster had used in his debate with Robert Hayne. The Union was a creation of the people and not of the states. It was sovereign in foreign affairs, in question of war and peace, and in the exercises of power delegated to it. He carefully and with skill set forth that the Union was a perpetual entity, and his formulation of that concept was, as, Kenneth Stampp, the historian, states, remarkable for its incisiveness, coherence, and comprehensiveness.[42] He called for authority to use force.

Everett promptly wrote to his brother Alexander stating that the proclamation should be supported even though "our interests will be sacrificed to the nullifiers."[43] Daniel Webster, who was in Boston, spoke in Fanueil Hall praising the president's stand and calling for his support.[44]

While the president planned his next moves, Congress considered the Verplanck Bill that would slice tariff duties in half. Everett and Webster were appalled, but saw no way to defeat the measure. The Speaker of the House asked Everett to prepare a compromise bill. Everett and his colleagues from Massachusetts drafted a bill that would have resulted in modest decreases in duties but would have protected woolens.

That effort came to naught on 25 February when Clay introduced his bill providing that all duties should be lowered every two years until they reached a point no higher than 20 percent. Webster opposed the bill with all the rhetoric at his command. Henry Clay had proceeded with well-laid plans, holding almost daily meetings with protectionist friends in the Senate. Webster attended the first session and then parted ways. Once assured of the support of these friends, Clay communicated through an intermediary with John C. Calhoun who listened but suggested amendments. Knowing well that he was likely to be charged with surrendering to the nullifiers, he contended that nullification was already dead, and the Carolinians no longer sought a showdown. Clay was equally ready to meet charges that his bill was a surrender of protectionism. The proposal would assure the manufacturers of stability. If enacted into law his proposal would bring peace between the sections. Calhoun, too, was brought into line, partly because he had no wish to carry nullification to the point of civil war and possibly because he had learned that Jackson was prepared to send him to the gallows if it became necessary to implement his Force Bill.[45]

Shortly after the passage of the Force Bill by a vote of thirty-two to one on 20 February, the Clay Bill passed the Senate by a vote of twenty-nine to sixteen. The bill had already swept through the House, as Adams put it, like a hurricane.

The House met until five in the morning of 3 March and then adjourned. John Quincy Adams and Everett drove home together, narrowly missing an overturn of their carriage as they rode down Pennsylvania Avenue. On reaching Everett's lodging, Adams alighted and walked home. Exhausted and dejected, he was nevertheless thankful "to the Supreme Disposer of events for the merciful dispensation of His providence in bringing affairs of the country to a condition more favorable to peace and union than it has been of late, and though surrounded with dangers."[46]

The response to Clay's measure among the businessmen in Boston was mixed. P. C. Brooks looked upon it as a disgraceful surrender and so did Harrison Gray Otis, but Otis thought the compromise would secure the manufacturers better protection than they had been led to think possible. It would, be said, enable the existing establishments "to indemnify themselves against the consequences of the reduction intended in 1842, by giving them almost a monopoly in the meantime—as the inducements to institute new establishments would be feeble."[47] Nathan Appleton had said a year earlier that his large woolen goods company was not dependent on the tariff. Prosperity in the New England textile industry coincided with the debates in Congress and quieted criticism of the compromise. Less than a month after the passage of the bill, Abbott Lawrence wrote to Clay that the manufacturers believed the new law was wise and fair.[48] Everett lost interest and was pleased to have the divisive issue set aside.

* * * * *

Congress had no sooner passed the tariff bill in June 1833 than the heated debates over rechartering the Bank of the United States came to a close and the bill went to the president. He delivered a veto message that, from Everett's viewpoint, was a call for warfare. He denounced rule by the rich, charged that the bank was guilty of corruption, and had failed to establish a sound and uniform currency, and he held the bank unconstitutional. To this he added that the president had an equal right with the Supreme Court to rule on constitutional questions.

After his victory in the election Jackson determined to make certain that the bank could not, at some more propitious time, again ask for a new charter. What the alternative would be to the bank was not clear, but at the time Jackson faced the immediate problem of where to place government deposits. He appointed Amos Kendall, an opponent of the bank, to investigate which banks could be entrusted with the funds. By September 1833, he was ready to launch the country on a new course and announcd the removal of government deposits from the Bank of the United States.

In his message to Congress in December, Jackson defended his removal policy. He explained that he did so "upon the highest consideration of public interest and public duty" and pronounced the bank an electioneering engine. The question, he said dramatically, was whether there was to be a democracy or a moneyed aristocracy, "whether the people of the United States are to govern through representaives chosen by their unbiasted suffrage or whether the money and power of a giant corporation are to be secretly exerted to influence their judgement and control their decision."[49]

Everett, in a speech he wrote but that he did not have the opportunity to deliver, charged that the withdrawal went beyond the law and that to suddenly withdraw $8 million dollars from the bank was an act of injustice. Time and again Congress had expressed its confidence in the bank. Legislative committess, after laborious inquiries, had cleared it of wrongdoing and affirmed that the bank was a necessity. In defiance of the law in the bank's charter, Jackson had ordered the withdrawal of deposits. "Under the present administration," Everett wrote, "the Executive is everything and Congress nothing."[50]

As Jackson's biographer acknowledges, the president was ignorant of financial matters and had a "total lack of appreciation for the B.U.S. [Bank of the United States] and its importance to the American economy."[51] Only such a man could have reduced the pros and cons of the complicated question of centralized banking to this simple moral dimension, but it was his presenting the issue in these moral tones that won him popular support and enabled him to kill the bank.

Everett, and leaders like Henry Clay and Daniel Webster, were convinced of the necessity of a centralized banking system that was able to exercise some control over credit and to moderate the violent swings from overexpansion and speculation to periods of bank failures and economic collapse. Indeed, Jackson's own cabinet had been greatly dismayed when he first presented his plan to them.

That Nicholas Biddle misused his power before the bank war appears doubtful. Historians have refuted the charges of improper uses of the bank's funds. Bray Hammond, in his study *Bank and Politics in America from the Revolution to the Civil War,* and

Thomas Payne Govan, in his scholarly biography of Nicholas Biddle, after careful and detailed examination of the evidence, concluded that the charges against the bank were unwarranted. Govan found that Biddle sought to stay free of politics before the bank war and that he extended more loans to the followers of Jackson than he did to National Republicans.[52]

Once the bank became a focal point of politics, however, the various investigations of the bank's wrongdoings were not directed to the facts or to serious studies of the problem of how to recncile the necessity of central banking with the protection of the public interest.

Everett served as one of two minority members of the last committee to investigate the bank. The meetings of the committee of the House with the committee representing the bank were reduced to fiascoes. The House Committee demanded that the bank turn over its books and that these books be delivered to the committee's hotel rooms. The bank was willing to open the books but would not permit them to be examined except in the presence of the bank. The visiting committee then issued subpeonas ordering the bank's representatives to permit the investigating committee to take the books to the hotel and to examine the books free of the presence of the bank's representatives.[53]

The majority of the committee presented a report calling for issuing subpeonas to each member of the committee that had represented the bank charging them with contempt. The rash and indiscreet recommendations of the majority presented Everett with the opportunity to expose the majority to an exhibition of their errors. Everett's charges reduced the majority report to a hastily and ill-conceived accusation.

Everett held that the committee could only investigate what the bank's charter authorized Congress to investigate. The charter only authorized investigating violations of the bank's charter. It had no authority to go beyond this limitation. The five points raised by the majority as a basis for charging the officers of the bank with contempt were points that were beyond the authority of the committee. The committee was wrong in demanding that the books of the bank be delivered to their hotel rooms, and the banks refusal was wholly reasonable. The bank committee had given adequate reasons for refusing. The bank's action provided no grounds for contempt proceedings. The insistence by the bank's members that they be present at the examination of the books was reasonable, and it was equally reasonable that they asked for the charges against the bank. Everett held that there was no basis for charging contempt,

Everett's Role in Politics

and to call the officers of the bank to stand trial before the House of Representatives was wholly unjustified. To substitute "for the course of procedures prescribed by law the uncertain process of this body, to drag the respondents from the bar of the impartial tribunal of the country and place them at this bar where we ourselves are the party offended, the judge, jury, and executioner" was unwarranted.[54]

* * * * *

Everett gave close attention to voters in his district, and he was reelected five times with majorities of two to one. Many of his constituents were engaged in shipping, and many of those had spoliation claims including P. C. Brooks, his father-in-law, that dated back to the wars of the French Revolution and the Napoleonic Wars.

The first set of these claims grew out of French attacks on ships during the Undeclared War with France under the administration of John Adams. In the treaty with France negotiated in 1800, it was agreed to surrender spoliation claims against France. This left open the question as to whether the federal government was liable for the losses suffered.

On his election to Congress, Everett became the chief spokesman for the claimants. There was strong opposition to paying the claims led by Abljah Mann of New York and later by Churchill Cambreleng, both Jacksonians. Mann contended that many of the claims were dubious.[55] Others held that the treaty did not cancel claims. Everett, in a speech in the House, presented a convincing case to the countrary, contending that the United States in surrendering the claims against France assumed the obligation. The opposition cared little about the losses suffered by New Englanders; the losses, they said, constituted no more than a contribution to the war effort. In many instances, the opponents held, the losses had been covered by insurance. Everett affirmed that the claims could not be set aside by such arguments. "If something be not due to the claimants under this state of facts," he said, "the national principles of rights are illusory, and the provision of the Constitution is worthless, which prescribes 'private property shall not be taken for public use without just compensation.'"[56] Politics overruled Everett's principles, and his bill in the House met defeat. Not until 1846 did the House pass a bill providing for payment, and then President Polk buried the long-lost cause of the claimants with a veto.

A second set of spoliation claims against France related to American ships destroyed during the National Wars. At the close of those wars France labored under a staggering debt, and the United States agreed to wait before pressing the claims. Not until 1831, and then only after peremptory demands by the American minister, William C. Rives, did France agree to pay $5 million, a sum the French held with good reason to be in excess of what was due.

France made no payment for the next five years. The political situation in France after Louis Philippe ascended the throne in 1830 caused the delay. The French population was divided into powerful factions of reactionary Royalists, admirers of Napoleon, and republicans. Uprisings against Louis Philippe were frequent, and the king could complain with some accuracy that he was the fairest game in the kingdom. The treaty with the United States was unpopular, and it was a useful weapon to use against the king. The dissident parties controlled the Chamber of Deputies and refused to appropriate the money to pay the United States.

The opposition to paying was strengthened by hostility to the United States based on fear that the rapidly growing and prosperous republic portended future danger. A combination of the two English-speaking nations meant complete control of the seas. France did her best to enlist the cooperation of the British, and these efforts only served to alienate the United States where there was fear that the two European powers would combine to curb American expansion.[57]

Relations reached a crisis in the summer of 1835 when, after protest by the American minister in Paris, Edward Livingston, the Chamber of Deputies once again failed to make the necessary appropriations. Livingston decided that the time had come for reprisals and recommended the shutting off of trade. Andrew Jackson reasoned that cutting off trade would impose great losses on the United States; instead he recommended the sequestration of all French property. This raised the prospect of war. The president had overruled his advisers who favored a milder tone. The cry now went up that the country faced a multimillion dollar war over a paltry $5 million claim.[58]

In January, only a month after Jackson's message, the Senate unanimously adopted a resolution declaring it inexpedient to adopt any measures. No such unanimity marked the debates in the House of Representatives. The House Committee on Foreign Affairs was no less anxious than the Senate to avoid war, but there still remained the difficulty of framing a report. The chairman of the committee, Charles Cambreleng of New York, called for three resolutions.[59] These recommended that there be no further negotiation, that the committee be discharged from further consideration of the question, and in the contingency preparation be undertaken to meet any emergency. Everett, leading Whig on the committee, was unsuccessful in eliminating the recommendation that there would be no further negotiation, and wrote a minority report opposing the recommendation of all three resolutions. His effort to reach a compromise with Cambreleng having failed, he now returned to his preference. Everett maintained that it was unwise to adopt resolutions when the future was changing from day to day. To pass resolutions posed the danger of saying something that had better not be said.

The Whigs in Massachusetts were appalled by Jackson's message and the prospect of war. The French Chamber was scheduled to meet and might meet the American demand. In any case, this was no time for hasty action. These were Everett's final days in Congress, and he was to deliver his final speech. He arose to speak, he said, for the purpose of addressing the president, and he wished it understood that what he would say was not motivated by any vindictive spirit toward the president. An international crisis was no time to seek party advantage. He made a plea for peace:

> Let us adjure the President to exercise his vast power to preserve the peace of the country. Let the last years of his eventful life, already crowned with a variety of success and honor, be signalized by the glories of a war, not gallantly braved but honorably avoided.
> . . . I, too, sir, with my distinguished colleague [Mr. Adams] will admire the President's spirit. But spirit is not all that is wanted in great affairs. There must be prudence, there must be moderation, there must be wisdom.[60]

John Quincy Adams now delivered what was to be labeled a "furious war speech." He attacked the Senate for failure to act. It was guilty of dodging the question. He spoke bluntly of the possibility of war. Adams acted on the belief that in a time of danger it was important to present a united front. The speech alienated the Whigs at home where the legislature was in a deadlock over the selection of a senator. John Davis, the governor, had agreed to run at the behest of Webster. John Quincy Adams was also a candidate. Adams had a majority in the state Senate, but Davis had a slight majority in the House of Representatives. The outcome of that election would determine whether Davis would continue as governor or go to the Senate. If he went to the Senate, then Everett would be free to begin his campaign for governor.

War was avoided only after the French minister in Washington had been recalled and Edward Livingston had left his post in Paris.

Neither country wanted war, but France demanded an apology from Jackson. The question of peace hung on the issue of national honor.

Once again European rivalry played into the hands of the United States. France had reason to fear that recent moves by Russia could lead to war. The British, allied to France, in the event of war with Russia, did not wish to have her ally bogged down in a war with the United States. The British, by means of delicate and quiet diplomacy, eased the way to a solution.[61]

* * * * *

The power of Jackson jolted Everett. That power was based on the president's popularity, the cohesiveness of his party, and the general but vague discernment of a large part of the public that conditions were no longer what they had been and that all was not right.

Amid the kaleidoscopic changes stood Andrew Jackson and the Whigs. Their incapacity to confront a new age in a constructive manner constituted a tragedy. Andrew Jackson was a great leader but the path he chose led to a past constructed out of dreams and spiced with filial piety. On the other side were Everett and the Whigs, more attuned to the new age, but out of tune with the frustrations and the concerns of the mass of the populace. The Whig party, established in 1834, was composed of remnants of factions critical of Jackson for different reasons. The party was as divided as the age itself, and it was rendered more so by the rivalry of its two great leaders, Daniel Webster and Henry Clay.

These weaknesses were added to by the conflicting sectionalisms. Both parties found it necessary to win support in all sections. To be successful in gaining power each party carefully avoided measures that could only win them more enemies than friends. The most frightening of these was the slavery question and the Bank of the United States. On these questions they were strictly exparte, and their adversarial relationship aborbed most of their energies. Only rarely as when Henry Clay laid the tariff issue to rest for ten years with his compromise of the tariff, thanks to the fears inspired by the nullification movement, did a statesman come forth and break the log jam.

Jacksonianism was a product of the new frustrations and fragmentation of society. It clashed with Everett's view of the states as a community of interdependent people who were free to think and were not subordinated to party dictates, or who chose to follow a leader simply because he was popular. Everett believed that all great literature, the discoveries of science, and the improvements in technology were triumphs of human thought and evidence of the genius of the human mind when left free to think. He applied this to politics as well, and therefore he could write that a rightly organized state was the greatest engine of moral power known to man and the ingenius discoveries and the wonders of art were "as nothing, compared with the collective, perpetuated influence on human affairs and human happiness, of a well-constituted, powerful commonwealth." In this Everett demonstrated that his ties to a bygone age remained strong.

The methods of Jackson and the passions of party politics left Everett disillusioned. After the close of the twenty-second Congress he spoke in Salem. "The terrific force of party discipline, the personal popularity of the President," he said, "have wrought a practical Revolution." The legislators "not only support the chief of their party, in measures which they know to be highly injurious, but support him in such a way, as to make him think they really approve those measures and admire and reverence him for pursuing them."[62]

* * * * *

Everett's experience in Congress was not unrewarding in terms of the reputation he earned as a hard-working member and an able speaker, but the administration in office won all the battles. Not one of the major aims of Everett and the Whigs came to fruition. The party they represented was constantly on the defensive, whereas the Jacksonians controlled centre stage. As Everett saw the political situation the government had fallen into the hands of a party that won public support by demagoguery. Its success, however, lay in large part in the charismatic leader who was able to identify himself with the people. Jackson was a Nationalist, but he did not see as his mission that of enlarging the role of government. He enjoyed wide support, and, in the eyes of the public, was a hero and an uncompromising defender of the country's interests. Unlike the Whigs, Jacksonians were aggressive in building a party organization and in welcoming aboard new support, more particularly the rapidly multiplying immigrants.

The political scene in Massachusetts by 1835 was honeycombed with ill feelings. Not all Whigs closed their minds to the party's need for embracing a more open policy and a willingness to listen to dissident voices, but the oligarchy of the party held on to power with tenacity, and they bitterly attacked the most mild of dissidents. Anti-Masonry was viewed as a potential enemy that would undermine control by the elite and the stalwarts, and revolutionize the state. Everett became a target of distrust because he sought to work with the Anti-Masons. To correspondents who raised questions as to his party loyalty, Everett explained that the only hope of displacing the Jacksonians lay in cooperation with the Anti-Masons. This failed to allay the distrust.

When George Bancroft entered politics, he drew on his historical studies. In his first volume of the history of the United States there was a strong note of filial piety and admiration for the American people who had overcome each obstacle along the way. It was the people who pulled together and pooled their combined wisdom that had made the United States great. This was not offensive to the reading public, but when he applied it to the politics of his own day, joined it with observations that there was a growing gap between rich and poor, and that the solution to the banking crisis lay in abolishing the Bank of the United States and restoring free competition, he alarmed the conservatives. The attacks surprised Bancroft who considered himself a loyal Whig. He was in agreement with Whig principles, but he also saw his role as an intellectual to stand aside and share his learning with the people who would eagerly grasp for truth.[63]

Bancroft and Everett had much in common. They had been friends for years and remained friends throughout the political upheavals. Like Everett, Bancroft came to believe that his ability to sway audiences testified to the political validity of his writings and his oratory. The two friends differed in that Everett knew well that to challenge Daniel Webster or the oligarchy could result in political suicide. In April 1833, Everett had warned his brother, Alexander, who was anxious to be elected to Congress, that he would be embarrassed if he did not support Webster for president.[64] Alexander soon learned that Edward was correct.

Bancroft's lengthy publication on the bank question suggested to the Boston Whigs that Bancroft would support Jackson. Bancroft promptly denied this, but he did not back down on the bank question. The Whig newspaper in Boston, *The Atlas,* charged that Bancroft had been contaminated by German philosophy, that he was no longer an orthodox-believing Unitarian, and that only the idle "in the halls of infidelity and atheism, the dram shops and the dram cellars" who "lives off the earnings of other industrious people," would vote for such a man.[65] Shocked by the attacks, he wrote to his friend Edward Everett, "The Community was made to believe that there was danger the Bible would be taken out of their hands. . . . Democracy was said to be a branch of atheism . . . a perfect fever was got up."⁶⁶ His candidacy for the General Court was a decisive failure.

The alarmist cries of the Whig newspapers and Whig harassments of dissenters did not elicit vindictive charges from Whig leaders such as Everett or John Davis. Daniel Webster, however, had no intention of permitting the independents to wreck his Whig party in Massachusetts. He had long since distrusted John Quincy Adams who was among the very few who did not hesitate to take issue with him. Webster entertained no fears as to Everett's loyalty, and took comfort in the fact that Everett was not a man who would lend himself to be used by mischievous men to divide the party. Everett's flirting with the Anti-Masons does not contradict this. In his dealings with the Anti-Masons he always put first the interests of the Whig party. His close association with John Quincy Adams and their friendship remained, but Everett was a follower of Webster and not of Adams. It was Webster and not Adams who called the tune in Massachusetts politics.

John Quincy Adams's son, Charles Francis, was as yet an outside observer of the Whigs, busy editing his grandfather's papers, and trying to put the family's finances in order, but he was a gadfly by inheritance. He spurned the Jacksonians as men of ignorance and charlantry. Adams was a Whig, but he had contempt for the ruling Whig oligarchy in Massachusetts. The ruling Whigs, he charged, closed their eyes to the evil of slavery and failed to deal intelligently with the banking and currency questions. The merchants dominated the Whig party, and merchants, said Adams, invariably thought the only thing at stake was their own fortunes. He deplored the failure to stand up to France on the payment of debts. The nation's dignity received no consideration. Merchants feared their profits would be endangered.⁶⁷

Because Everett and Charles Francis Adams were married to sisters, the two men were thrown together. In the 1830s, it was a torturous relationship. After a meeting with Evertt in 1833, Adams wrote: "Mr. Everett is one of the most unpleasant men in private society I have ever met. He strikes me as artificial, rarely expressing sentiment of any kind and never one from his heart, and covering everything with a perpetual tone of persiflage. I do not like him."⁶⁸ After hearing Everett speak at a memorial service in honor of Lafayette, Adams wrote in his diary, "His modes of hitting the audience remain the same, but there is no depth of maturity of thought, no greatness of view, no ingredients that make the Statesman or the Philosopher. As a popular festival orator he will be unrivalled, but I doubt his success as a name for futurity."⁶⁹

The relationship was further poisoned during Everett's final months in Congress. John Quincy Adams was a candidate for the vacant seat in the Senate. Webster maneuvered to avoid having Adams as his colleague in the Senate. In December, after Everett resigned, but while he was filling out his term in the House of Representatives, Webster, unbeknownst to Everett before this time, conferred with John C. Davis, candidate for governor in Massachusetts, and persuaded Davis to be a candidate for the Senate. In this way it might be possible to defeat John Quincy Adams. The contest between Adams and Davis was close. Webster looked on Adams as the Anti-Masonic candidate who should be defeated so as to put an end to the quarrel between the Whigs and the Anti-Masons.[70]

Charles Francis Adams took a sinister view. He saw it as a maneuver on the part of Everett to become governor. The facts appear to be that the contest in the General Court of Massachusetts could have gone either way, but reports of John Quincy Adams's fiery speech in the House calling for a bold stand against France on the debt question alarmed Boston. Adams called for full support of Jackson and held that national honor was at stake and must be upheld even if it meant war.

Reports of Adams's speech turned the tide against Adams.[71] Davis went to the Senate, and the way was now open for Everett to be nominated for governor. He faced the division between the Whigs and the Anti-Masons. He had already demonstrated sympathy with Anti-Masonry and, in a postelection speech in 1834, had expressed hope for a coalition.

Charles Francis Adams believed his father was being robbed of a Senate seat by Webster and Everett. Certainly the maneuver originated with Webster. It is equally true that Everett raised no objections. Charles Francis Adams now sought to put Everett in a dilemma by suggesting to the leaders of the Anti-Masons that they nominate Everett first. They did, but the Whigs, despite some opposition by Masons, also nominated Everett. Adams noted that Everett's support among the Whigs came from Boston and that there was strong opposition in the western part of the state. The Masonic Whigs refused to vote for the Anti-Masonic candidate for lieutenant governor and nominated another man for that position. The episode prompted Charles Francis Adams to write in his diary concerning Everett: "He is a double hearted man if there is one on the face of the earth."[72] Adams never appears to have withdrawn the charges against Everett, but their personal relations greatly improved in the future. Everett, with equal vehemence, denied that he was guilty of maneuvering so as to get the nomination for governor. Everett was not, at least, directly responsible. What occurred was in large part due to the resentment felt by Masonic Whigs because he had been willing to run on the Anti-Masonic ticket in 1833. At the time Everett probably made the mistake of failing to take Charles Francis, who was thirteen years his junior, seriously. In 1838, only three years later, Adams, though still disliking Everett, observed that Everett was showing him respect that he had not formerly shown.

Everett's difficulties were not to end with his election as governor. Both the Whigs and the Democrats were approaching a stage when they would achieve full status as political parties, but the divisions among the Whigs continued.

His difficulties stemmed from his willingness to play Webster's handy man. In 1834, Everett took the lead in asking wealthy industrialists to contribute to a fund to support Webster, who once again was in financial difficulty. He asked for contributions of one thousand dollars each; how much he raised is not known. It was Everett, who in response to instructions from Webster, agreed to launch a movement to nominate Webster for president. In each instance he defended Webster as the one man who could save the country from the levelers, the only man who had fought consistently the battles of property, order, and law. Webster was a hero in Massachusetts, but he was also deeply distrusted as reports revealed that at the same time he was defending the Bank of the United States he was rendering legal services to Nicholas Biddle and collecting fees from Biddle.

3
Governor of Massachusetts

In his four terms as governor of Massachusetts, Everett proposed constructive programs and demonstrated concern about the widening gap between the rich and poor, the desperate need for reform of public education, the banking and currency problems, and other of the new reforms that were being widely discussed. He, at the same time, confronted the serious difficulty of presiding over a legislature that was sharply divided. Conservative Whigs could not forgive him for his consenting to the nomination by the Anti-Masonic party. These same Whigs failed to support many of his proposed reforms. At the same time many Anti-Masons, led by Benjamin F. Hallett, charged Everett with betraying them.

The election campaign erupted in such sharp divisions that Everett expressed regret that he was a candidate. No sooner had the Anti-Masons nominated Everett than they passed resolutions endorsing Van Buren for president and nominated their own man for lieutenant governor rather than going along with the Whig nominee. Everett was firmly committed to supporting Daniel Webster for president.

In the election, many Whigs deserted Everett. He won the election by 37,555 to Morton's 25,227. Everett held that a great many Whigs in Boston had deserted him and that he had won because of Anti-Masonic support. Hull, the Whig candidate for lieutenant governor won over the Anti-Masonic candidate, William Foster, who was first nominated by the Democrats, by only 32,683 to 30,683. Everett polled up 2,330 more votes than Hull. Foster received 6,456 votes more than Morton. Given these figures, the historian, Ronald P. Formisano, concludes that in all probability many Anti-Masonic voters supported Everett. In the course of the campaign, Webster, anxious to win over the Anti-Masons, "led a behind the scenes movement for Everett."[1]

The strong feelings against Everett on the part of Masonic Whigs during the preceding months and the harassment of Everett by Hallett, leader of the Anti-Masons, caused him great anxiety. He confided in his brother, that he did not care if he won or lost. If he did win, he faced the "prospect of an Adm. [administration] rendred by the same causes, the source of eternal perplexity and torment. My only consolation is that I am rendered indifferent to the event, which is no unlikely result of the schism which has sprung up between the two parties who nominated me."2

Family tragedy followed victory at the polls. Two days before he took office his daughter Gracie died. He went directly from the burial to assume his duties of governor. Charles Francis Adams now could not help but be sympathetic. He was moved to write, "My heart is now softened towards him. He has miseries which make him a pitiable object."3

Everett's inaugural address called for a series of reforms, each of which had been widely discussed. The welfare of the people, he said, was the sole object of government. With that as a keystone he presented a program more liberal than many Whigs were ready to accept. To preserve political and social institutions required more than merely holding fast to that which is good. It was necessary to introduce "those improvements and reforms, which may be demanded by the growth of knowledge in the science of government; by the elevation of the standard of public morality; and in general by the lessons of experience." The people of America should be the last to blindly resist change. It was a duty "to imitate our forefathers in the great trait of their characters, the courage of reform."4

To a later generation this might seem like no more than a firm grasp of the obvious, but Everett knew only too well—and his tenure as governor was to confirm it—how resistant to change the public could be. Everett was not the originator of what needed to be done, but the instrument by which ideas already under discussion might be implemented. An asute politician, he reached only for the possible.

He called for a law code to replace the common law, a reform that enjoyed stronger support among the Democrats than among the Whigs. Once again he gave his opinion on secret organizations that held that they should abandon their secrecy. Three years earlier the legislature had narrowly missed outlawing them. He called for the total abolition of imprisonment for failure to pay debts. John Davis had urged this reform in 1833, and in 1835 the Democrat, Robert Rantoul, introduced a bill providing the same. Everett also recommended the abolition of capital punishment except for murder. The banking system, already subject to severe criticism, also received attention, and Everett recommended an investigation. The existing law limited the rate of interest a bank could charge, but the law, he said, was being evaded in many ways. He also proposed that the existing tax of 1 percent of a bank's capital be changed to a tax on its income. Everett had long been friendly to the state building railroads, but he called for further support.[5]

To provide the leadership necessary to get this program adopted posed a challenge, given the situation in the legislature. The House of Representatives had no less than six hundred members, and it was almost hopelessly unwieldy. The Whig majority in the Senate was sharply divided. It balloted eighteen times before agreement was reached on a chairman.[6]

In addition to the difficulty created by the divisions in the Whig party, Benjamin Hallett continued to make trouble. In an editorial in the *Advocate* just before Everett took office he launched a campaign phrased in Jacksonian rhetoric. The legislature, said Hallett, should devote itself to building up "Anti-Masonic Democracy." The lines, he continued, must be distinctively drawn between Aristocracy and Democracy, monopoly and antimonopoly. "Let the lines be drawn here, distinctly, and the people will assert their supremacy and take the state from the hands of Masonic Whig Aristocracy, who have so long ruled it with a rod of iron."[7] Two days later, Hallett again called for a people's war against the Whigs.

When the legislature took up Everett's recommendations for an investigation of banks, Hallett charged Caleb Cushing with seeking to scuttle the proposal and predicted that the investigation would end honoring the banks. Cushing had been critical of several practices of the banks. When a committee was appointed to investigate the banks, Hallett dismissed it as a fraudulent gesture. The committee, Hallett said, was dominated by Whigs friendly to bankers selected by the president of the Senate. The Whigs, he declared, "have the power yet, and the people must submit to the rule of money over men, for one year longer."[8] At the same time Hallett devoted his columns to supporting Martin Van Buren.

Hallett shortly launched a battle cry against Everett because some of his appointments were Masons, and he charged Everett with violating a pledge. Everett protested that he had never made such an agreement, and that when he made appointments he did not inquire as to whether a well-qualified man was or was not a Mason. Hallett's campaign placed Everett in an embarrassing position, and he noted in his diary that "never was a man so grievously wronged."[9] Webster sought to comfort him and advised that he take up his pen, publish anonymously, and destroy Hallett "who is a vile fellow."[10] On his brother Alexander's advice Everett decided to ignore Hallett. He concluded, "there is a darkness of heart evinced in what he says of me in his paper of the 8th, which bids defiance to reply from anyone less of a brigand than himself."[11] He attributed Hallett's bitter attacks to the fact that he refused to support Van Buren.

The attacks on Everett, usually phrased in Jacksonian terms, was actually directed less at Everett than at Daniel Webster. Everett saw through the campaign that was carried on in the daily press. To his trusted colleague John Davis, he raised the question as to whether Massachusetts should continue to support Webster's candidacy for the presidency given the fact that at best he could probably carry only Massachusetts.[12] It was a cynical game. He suspected, with near certainty, that the Anti-Masons had nominated John Quincy Adams two years before because they hoped to thereby weaken Webster.[13] Everett thought that Webster could only win in Massachusetts by a very narrow margin. "When you wish to whip a dog, any hedge will furnish a stick," he wrote to Hallett.[14]

During his first months in office, Hallett hounded him with charges of betrayal. Everett, in making appointments, chose not to ask whether a man was a Mason. Whenever he did appoint a Mason, Hallett seized on it. After appointing Timothy Reed, Everett learned with regret that Mr. Timothy Reed was a Mason.[15] "I say with regret," Everett continued, "because the appointment of Masons to office furnishes those who wish to carry over the Anti-Masons to Van Buren with a plausible pretext for assailing my administration, with which under present circumstances the success of the Webster electoral ticket is identified." It was obvious to Everett that the appointment of a Mason played into the hands "of those who want to destroy E E's [Edward Everett] administration in order to defeat Webster."[16]

* * * * *

That as governor he would call for strengthening the public schools seemed inevitable. In his own life, education had opened doors to a career, but more important, his schooling had enriched his life with the finest literature, a knowledge of history, and given to him rich resources to draw on in finding meaning and broadening his horizons. His reading bestowed new perspectives and gave him a vantage point from which to view rapid change and to sense that the changes of his day heralded a new era. It had given shape to his personal philosophy.

Those who live from day to day within the narrow circle of family and neighborhood were, for Everett, the underprivileged. Everett's philosophy included myths that he lived by and saw as absolute truths, but true or not they gave meaning to his life. That truth was ever-changing, the philosophy of relativism, which was to capture the twentieth-century mind, was far beyond his ken and yet to be formulated; however, he appears to have dimly recognized it when he commented that the new truths of each generation of scholars existed only to be corrected by the next generation. He must first awaken his constituents to the existing state of public education. Therefore he cited the sad facts—bare and ill furnished one-room school houses, without books, where teachers, many of whom were there because they had failed to make the grade into the professions, who could do no more than transfer a thin slice of their own limited knowledge to their pupils during a four-month period in the winter.[17]

In 1837, Everett recommended to the legislature that the $2 million recently received by the state in payment for the expense of the state militia in the War of 1812 be allotted on a matching basis to each town's expenditures for education. This common sense proposal was rejected by the legislature but only after prolonged debate.

Everett did succeed in winning the legislature's support to create a board of education. Two of his appointments are of special interest, namely Horace Mann and Robert Rantoul. Horace Mann was not well known at the time, but he had demonstrated both energy and ability in the state legislature. When he was elected chairman of the board, Mann promptly launched a crusade. He traveled to all parts of the state on horseback campaigning for support of education, and he, more than anyone, deserves credit for what occurred.

Robert Rantoul of Gloucester, who had served only one term in the legislature, was a Democrat. In several respects Rantoul and Everett had much in common. Both had been brilliant students, both had a zest for historical studies, both wrote poetry and excelled in prose, both were lovers of books. Rantoul was a lawyer and made a reputation in the courts. Rantoul, as a member of the minority party in a state dominated by the Whigs, was a fiery critic of many Whig policies, however. Conversely, Rantoul and Everett on occasion found themselves in basic agreement. Both men were opponents of capital punishments, and although they disagreed on the paper money question they did recommend, in part, some of the same reforms. Rantoul was not a man who could be dismissed easily for he was a master of the subjects on which he proposed to speak. Webster vetoed the proposed appointment of Rantoul. A third member of the board of education was James G. Carter, who had already been active in promoting school reform.

Everett turned to educating his audiences on why universal public education should have the highest priority. Here he was at his best, partly because he was wholehearted on the issue and partly because he knew a great deal about education. Speaking at the commencement at Williams College 16 August 1837 he said, "It is at once melancholy and fearful to reflect how much intellect is daily perishing from the false direction given it in the morning of life."[18] Intellect, he said, was a faculty in need of nourishment and discipline; without that it would sink down and die before a man's natural death. "Trained and instructed, strengthened by wise discipline, and guided by pure principle, it ripens into an intelligence but little lower than the angels."[19]

Even in Massachusetts, charged Everett, "there exists . . . a woeful waste of mental power, through a neglect of education." The time spent in school was too limited, teachers were often incompetent, and able teachers were deprived of maps and the necessary books. Too often "the training of the young is entrusted to the cheapest hand that can be hired to do the work—to one who is barely able to pass a nominal examination, by a committee sometimes more ignorant than himself."[20]

In Europe, Everett said, states waste their resources, "too often wrung from their rightful possessors," on palaces, massive fortifications, mighty armies, and overgrown navies. Those countries, given the condition of European politics, would probably not escape from the system, but "with us on the contrary . . . there is nothing to prevent the appropriation, to moral and religious objects, of a great part of those resources which are elsewhere lavished on luxury and war." What existed in Europe was "a monstrous perversion of human energy."[21]

Education, said Everett, held the key that opened the door to appreciation and understanding of the history of man and the wonders of the material universe. What was needed was the raising of the human vision. "A mere book worm is a worthless character, but a mere money getter is no better."[22] In a public where people vote, influence decisions in major disputes, and serve on juries, education of the electorate is indispensable.

At a school dinner in Faneuil Hall, Everett pleaded for more adequate support of schools. The support of schools, he said, was too often regarded as simply another item in estimating a year's budget, "like lighting or paving the streets."[23] People were free to decide whether money should be spent for street improvement, new buildings, or improved water supply, but it was not so with education. Education was too important to be treated in this manner.

The campaign to improve schools brought to the surface the need for training teachers. A member of the board of education, James Carter, took the lead in the state legislature. In 1838, the legislature voted to establish four schools to be called normal schools. When the one in Barre in Worcester County opened, Everett spoke. Teaching, he said, ought to be a major profession. Teaching, he contended, called for special preparation quite as much as did the other professions. The duties of a teacher were as "important, complicated, and arduous" as the practice of law, the ministry, or medicine. It was not a mere piece of job work to which any one could turn his hand. It was a professional calling, which required knowledge, judgment, and experience.[24]

Anticipating the query as to why training was now required when it had not been necessary in the past, and the assertion that there were fine teachers who had never had such training, he acknowledged that there were uniquely talented people. Even they would have benefited from further study of the art, however. Teaching had become a lifetime profession, whereas formerly men had taught for a year or two and then, if talented, moved on to one of the established professions. Some teachrs learned by their early experiences at the cost of their pupils, others failed to profit by their mistakes. "We are," he said, "brought to the necessity of some specific preliminary preparation for the office of teacher."[25]

What was necessary to success in teaching? A teacher ought to know much more than the learner can be expected to acquire. He must see the truth in all its aspects "or he cannot present it in just that shape in which the young mind can comprehend it. He must, as he holds the diamond up to the sun, turn the facets round and round, till the pupil catches its luster. The teacher must almost know what the student has to unlearn. He must determine what the student must do for himself and what the instructor may do with him and for him. He must learn the art of discipline, how to control youthful spirits."[26]

* * * * *

A second major aim of Everett as he took office was codification of the common law. Since 1820, the movement had gained strength by insisting that common law was judge-made law.[27] The preceding year, in 1835, Judge Joseph Story published his article praising common law, but he also acknowledged that a code for a particular area of law was practical.[28] Advocates of a code were generally Democrats, foremost among them Robert Rantoul, who attacked common law as judge-made law.[29] The advocates contended that the public had a right to know what the law was and that the law should be stated so that every citizen could understand it. Everett shared the view. In his student days at Göttingen he had studied the Justinian code. Now he found that members of the legal profession had great doubts. Among these was Judge P. O. Thatcher. Everett wrote to him stating that if Justinian and Napoleon could construct a code it certainly was not an empty dream. He told Thatcher that he would be willing to take advice, but he also expected his friends to tolerate in him "a little freedom in occasionally expressing an opinion which they may deem too liberal."[30]

The legislature acted promptly in approving a commission to study the feasibility of codification. Everett appointed Justice Story to chair it and gave thought to appointing Rantoul, but Webster discouraged naming him.

Justice Joseph Story, one of the foremost judicial figures in American history, professor of law at Harvard since 1829 and the man most responsible for the preeminence of the Harvard Law School, distinguished by his extensive scholarly writings, and whose decision revealed a remarkable breadth of learning, was an intimate friend and an admirer of Everett. Story was reluctant to accept the appointment, and he had serious doubts about codification. He wrote to an English friend that he did not approve "but the present state of popular opinion here makes it necessary to do something on the subject."[31]

Story wrote the report of the commission. It began by stating that the answer to the question as to whether codification was practical involved two different propositions. The answer was in the negative if what was sought was "not only all the general principles of that law, but all the diversities, ramifications, exceptions, and all the qualifications of those principles, as they ought to be applied, not only to the past and present, but to all future combinations of circumstances in the business of human life." To make a code adequate to the business and rights and modifications of property in any one single age and foresee the future called for a degree of wisdom and foresight that "belongs not to any human beings."[32]

A more limited codification, the report stated, was possible, however. The common law regarding trials and punishments of crimes could be codified, and the commission thought it highly desirable to codify the law with respect to civil rights and duties of persons in social relations.[33] The legislature thought otherwise. It only approved the drafting of a criminal code, and when that was completed and presented to the legislature, it was rejected.[34]

* * * * *

In his message to the legislature, Everett deplored the fact that there were one thousand individuals in prison for debt. The evil first came to the attention of Everett in 1826 when his brother Oliver was placed in jail for failure to pay his debts. Oliver and his family lived on a farm near Fitchburg. Illness and an absence of good management of family finances reduced the family to a near subsistence level. Edward and his brother Alexander were the sole supporters, and they furnished funds on a regular basis, but in August 1826, Oliver failed to pay some debts and was put in jail. Everett protested to the local official, Josiah Loring, asking what was to be gained by placing a husband and father in jail who had a sick wife and several children.

The movement to abolish imprisonment for debt owed much to Louis Dwight who had founded the Boston Prison Discipline Society in 1826. Dwight's reports, describing in detail the condition of prisons, made a major impact not only in New England, but in New York, Pennsylvania, and Ohio. Imprisonment for debt had been abolished by 1829 in Ohio and Kentucky. New York did so in 1831.[35]

The practice of imprisonment for debt offered a glaring example of the public's willingness to dismiss poverty as a result of individual depravity. The impracticality of the policy was illustrated in the fact that debts remained unpaid by a ratio of eighty-six to one. Most of those imprisoned had only small debts. A study by the Boston Prison Discipline Society revealed that in fifty-three prisons the entire number imprisoned for more than one hundred dollars was 416, or as a ratio of one to seven, compared with prisoners owing twenty dollars or less.[36]

In the 1830s, imprisonment for debt had largely given way to reform. The practice was in conflict with the humanitarian spirit of the decade. Imprisonment for debt had become in some degree nominal. Thanks to the rise of the market economy the greater number of debtors were not delinquents but the victims of the business cycle and changed business conditions. Courts had ruled that the imprisoned debtor should have the freedom of the jail yard during the day, and the yard was finally ruled to be coterminous with the towns.[37] In 1834, the state legislature enacted a law abolishing imprisonment for debts contracted after that date. Social change had brought amelioration but not complete reform.

Everett found it useful to appeal to Whig principles of economics. At present, he observed, indiscriminate credit is given "and a great reason for it is that the creditor has the power over the person of the debtor, and if he can get his money no other way he can put him in jail and so compel the poor person to borrow from some friend or of his neighbor to pay, which they often do rather than see a poor family made wretched by the absence of the father." If imprisonment for debt were completely abolished, then credit would greatly diminish, and the poor "will get along the better for it. They will be put on their own exertions more, they will be more careful of their money, they will behave so as to deserve the aid of their friends."[38] This was part and parcel of the Whig view that overexpansion of credit was the factor that created the business cycle.

In 1838, Everett pointed out to the legislature that the law of 1834 had been evaded and should be revised. His proposal met the strongest opposition from lawyers in the Senate. In his final message to the legislature in 1839, he cited the fact that more than one thousand were in prison for debt, most of them being seamen who had been defrauded.

In his first message to the legisalture, Everett called for the abolition of capital punishment except in the cases of murder; Massachusetts law prescribed the death penalty for six offenses: murder, arson, rape, treason, armed robbery, and armed burglary. In February 1836, the House debated a bill to bring about reform. The bill's strongest supporter was Robert Rantoul, the influential Democrat. There appeared to be some hope of a modest change when a minority of the committee reported in favor of abolishing public executions, and eliminating capital punishment in cases of armed robbery and armed burglary.[39] In March, the House passed a bill including these reforms,[40] but there was a long delay. Opponents charged that the laws against these crimes would be useless if the death penalty was not imposed.[41] In the Senate critics ridiculed the governor's proposal as that of a dreamy philanthropist, and the Senate rejected the House bill.[42] In 1837, and again in 1838, Everett's proposal was rejected, but the following year capital punishment for armed burglary was abolished.[43]

In his inaugural message Everett took note of the changed nature of banking. He recommended the creation of a board to investigate the problem; that problem would emerge as a crisis two years later. There were 138 banks in the state. By the close of 1826, 32 had either failed or surrendered their charters. Those failing had assets of $5,500,000 and liabilities of $11,283,000. Shareholders lost $2,500,000. Many of the newer banks had begun with borrowed capital. As Everett was to say when the crisis came, the legitimate function of banks was to provide funds for borrowing, but now banks were started not to loan funds but to borrow funds. There were those who went into banking who borrowed enough specie for one day to meet the state requirement, and after the bank had been examined by the state bank commissioners the specie was returned to the lenders, although the directors had signed an oath to hold it as capital stock. Banks at large, an ever-larger number of them, held only limited specie while they circulated notes that they could not redeem. In one instance, a bank that failed closed with $110,000 in notes outstanding and only $36.71 in cash.[44]

When Everett's proposal came before the legislature the Whig newspaper, the *Columbia Centinel,* dismissed the question of giving the commission authority as no more than another cry against banks.[45] No question at the time aroused more heated feelings. Not until April 1838 did the legislature establish a bank commission. Because of the furor, Everett delayed appointing bank commissioners. When he did seek to make appointments, the first eight choices declined. He wrote in his diary, "Oh that I had wings of a dove." On 18 April he nominated three. The council rejected two and suggested two others. Everett accepted the council's suggestions, and the three were confirmed.[46] Great excitement ensued when the officers of a state bank refused to appear before a joint committee of the legislature. The committee then voted to issue subpoenas. The following day the Senate chamber filled to capacity. The officers of the bank had no choice but to appear.

In 1836, the Jackson administration issued the specie circular requiring that all sales of public lands must be paid for in specie. This move to curb the wild speculation came too late. To add to the difficulties the recent enactment of a bill providing for the distribution of the federal surplus among the states forced many banks to surrender their federal deposits. First the New York banks suspended specie payments. The panic spread to Boston where several banks failed.

The suspension of specie payments immediately became a political issue. The Democrats seized on the issue, charging that paper money was being foisted on the people and that the crisis was a result of Whig legislatures granting banks permission to increase their capital.

On 9 January 1838, in his annual message to the legislature,

Governor of Massachusetts

Everett discussed at length the causes of the banking crisis, held that the banks either had to suspend specie payment or go bankrupt, and proposed new legislation. He did not spare the banks from criticism. He recommended that banks be required to issue monthly public statements listing their investments. Their loose practices were one cause of the difficulties.[47] Of course, he did not fail to contend that the policies of the Jackson administration were basically at fault.

The governor's speech defended paper money when it was based on an adequate specie reserve. Bank notes were the only convenient way to transct business. The Democrats were quick to the attack. Robert Rantoul argued that it was the issuing of paper money that transferred the fruits of hard labor from the poor to the monied aristocracy. Rantoul proposed that when a bank was in difficulty the depositors who lived nearby were able to withdraw their savings, but the innocent noteholders scattered far and wide were the victims.[48] In contrast, Everett acknowledged the evils that had sprung up, but he held that a modern economy built around trade and commerce required banks and a convenient paper currency. The differences between Everett and Rantoul were not as great as the rhetoric appearing in the press suggested. Rantoul was not an enemy of banks, nor was he opposed to bank notes if the banks were required to hold sufficient specie to redeem those notes at any time.

By May 1838, many banks had resumed specie payments, and Everett could announce that the crisis was over. The legislation enacted did not wholly fulfill his recommendations but did so essentially.

* * * * *

The antislavery movement was soon to become of central importance. Everett clung to the view that the Constitution barred the federal government from interfering with slavery in states where it already existed. He firmly believed, however, that the federal government did have the power to prohibit its extension and that it likewise had the power to prohibit the slave trade in the District of Columbia. Slavery, he said, was a great evil, but the question must not be permitted to lead to a destruction of the Union. In these views he did not differ from Robert Rantoul. As Rantoul put it, "he who should so conduct an ill-advised and unsuccessful attempt to liberate three million human beings, as to render asunder the Union, and thereby bring down upon fourteen million education to the enjoyment of freedom, the miseries of political slavery, destroying the noblest fabric of free government that human wisdom ever erected, would incur a fearful weight of responsibility, leaving out of the account the gloomy possibility of civil and servile wars, with their manifold and varied horrors."[49]

In 1837 the state legislature passed resolutions condemning slavery and calling for the abolition of the slave trade in the District of Columbia. Everett signed the resolutions. At the same time he condemned the abolitionists as disrupters of the Union. His stance placed him in the ranks of those who chose a middle course, but political enemies still trotted out the speech he had made in Congress twenty years before. During the election campaign of 1837 one of his constituents wrote to Everett asking if he defended slavery. Everett replied slavery "is a social, political, and a moral evil of the first magnitude." The slaves should be emancipated as soon as it could be done peaceably "and in a manner to better the condition of the emancipated."[50] He cited the resolutions of the legislature denouncing the slave trade in the District of Columbia. The conditions of the slave trade in the nation's capital, he said, were the worst in the entire South, and it should be abolished.

The Texas question put the problem in a new light for Everett as well as for a large part of the North. The Constitution, he wrote, did not countenance an extension of slavery. He cited William Ellery Channing's bristling letter to Henry Clay denouncing the moves to annex Texas and extend slavery. That letter received his uncompromising approval. If we countenance an extension, Everett warned "we will stand condemned before the civilized world." To do so would render our pleas that the Constitution stood in the way of emancipation hollow. "It would be thought and thought justly, just lust of power and lust of gold had made us deaf of the voice of humanity and justice."[51]

Everett's views on emancipation changed after the British abolished slavery in the West Indies and instituted an apprenticeship system. He no longer dismissed general emanciptation as impractical. He still believed it could not be achieved immediately, probably not until 1876, when the country would celebrate the one hundredth anniversary of the Declaration of Independence. The slavery question would not go away, however, and it would soon make pale the many other reforms of the period. Everett would appear as a bystander in the face of the greatest moral issue of his generation. His horror of war and his commitment to the Union counterbalanced his moral convictions.

* * * * *

As a governor, Everett took advantage of the opportunity to promote use of state resources for the building of railroads. The Boston and Worcester railroad was completed in 1835, owing in part to the strong support from Everett's brother-in-law, Nathan Hale, editor of the Boston *Advertiser*. In 1832, the legislature granted the charter despite stiff opposition. Sufficient capital was raised by the sale of stock, and when completed the line paid 6 percent dividends.[52] Its success almost immediately led to a campaign to extend the railroad from Worcester to Albany. It was estimated that the extension would cost at least 3 million because it was almost twice the length of the original road, and the terrain often steep and rugged. Raising the money seemed an ever-greater challenge than building the railroad.

When the sale of stock fell far short of raising the capital necessary, interested manufacturers and merchants, led by Hale, called a meeting in Faneuil Hall for 7 October 1835. Everett urged the canvassers to miss no one in the sale of stock from "capitalist to carman." He paid tribute to the people of Massachusetts for their industry and energy and declared, "But the great thing wanting to the prosperity of Massachusetts is COMMUNICATION WITH THE WEST." The destinies of the country, he affirmed, "run east and west." Because the state's rivers ran north and south, Massachusetts was deprived of commercial relations with the West and Boston was isolated from the interior of the state. A railroad from Boston to Albany, with lateral routes, would place the capital city in its "natural position toward the interior." West of Albany was the Erie canal, the Great Lakes, and a chain of canals. "The entire west is moving to meet us. . . . But is there nothing left for us to do? Next to nothing, sir." A few miles more of railroad would give "to Massachusetts, to Berkshire, to Old Hampden, to Worcester, to Middlesex, to Boston, to our whole manufacturing, commercial, fishing interest, the benefit of a direct connection with the illimitable west."[53]

The drive was a success, but the shareholders recognized that more capital was required, and they turned to the state for assistance. The state legislature acted promptly and enacted a law that allowed the state to purchase $1 million in stock and appoint three directors to protect the public interest. Everett, as governor, signed the bill. To pay for the shares the state issued scrip, which they sold in London. One year later, having discovered that construction would cost $4 million, the state underwrote a bond issue for $2.1 million. The directors of the railroad then negotiated with Baring Brothers in London for the sale of the bonds.[54] Shortly thereafter Everett's administration promoted a series of other railroads that would converge on Boston.

Everett firmly believed that the state should help business. The accumulation of capital, the protection of property, and the availability of credit were the wellsprings of the community's well-being. Wealth in this country, he said in an address in September 1838, "may be traced back to industry and frugality; the paths which lead to it are open to all."[55] Factories, railroads, and steamboats, vanguards of the new age, could be constructed only at vast expense. "Strike out capital invested in manufactures, and you lay upon the society the burden of doing by hand all the work which was done by steam and water, by fire and steel, or it forgoes the use of the articles manufctured."[56] Credit was no more than the distribution of capital and served a necessary function; it benefited both the borrower and the public.

Everett, always the advocate and practitioner of prudence, also warned that the overextension of credit was "the disease of the age and country in which we live." He urged his Mercantile Library Association friends: "Never let the mere acquisition of wealth be an exclusive pursuit." Wealth, he warned, "is ennobled only in its uses."[57]

The completion of the railroad as far as Springfield in October 1839 called for a formal celebration, and Everett was invited to attend and give an oration. In a day when oratory could still thrill an audience, Everett had few equals, and that day in Springfield he delivered an oration celebrating the new age in transportation.

He had traveled from Boston that morning on the railroad he was to honor. For Everett it was a trip "over the noble embankments, and through the grand corridors of solid rock." He had seen the road "following the sparkling footsteps of the river through the highlands," and the "entire railroad, with its cars and engines," was one vast machine. "What a portent of art! Its fixed portion a hundred miles long; its moveable portion flying across the state like a weaver's shuttle; by the sea-side in the morning, here at noon, and back in the compass of an autumnal day!"[58] Railroads, he said, would bind the East and West and provide channels for the free flow of commerce.[59] Those who objected to the state granting funds for the building of the road were mistaken.

* * * * *

For several years the temperance movement had been gaining in strength, and in 1837 many of the temperance advocates were elected to the legislature. The reformers focused their attention on the state's license laws. Their crusade had no success until the closing days of the legislative session in April 1838, when with unexpected suddenness the fifteen-gallon law, which limited purchases to fifteen gallons or more, was passed. The law was aimed at dram shops serving liquor by the drink. In effect it discriminated against the poorer classes. The law, hastily conceived, did not apply to apothecaries and did not apply to wine. Almost without debate the bill passed the House by a vote of 229 to 106 and the Senate 24 to 9. This coup by the temperance people was facilitated by the provision that it would not go into effect until 1839. Because he disliked vetoing a bill passed by a large majority, Everett signed the bill but with great reservations. He was an advocate of temperance but not of abstinence.[60]

The hastily passed measure had all the weaknesses of a novelty drafted in a spirit of zeal untainted by either legal experience or realism. Ambiguities and contradictions within the law reflected the feverish moralism of its supporters. The critics were prompt in pointing these out in a widely publicized statement entitled "An Appeal to the Good Sense of the People of Massachusetts." The law rested on an invidious drawing of a line between the rich and the poor. The opponents asked if the prohibition of sales had as its purpose the common good why then should it not prohibit sales to the rich who alone could buy fifteen gallons. What was right for one class of citizens must also be right for another class. "One man goes into a shop, buys and drinks. Another man goes to his friend's house or his own sideboard, and takes and drinks. Where is the moral distinction to make one a crime and other not?" As the party seeking revision of the law charged, the law said that the rich person who could afford to buy fifteen gallons enjoyed the right to drink, but the poorer person who could not afford to do so did not have that right.[61]

When the critics published their report attacking the law, the law's defenders dismissed it as no more than bias and the self-interest of the seller. Those calling for revision of the law said it was the work of deluded men and warned: "We might reply that nothing renders men less impartial and more in danger of falling into a perverse judgment, than the 'occupation' of a great reformer; one of your self-complacent 'stand-thou-aside-I am-holier-than-thou' men."[62]

The law did not apply to wine, and wine could be purchased in any size bottle. This left the license law open to the charge of inconsistency. In the legislative debates one ingenious member proposed that wine also be prohibited. *The Statesman* saw this as a clever move to turn the upper classes who drank wine regularly against the law.

In the spring of 1838 when the law was enacted, it was not a party question. The election of county commissioners at that time offered no mandate in favor of the fifteen-gallon law, and public opinion was divided. Once the law had been enacted and the public became excited, however, then it became a party question.[63] The Whigs were not held responsible. The strongest opposition to the law also came from the Whigs. The Whigs in Boston who opposed the law formed a separate slate of candidates for the party convention where they could hope to pass resolutions calling for its repeal.[64] The Democrats were prompt to see that the law's unpopularity offered them the opportunity to exploit a popular issue.[65] Marcus Morton, the Democratic candidate for governor, promised that he would support repeal. The Whigs split on the issue. As a result, when Everett at the next session of the legislature recommended reconsideration, he could not count on party support.

The advocates of repeal protested that "small quantities of spiritious liquor, prudently taken, are not injurious." To prohibit its use was to invite legislation controlling private morals and to this there would be no end. Eventually it would lead to replacing the people "under a universal guardianship." It would draw "Matters of prudence & private judgment . . . into the vortex of legal prohibition."[66]

In his message to the legislature in January 1839 Everett invited reconsideration of the law. The newly elected legislature, he observed, would bring the views of their constituents on the law. He cited the fact that when the law was passed it provided that it would not go into effect for a year, indicating that the legislature thought there might be occasion for amending it. A law of this kind could only be successful if it had the full support of public opinion. "It will be for the two houses," he said, "to decide, under all the circumstances of the case, whether the great body of the people approve the law as a useful practical measure and will aid the magistrate in enforcing it, or whether there is ground to apprehend, the opposition to it may continue and increase, to the injury of the cause which the law itself was designed to promote."[67] He warned the law would produce unintended results.

In the midst of the controversy Everett received an invitation to attend a dinner of a temperance society. He refused to attend because he saw it as clearly a political meeting, "a rally in favor of the license law." Writing to Robert C. Winthrop, he declared the current fad in favor of total abstinence was a form of asceticism that was "all right for a sect but its adherents would always remain a sect."[68]

The legislative committees could not produce a compromise satisfactory to a majority. The temperance advocates were unbending. Those favoring repeal were divided. The House committee presented a majority report setting the limit at five gallons but extending the law to include wine. The whole Boston delegation supported the compromise, but the representatives from Worcester County were almost unanimously opposed. The legislature of 1839 adjourned without a solution.[69] When the law went into effect, it created an uproar.

The Democratic party had recently undergone a major change. The former leader of the party, David Henshaw, lost control after his bank failed, and the Van Buren administration shortly appointed George Bancroft Collector of Customs in Boston. As the distributor of patronage Bancroft gave the party new life, and he sent out word that the license law should be attacked at every opportunity. Benjamin Hallett found the license law an ideal target. Hallet was a master of ridicule, and he declared, "I cannot detect by what conjuration of necromancy our grave and reverend legislature have arrived at the grand discovery in voluntary morals, that the Imp of the bottle is to be found only in the gill cup and the angel of temperance in a fifteen gallon jug."[70]

Everett assured Webster that he would be reelected but he confessed to a dread of "the dead weight of the Government patronage and the apathy (of the Whigs) produced by long and unsuccessful struggles against it."[71] He greatly underestimated the losses that resulted from the fight over the license law. Morton, the Democratic candidate did not get a majority of the vote so the choice went to the legislature where Morton was elected by a margin of two votes. His brother Alexander, for the past several years an enthusiastic Jacksonian and member of the legislature, voted against Edward.

Everett acknowledged that the license law was the major factor in his defeat, but Democrats in other states preferred to believe that it was simply a long overdue victory of the people over the monied aristocracy. As one biographer of George Bancroft put it, "Bancroft knew very well that his party had won because the Boston mechanic liked a drink at the corner saloon and would not have it taken away from him."[72]

Judge Story wrote a warm and flattering letter to Everett stating that his defeat was no fault of his, "it is one of those odd and strange outbreaks of popular caprice and popular delusion, brought on by the rashness and indiscretion of the legislature, for which you were not, and ought not to be, in any degree, responsible." To this he added that when he looked back on Everett's administration he did so with feelings of lofty pride and unmixed pleasure. He added a bit of advice. Everett, he thought, should now meditate some great work for posterity, "which shall make you known and felt through all time, as we, your contemporaries now know and esteem you."[73]

During the controversy opponents of the law had questioned its constitutionality. In 1847 three license cases came before the Supreme Court testing the law regulating the sale of alcoholic beverages in Massachusetts, Rhode Island, and New Hampshire. The major question was whether retail sale of liquor violated the commerce clause of the Constitution. The justices agreed that the law in Massachusetts was a constitutional exercise of the state police power.

In February 1840 the Whig convention renominated Everett for governor, but he declined. "But in truth," he wrote, "the office of Governor, in my view of it, is not that of a political theorist or champion. It is a business office. There is little beyond the quiet routine of prescribed official duty, mostly within the walls of the Council Chamber, with an opportunity to expressing opinion and recommending measures to the Legislature, in the customary Annual Address." He confessed he was bitter because the sins of the legislature were placed on the governor, but he also took satisfaction in having recommended sound measures and rejoiced in the support he had received from the board of education.[74]

Everett, however, enjoyed the years as governor. The position gave him the freedom to enjoy his family and to catch up on the reading he so much enjoyed. In the summer the family left Boston and vacationed in Waltham. There he enjoyed the pleasure of renewing his friendship with Theodore Lyman, a neighbor, who had been his traveling companion in Europe twenty-two years before.

At the summer retreat he gave time to his children, both in play and in helping them with their lessons. Nothing pleased him more than picking peas in the garden and wild strawberries in the nearby woods, riding his horse in the company of his children, and taking walks with his wife Charlotte, whom he affectionately called Charlie. These were the pleasures he had longed for while in Washington.

There was also time for reading, and he read with a critical eye. Dante, Shakespeare, and Milton gave him pleasure. He read George Bancroft's *History of the United States*. Although it pleased him, he thought "The purpose of reducing everything to a system, to find on all occasions the operation of certain principles is the adverse to calm historical truth. But it is a production of surprising vigor and spirit."[75] His close friend William H. Prescott's *Ferdinand and Isabella* delighted him, and he concluded that it was not surpassed by anything in the same category of English literature.[76] After reading Longfellow's *Hyperion* he wrote, "It evinces great ability, but the continued effort at effect fatigues me, nor is the abrupt fragmentary style to my taste." Ralph Waldo Emerson left him with ambivalent feelings. After hearing Emerson preach he wrote, "Mr. Waldo Emerson preached with great ingenuity and beauty, but in a style so wrapped up in mysticism as to be nearly unintelligible."[77] His only comment on Emerson's Divinity School Address in his diary was "entirely in strain of Carlyle." Three days later, commenting on what he called Emerson's productions, he remarked that they contained brilliant and profitable thoughts, but they were mingled with much nonsense.[78]

Everett's administration saw the beginnings of school reform, the first regulation of banks, the advance of railroads with state support, and the first moves toward legal reforms. Everett was in advance of the rank and file of his party.

Time and again his own party failed to support his measures. On the eve of the election in 1839 he correctly predicted the victory depended on "10,000 lazy Whigs who will stay at home on the 11th of November one on his farm and one at his mercantile and allow the battle to go against us."[79] The Massachusetts Whigs controlled the state so long that they were apathetic and Everett was not successful in invigorating the party.

The new leadership of the Jacksonians gave life to that party. The exuberance and dedication of George Bancroft channeled general discontent into support for the Democrats. Bancroft enjoyed the advantage of being able to exploit the popular issue of the fifteen-gallon law, but the Democrats aroused popular interest in the issues of the day. No issue was more important than the abuse by the banks of freedom to issue paper money and the readiness of the state legislature to grant corporations charters extending privileges to private firms that were in conflict with the public interest.

The differences between the Whigs and the Democrats in Massachusetts, however, were not as great as historians have sometimes made them. George Bancroft and Robert Rantoul were both conservatives.

Everett had come to the conclusion that it was a waste of time to fight for the establishment of a central bank. The opposition was too strong, and if one were established that was under government control, given the public feelings, it would soon become an engine of politics. His thoughts now extended to the broader question of whether manufacturing would prove a blessing or a curse. He wrote to a correspondent:

> I have looked with anxiety to the possibility that our large manufacturing towns may eventually resemble those of England and the European Continent generally in becoming the abode of the uneducated, physically degenerate race and I should think the seasonable adoption of measures calculated to prevent so deplorable a result one of the most signal services which philanthropy could perform.[80]

4
Everett's Debut in Diplomacy

Everett's entry into the field of foreign relations coincided with the approach of a crisis in Anglo-American relations. The many factors at play in the tangle of relations produced complexity. If the disputes were not resolved, they would become immersed in party rivalry, national honor, and the question of state rights. There were four points of conflict: the *Caroline* affair, the northeastern boundary question, the question of the boundary between the western end of Lake Superior and the Lake of the Woods, and the Oregon question.

In 1837, with the outbreak of insurgency in Canada, Americans along the border took the side of the insurgents supplying them with arms. An American ship, the *Caroline,* carried arms from Buffalo to insurgents on an island in the Niagara River. To put an end to this, a contingent of British troops crossed the border and destroyed the *Caroline*. This promoted further hostility on the frontier. Complicating matters further, a member of the British armed force, Alexander McLeod, was arrested and charged with having killed an American on the *Caroline*. The British protested that as a member of an armed force, under the laws of war, he could not be punished for acting on orders. As the case dragged on and appeals from Washington to the state of New York to release McLeod, there was danger of a break in the diplomatic relations between the two countries; the British Foreign Office instructed its minister in Washington to leave his post at once if the court found him guilty and sentenced him.

The long, unsettled, northeastern boundary dispute came to the fore in 1838 when New Brunswick provincials entered the disputed area and began lumbering. When the governor of Maine dispatched an agent to check on this activity, the agent was arrested and held by the New Brunswick authorities. Governor Fairfield of Maine, in a knee-jerk reaction, issued a call for ten thousand volunteers to uphold Maine's claims. At the same time the legislature in Augusta passed resolutions declaring that the federal government could not cede the territory within a state to a foreign power. These resolutions were forwarded to the Massachusetts legislature in hope of rallying that state's support. The Massachusetts legislature did adopt the Maine resolutions. Governor Everett, however, consulted with Justice Story who advised Everett that if the proposition was true "it would stand in the way of making peace if any territory were conquered in a war and to make peace the enemy demanded a cession." Everett refused to sign the resolutions.[1]

The absence of fortifications in Boston caused anxiety. One fort had been taken down, and the second was not yet completed. Everett warned that Boston was literally without a gun.

Everett's studies of the history of the controversy led to the conclusion that the United States had a strong claim. What he lacked in his study were the British documents connected with the question. He complained that although the United States had made public all of the correspondence, the British had released none of theirs. In February 1839 he wrote a lengthy letter to the Marquis of Lansdowne, son of the Earl of Sheffield, who had been a British representative at the peace negotiations of 1783. He explained why he thought the present situation could erupt in a war that was to be deeply regretted. It would be helpful, he said, if Lansdowne would use his influence to make public the British documents.[2]

Disturbed by the failure of the Van Buren administration to take any steps, he wrote two letters to Joel Poinsett, the secretary of war.[3] In his first letter he explained the helpless situation of Boston in the event of war, and he pleaded for assistance.[4] A short time later he wrote again, this time explaining the origins of the controversy.[5] It began when the controversy was submitted to a commission in 1798. The commission ruled that the treaty of peace was mistaken in its assumption that there were highlands from which rivers flowed east and west. No highlands had been located according to the commission. Governor Sullivan of Massachusetts made a grievous error in agreeing to this interpretation, and Secretary of State James Madison accepted Governor Sullivan's ruling. It made no difference, Everett stated, that there were no highlands. There was a high broad morass in which the rivers originated. The essential fact was that some of these rivers flowed into the St. Lawrence and others into the Atlantic Ocean. The morass was clearly where the boundary should be drawn.

The heart of controversy, Everett added, was the existing British control of both sides of the St. Johns River. In the course of the War of 1812 the British decided that they must have a road from New Brunswick to Quebec because the St. Lawrence River was frozen over in the wintertime leaving the city isolated. Not until that war did British maps indicate that the boundary between Maine and New Brunswick was west of the St. Johns River. This was now of importance because British control of the river meant that American lumber from the North could not be sent down the river and to sea. The British based this boundary on the assertion that the St. Johns River emptied into the Bay of Fundy and not into the ocean, and the treaty of 1783 specified a river that entered the Atlantic Ocean. Everett charged that this British ruling was pretentious. The Bay of Fundy was clearly a part of the ocean. The passageway from the Bay of Fundy to the open sea was much too wide to justify the claim that the bay was not part of the ocean.

He also informed Poinsett that a friend, who refused to have his name mentioned, told him that he had seen documentary evidence in the papers of the Marquis of Lansdowne, signed by Richard Oswald, that supported the American claim. The friend, Professor Jared Sparks, was committed to Lansdowne not to make available anything in the papers detrimental to British interests. Sparks, however, turned over to Everett a large bundle of copies of the papers. What little they revealed did not meet Everett's expectations, but he suggested that even this little could be used in questioning the British authorities and in encouraging them to make a further search.[6]

Alarmed, Everett wrote a series of letters to President Van Buren, pressing on him the dangers that some incident could occur that would plunge the two countries into war. The source of greatest danger was in the heated party strife in both countries. He cited the great excitement in Maine that had been generated by the politicians of both parties. It was quite likely that this excitement could not be kept under control.[7]

The political situation in Great Britain was equally fraught with danger. Only yesterday he had received a report on the speech from the throne and the heated debate that followed. "It seems plain to me," Everett wrote, "from the tone of the Duke of Wellington and Sir Robert Peel on the one side and Lord Melbourne and Lord John Russell on the other, that there will be a rivalry of patriotic ostentation between the outs and the ins when the intelligence of recent events arrives." Once that was underway and national honor came to the fore, it would be too late to negotiate. Therefore, Everett proposed that the president immediately send a special mission to London.[8]

Everett also advised the president that there was no hope of the British giving up their pretensions in the Northeast. That controversy must be linked to the other three conflicts that existed: the *Caroline* affair, the unsettled boundary between Lake Superior and the Lake of the Woods, and the Oregon question. Negotiations should include all four. As the price for avoiding a disastrous war, the United States should concede all of Oregon north of the Columbia River to the British (although the United States had a strong claim), and the British should concede to the United States its claim along the northeastern boundary.[9]

The excitement in Boston far surpassed the feelings in Washington where Secretary of War Joel Poinsett had failed to release money for the construction of new defenses. On his way to New Brunswick General Winfield Scott, on his mission to seek a truce, called on Everett. Everett noted in his diary that Scott "leans, I think, to my opinion that there will be war."[10] At the close of March, Everett called both branches of the state legislature into a secret session, and he addressed them on the defenseless condition of Boston.[11] A few days later both houses passed a bill for appropriating funds for fortifications with the understanding that the federal government would later reimburse the state.

This was already, more than a year before the next presidential election, but there was talk of sending Webster on a special mission to London. Abbott Lawrence called on Everett and advocated a mission. Webster, too, gave it thought, and, in March, he drafted a lengthy memorandum on the basis for a settlement. He did not share Everett's alarm, and he doubted that there would be war. He proposed that efforts should be made to settle the question on the basis of the treaty of 1783. If that was not successful, then an effort should be made to arrive at a conventional line that met the requirements of both nations. He considered the British aspirations for a road from New Brunswick foolish. Even if they were in possession of that strip of land, in the event of some future war in the distant future, American forces could attack Quebec. As for the road, it was not a matter of concern. It would take fifty years to complete it. Webster urged that negotiations should get underway as soon as possible.[12]

The state of alarm came to an end in April when Scott was successful in negotiating a truce, and quiet returned to the state of Maine where the public was left to contemplate the cost of the expedition to Aroostock by the Maine volunteers.

The moderate tone that Everett and Webster introduced in the discussions on this side of the Atlantic was to have a good effect in London where the flamboyance and excess of American protests had so recently served to dampen any prospects of negotiation.

Andrew Stevenson, the American minister in London, exhibited a combative spirit that was met with an equally combative spirit by the British foreign secretary, Lord Palmerston. Stevenson focused all of his attention on the British interfering with American shipping in African waters. Between the two a battle raged over the British assertion of the right of visit and search of American ships to determine if they were engaged in the slave trade. Daniel Webster's long visit in London in 1839 undid some of the damage. He won the confidence of his hosts, and showed them that there was a strain of moderation and reasonableness among Americans.

Everett was alarmed by the dangers as he saw the situation in March 1839, but two months later he confided to his old friend Robert Walsh, the journalist, "Our troubles for the present are over." Lord Palmerston, he wrote, "has sent out the draft of a convention, the provisions of which have not been leaked out."[13] It appeared, however, that there was to be a new survey. At least this indicated that the British were not prepared to take immediate action, but, said Everett, it could not lead to any settlement of the controversy. There had been several surveys already, and there was no need for another. The controversy, said Everett, "all grows out of the pretension of Great Britain that St. Johns is not one of the rivers that empty themselves into the Atlantic."[14] The survey undertaken by the British only served to stir up more distrust. Albert Gallatin, who was in command of the facts, charged that the British surveyors had failed to make a careful and accurate survey, and their findings were skewed to serve British interests.

In the absence of an immediate crisis, both Webster and Everett arrived at the conclusion that it would be most useful to play down the controversy and encourage faith in a satisfactory settlement by negotiation. In an editorial that expressed Everett's view, his brother-in-law, Nathan Hale, editor of the *Advertiser,* assured his readers that there was no reason to be alarmed. "The object in dispute is too utterly contemptible," Hale wrote, "to be made the cause of disturbing the friendly relations between the two countries even for the shortest period of time."[15] "It is said that honor is at stake. The two parties cannot recede from their claims without disgrace," which, he said, is ridiculous. "National honor requires, in a conflict with a foreign power, the maintenance of the essential rights and substantial interests of the country, but it no more interdicts the amicable compromise of a claim believed to be well grounded, even at the expense of yielding some part of that claim, when it comes in conflict with a claim that is confidently entertained by the adverse party, than individual honor, in private life, forbids a man from compromising a claim disputed by his neighbor."[16]

Hale contended: "We are clearly of opinion that all idea of an adjustment at present insisted upon by the state of Maine, that their whole claim is to be allowed, without modification or reserve, is utterly hopeless." Some adjustment might be required, Hale acknowledged, including an appropriation of money for its execution, and would therefore require the sanction of the House. What was necessary was to come to terms on a conventional line satisfactory to both parties.[17]

Hale's spirit was certainly conducive to a settlement. It was shared by Everett and Webster, but these two makers of peace were soon to encounter difficulties. Webster recognized from the beginning that Maine must be involved in the negotiations and its assent gained, or the treaty would encounter difficulty in the Senate. The *Caroline* question was still unresolved.

* * * * *

A significant turnaround occurred in 1840 when the Jacksonians met defeat in the election of that year. Before the campaign it appeared that Henry Clay would be the Whig candidate, but there were important people who doubted that he could win. Among these were Daniel Webster who was himself an eager aspirant. When the Whig convention met, Clay was set aside in favor of the military hero William Henry Harrison who had the support of Webster. To appease the disappointed followers of Clay, the convention nominated John Tyler of Virginia for vice-president. Tyler stood outside of the more general Whig pattern being a strict constructionist and an advocate of states rights.

The new president chose Daniel Webster as his secretary of state. Harrison died after only a month in office, and the Whigs found themselves led by a man who vetoed some of their most important measures. All except Daniel Webster shortly resigned from Tyler's cabinet, and the president sought the aid of leading Southerners who shared his enthusiasm for expansion.

The choice of Daniel Webster rested in part on his support of Harrison for the nomination, but it owed more to Webster's brilliance as a lawyer, his knowledge and understanding of the history of American foreign policy, and even more on the fact that Webster could be trusted to steer a middle course and avoid dangerous adventures. At the time of his appointment another consideration recommended him; he had given much thought to the Maine boundary question and was well informed on this, the most pressing problem faced by the country in the area of foreign affairs.

Everett and his family were already in Italy at the time of the election. Mrs. Everett suffered from asthma, and the severe winters of New England had long since led to thoughts of spending winter months in Europe. The family took up temporary residence in Florence where Everett took delight in the historical surroundings and pursued his studies in the rich library of the Grand Duke. It was at this time that he began work on a history of international law, a work he was to pick up from time to time but that he never finished.

The appointment of Daniel Webster as secretary of state almost assured Everett of appointment to a foreign post. In 1835 Webster, anxious to gain the presidency, had asked Everett to serve as his campaign manager, and Everett worked vigorously, though in vain, to elect Webster. The regular exchange of letters between the two men testify to a close friendship in which formality gave way to hastily written scrawls and frank exchanges. The Webster family entertained Everett frequently in Washington, and Everett's daughter, Gracie, was named afer the first Mrs. Webster. The two men stood as advocates of identical political programs. Webster had long known of Everett's great interest in European affairs. Most political leaders could not afford to accept a foreign post, but Everett, thanks to the generosity of his father-in-law, P. C. Brooks, was in a position to supplement a wholly inadequate salary.

In July 1841, Everett wrote to his close friend, Robert C. Winthrop, a leading Massachusetts Whig, stating that he had read in the newspapers that a John Sergeant had declined the offer of serving as minister to England. If the position "is still vacant," he wrote, "I hope there is no impropriety in my saying that I should prefer it to Paris, which Mr. W. (as you inform me) has, if the President approves, intended for me."[18] He suggested that his own intimate knowledge of the Maine boundary question would be useful and more especially his studies of the peace negotiations of 1783 would be valuable. He proposed that Winthrop discuss the matter with Webster.

Webster and Everett may well have discussed the possibility of an appointment before Everett ever left for Europe, but if they had not, Webster knew of his aspirations. Webster soon wrote to Everett and raised the possibility of diplomatic service; Webster also inquired of P. C. Brooks what he thought Everett would prefer. Everett felt close enough to Webster to speak frankly. Considerations of his wife's health ruled out Berlin or St. Petersburg because of their cold climate, but Tuscany, Turkey, or Paris would suit him. It was London that he preferred, however. Webster promptly arranged for his nomination to that post.

Then followed one of those disconcerting periods when politics held his confirmation in abeyance. Southerners wished to have a Southerner appointed who would boldly defend American ships against interference from the British and a reliable ally on the question of slavery. Everett, they thought, could not be trusted as word had leaked out that although he was not an abolitionist he did not condone slavery. In 1838 he had publicly endorsed bold resolutions of the state legislature condemning slavery and more particularly its extension. Winthrop wrote to a friend, "Alack, alack-a-day! E. E. is in the utmost jeopardy. I learn confidentially from Choate, that unless some change occurs, it is a hopeless case." Winthrop was dismayed. "The personal consequences of this proceeding to our friend are painful to contemplate. It goes nearer to a dissolution to the Union, than anything which has ever occurred."[19]

Shortly thereafter Fletcher Webster, son of the secretary of state, wrote to Everett explaining that Senate approval was far from certain. Everett expected the worst, at the same time reflecting on the fact that he had gone out of his way to be conciliatory toward Southerners. Webster wrote explaining that there would have been no objection had he been a candidate for France or Spain, but the southern partisans were worried about his position on slavery. In a preview of the sectional feelings of the future, the senator from Alabama angrily stated that if a man like Everett were confirmed then the Union would be dissolved. Henry Clay retorted that "if a gentleman so preeminently qualified for the position of Minister should be rejected by the Senate, and for the reasons given by the gentleman from Alabama, the Union is dissolved already."[20] The question finally came to a vote on 13 September, and Everett was confirmed by a vote of twenty-three to nineteen.

The tension and disillusion Everett had experienced came to an end when he learned from friends in London that he was now minister to England. He set out in great haste with his family, purchasing a large but ample coach in southern France for the trip to Paris where he enrolled two of his five children in school. He arrived in London the evening of 18 November, rode to the office where he found a month's accumulation of mail, opened and sorted it, retired to sleep, and returned to the office at six o'clock the next morning.[21] No one had been present in the office to handle business in the absence of the minister. Everett also found that his predecessor, Andrew Stevenson, had established no filing system, had not seen to it that the legation was furnished with a collection of congressional reports, and that he had departed a month before Everett's arrival leaving much ill feeling after having sent an angry message to Aberdeen—in his own words, a bombshell.

* * * * *

Everett's years in London were the high point in his career and probably the happiest of his life. His interest in literature and in the arts, his gentlemanly manners, and affable conversation won him lifelong friends in the upper strata of society. He was a guest at country estates and a breakfast and luncheon companion of Thomas Macaulay and other notables in the literary world. His appreciation of the best in British traditions contributed to making him an ideal appointment. He had long admired British political institutions, and in his many orations he paid tribute to America's British heritage as one of the country's greatest blessings.

His friendly attitude did not blind him to the grasping hand of that government nor to the perplexing social and political problems confronting the British. He resented what he saw as unjustifiable British claims in relation to the Maine boundary. In the course of the next four years Everett's understanding of British life deepened. Party politics raged as severely as at home, corruption was plentiful, British courts were not always dispensers of evenhanded justice, British naval officers at far-off stations acted high-handedly, and the British thirst for trade and territory in the Pacific and off the coast of Africa was unlimited. Alert to American interests in the Pacific, he reacted with vigor to British occupation of New Zealand. He warned that, if it went unchallenged, the British would probably seize the Sandwich Islands and Society Islands "and we shall be driven from all the convenient resorts in the Pacific."[22]

He was appalled by the disparity between the fashionable social life in London and the poverty in the manufacturing districts where wages were so low as to offer no more than the bare means of survival and in periods of decline of business the working class faced starvation. What he saw troubled him and caused him to wonder if there was any remedy short of a reconstitution of society. He wrote to an American friend: "There is great distress in England, thousands of workmen without employment and multitudes without bread. But the world of luxury and display, of wealth and power, of fashion and taste seems to move on unabated."[23]

He became a friend of Lord Ashley, later known as Lord Shaftesbury, who publicized the evils of rapid industrialization, and when he read Ashley's report on the physical and moral conditions of miners he wrote to the author, "I echo from the bottom of my heart your fervent wish, that my Country may learn wisdom from yours, in those things in which you have set us an example to be avoided." He told Ashley that in the free states at home "we have hitherto escaped most of the evils against which you have so nobly contended."[24] He was pleased by the report of a British clergyman who had studied conditions in the United States, and whose study of the female operatives in Lowell convinced him that their treatment was far better than in his home parish of Bradford.[25]

Conversely, Everett could also deplore American failures. When several American state governments defaulted on their obligations, more particularly Pennsylvania, Everett found it unforgivable. The extensive losses to British subjects created great ill will and seriously hurt the reputation of America, and Everett viewed the lack of responsibility as a disgrace. He wrote to his brother-in-law, Nathan Hale, editor of the Boston *Advertiser,* comparing the state of affairs in the two countries, "We, with all natural and political elements of prosperity in superabundance, reduced to a state of bankruptcy, by the violence and unscrupulousness of our factions. The English with an excessive population, a monstrous inequality of condition, a government and political system full of grossest abuses, yet enjoying the highest credit, and administering their affairs with a vigor and success, which are the admiration of the world."[26]

What he saw in England eroded his equanimity about the future, and he worried about the stability of the social order. A convulsion was probable, "for what motive is there to induce men, who have the physical power in their hands & who are actually starving, to obey the laws. Perhaps the real truth is, that the laboring classes have not the physical force. They have numbers, but the property holders are also numerous, and have arms, organizations, & funds, which together make up physical force."[27] As he viewed the early movement of the Chartists he wrote to Hale that England reposed on a volcano. He noted that the Chartists lacked a strong leader, however, and the two political parties controlled all the property and politics.[28]

Though pressed by official duties, he found time to read and discuss historical writings with eminent Britishers. He had dreamed of pursuing a literary career, and his fascination with historical works, and raw materials of the historical craft, and literature was very much alive. He was and remained an avid reader. He loved Tacitus and other classical writers, but his own literary aspirations gradually faded. The departure from political life and the means to support himself and his family in Florence, where the great libraries offered him a scholar's paradise, failed to reset him on the course of scholarship.

In both Florence and London he gladly lent a helping hand to those who did write history. He pursued research for the sake of helping his friends William Prescott and George Bancroft, and gladly investigated archival sources so as to assist them. He read history with a critical eye, and spoke of the historian as having a vast responsibility to "emulate the glorious impartiality of the great men of old, Thucydides & Tactius, who wrote even the annals of their own time, *sine via aut studio.*"[29] It gave him great pleasure to open the door for George Bancroft to examine papers in the hands of the British government and to send suggestions as to possible new sources. While waiting in a government office for an interview, he chanced to see fifteen folio volumes of bound manuscripts lying on the library table dealing with relations with the North American colonies before the Revolution. One was lettered "Massachusetts 1705–1774," a volume to which historians had not yet had access. He wrote to George Bancroft at once, "You may imagine the wistful glance I cast upon those precious documents, and the satisfaction with which I received the invitation from the gentleman in charge of them to come and read them as much as I pleased & mark anything which I wished to be copied."

Bancroft, author of the multivolume history of the United States, was like Everett a graduate of Göttingen, and they corresponded regularly on historical matters. He likewise corresponded with Jared Sparks, professor of history at Harvard, and John Romeyn Brodhead, whose collection on colonial material for the state of New York exceeded the collections of material gathered by representative of any other state. Everett took great interest in their work and assisted them in gaining access to British records.

He was no less enthusiastic about painting and sculpture, and he was a friend of Horatio Greenough and Hiram Powers, both of whom had been his companions in Florence. Powers became a close friend and once wrote to Everett that when he first met him he found him cool to which Everett replied, "I am very touched by your allusion to our first meeting in Washington. I then certainly undervalued you, or I should not have been so very cold. The truth is, I had not then got rid of some false notions of art which I brought from a former visit to Europe, and I was terrified with the old General's forehead and hair, not the first man in that respect. With respect to general coldness of exterior there is too much foundation for the remark, which has been made by many a one before though not always with your kindly qualifications."[30]

Powers, who had been working on a bust of Everett in Florence had discussed his plan for what later became his famous *Slave Girl*. When Powers had finished the work and sold it to a Britisher who displayed it in a London exhibition, it became a sensation. Everett, who greatly admired it, wrote to Powers of the enthusiastic reception it had received. At the same time he sought to help Powers by recommending him to a committee in Philadelphia reported to be considering having a bust made of Henry Clay. Everett lauded the work of both Powers and Horatio Greenough, by this time famous as a sulptor, and expressed the opinion that both were superior to any of the contemporary Italian sculptors. They were adornments to the nation and deserved support.

Only once during his years in London did he encounter embarrassment, and that was at Oxford in June 1843 when he was to receive an honorary degree. The festivities went well until Everett arose to receive the degree; then a burst of protest came from the audience. The Church of England was torn by the Tractarian controversy, and a group of churchmen in the audience called out in protest against awarding a degree to a Unitarian. The speech awarding the degree by the vice-chancellor could not be heard, but Everett received the degree as the protestors walked out of the theater. He later received a note of apology.

Tragedy struck in the fall of that year. His oldest daughter Anne had been ill for months with consumption and died in October. Everett was engulfed in grief. No one of the children had quite won his affection as had Anne who was highly talented, an excellent student, and a very sensitive girl who shared not only his interests but his religious feelings. He wrote to a close friend, "I have lost in her more than a dutiful affectionate child, for she has been for years, young as she was, my companion and friend. When these characters are found united with that of a daughter, I need not say to you what the separation is."[31]

* * * * *

Everett arrived in London at a time when Anglo-American relations were in disarray. The *Caroline* affair was still on the table for Lord Palmerston had denied the American request for an apology, and the exceedingly troublesome McLeod problem absorbed much of Webster's time in his early months in office. His efforts to have Governor William Seward of New York to release the accused to the federal government failed. That difficulty was not removed until October 1841 when the jury in New York found McLeod not guilty in less than twenty minutes.

Also pending was the settlement of a series of sharp disputes concerning British interference with American shipping off the coast of Africa. The British patrolled the waters in search for slave traders. It was against the law for Americans to engage in the slave trade, but Americans from both the North and South were involved in the trade. A part of the difficulty lay in the practice of ships, owned in Portugal, Spain, and Brazil, flying the American flag in the hope of evading capture.

Occasionally British naval officers, though more often friendly than not, vented their anti-American feelings on merchant ships even in instances where the merchant ship was free of guilt. The difficulty was complicated by American memories of impressment before the War of 1812. The British no longer practiced impressment, but they had refused to surrender the right.

The Maine boundary question posed the greatest threat to peace. That long-festering question required settlement before some new incident led to war.

In 1841 circumstances had so changed both in the United States and England that wise statesmanship could reconcile what had appeared irreconcilable. Daniel Webster as secretary of state was anxious for peace, and Everett, unlike his truculent predecessor, was conciliatory.[32] In London the change from Palmerston to Lord Aberdeen as foreign secretary in September 1841 provided an equivalent change in temperament, and England was now in a position where an accommodation with the United States was of great importance. The British had met disaster in Afghanistan, and there was deep concern as to the outcome of the Opium War in China.[33]

The relation between Aberdeen and Everett shortly became one of mutual confidence and cordiality. Both had a great interest in antiquity, both were cosmopolitan, both were of a conciliatory disposition, and both cherished warm friendships.

A great turn about in relations occurred when the new ministry of Sir Robert Peel seized the initiative and appointed Lord Ashburton to go to the United States on a special mission. Ashburton was a leader in the House of Baring, the great British banking concern that was heavily involved in American loans. Daniel Webster had spent time with him in 1839 during his long visit in England, and he was delighted with the appointment of Baring. The sending of a special mission would have sufficed to serve as proof that the British Foreign Office was serious, and the naming of Ashburton verified it.

Everett, without question, had anticipated with pleasure the prospect of negotiating on a question whose details he had mastered and one that was of major importance, but not a word of regret or disappointment crept into either his diary or correspondence. He immediately made use of the opportunity presented to him to contribute to the success of the mission when Ashburton called on him in December 1841 and then invited Everett to spend the Christmas holidays in his home. During three- and four-hour walks they discussed the questions that separated the two nations. Everett's mastery of the details and insight into what was central in the controversy strengthened his hand. Although he knew the legal side, he avoided legalisms and centered attention on what the United States could accept and what it could not accept.

His second opportunity to promote success came in the spring of 1842 in his interviews with Aberdeen, who contended that the instructions to the British peace commissioners in 1779 offered the best means for arriving at a correct interpretation of what the treaty of 1783 provided as to the Maine boundary. Everett refuted this, and a few days later, at a social levee on the queen's birthday, Aberdeen acknowledged that Everett was correct. Everett reported to Webster that Aberdeen was "now satisfied of one thing which he could never believe before, *vizt,* that we are sincere in thinking that we are in the right."[34]

In June 1843, during the Webster-Ashburton negotiations in Washington, Everett wrote to Webster that "he could not divest himself of the belief, that they have in their archives a copy of Mitchell's map on which Strachey and Oswald laid down the boundary settled by the treaty."[35] Webster complimented Everett on a note he had sent Aberdeen, but not knowing about the Oswald map, he advised Everett not to press the search for the missing map, for "Our strength lies in the treaty."[36]

Two factors favored success in the negotiations. Ashburton had only one major objective on which there could be no yielding, a passageway from New Brunswick to Quebec. Webster accepted this as wholly reasonable. There was nothing to fear, he said, for it would take fifty years to build the road. Second, both sides were anxious for peace. Halfway through the negotiations the Duke of Wellington intruded and added to the British demands. Ashburton promptly responded that to change his instructions would make success impossible, and Aberdeen set the military hero's proposals to one side. In July he instructed Ashburton, "I only wish to say that the importance of a successful result is so great, as almost to justify any sacrifice compatible with the safety of the North American Province."[37]

The only hope in settlement lay in drawing a conventional line of compromise acceptable to both sides, but this did not throw aside the treaty of 1783 as a guide. Webster fell back on that treaty that had espoused fifty years of miserable controversy, a treaty that as Webster said left both the British and Americans sincere in affirming that the treaty supported their claims.

Webster argued that while the treaty included only a few points of certitude that were beyond debate, the treaty did, beyond question, specify that the boundary should run, first, north and south and then east and west to meet the elevations from which rivers flowed north and south. This left open the question of where the north and south line should be drawn. Everett had long since concluded that the St. Johns River was a river flowing into the Atlantic and the river referred to in the treaty. Webster differed; he would make the river the western boundary of New Brunswick, and he insisted that a strip of land west of that river must be granted to the United States as an equivalent for the United States agreeing to the granting of a land route from New Brunswick to Quebec.[38]

The clearheaded Ashburton, accustomed to business affairs, was baffled by the tangled web of American politics. In an early dispatch he referred to "this ungovernable people."[39] Here was a nation where he dealt not only with the secretary of state but with the commissioners chosen by the legislatures of Maine and Massachusetts. There was also, in the words of Ashburton, "the singular state of parties here which makes them powerless."[40] The Whig president, he was told, did not have the support of the Whigs, and the American minister in Paris, Lewis Cass, was at work stirring up anti-British feelings in the hopes of advancing his chances for the presidency.

Arranging the northeastern boundary ran into the conflict of views between the representatives of Maine and those of the authorities in New Brunswick. The former were adamant on drawing the line immediately east of the St. Johns River. The officials of New Brunswick held that the boundary must be west of the river. The question of Madawaska north of the St. James River stirred up even deeper feelings, and on this question Ashburton felt strongly. Discussions on the boundary question continued until the close of July before agreement was reached.

The question of the northwestern boundary, conversely, was resolved with ease. Not much was known about this remote area in the Northwest. Neither Webster nor Ashburton were aware of valuable iron deposits that were to prove of great value in the development of the iron industry in the late nineteenth century. This was the area between the western end of Lake Superior and the Lake of the Woods. Ashburton readily agreed to accepting the American claim.[41]

In the course of the negotiations Webster had to be concerned about obtaining the agreement of Maine to the boundary settlement. He resorted to questionable tactics. A propagandist from Maine, Francis Smith, was paid out of secret service funds to promote a campaign that would make public opinion amenable to acceptance of a compromise line. He also made use of one map in his own possession and one in the hands of Jared Sparks, both of which showed a boundary that supported British claims. Sparks was sent to Augusta to show the maps to the Maine commissioners. Whether they saw this map as authoritative or not is not clear, but should negotiations fail and the boundary dispute be submitted to arbitration Sparks's map would receive consideration. Webster made use of his map in discussions with members of the Senate.[40] It was not the use of these maps, however, that carried the greatest weight in influencing the Maine commissioners. Should the negotiation fail and the dispute go to arbitration there was danger of a greater loss of territory. Most important in gaining the support of Maine was Webster's ingenuity in involving Maine directly in the negotiations with Ashburton.

Concurrent with the border negotiations Webster and Everett faced two other differences with the British. If these were not resolved the forthcoming Webster-Ashburton Treaty would probably not be ratified by the Senate. The first of these involved the British efforts to put down the slave trade on the coast of Africa. The second concerned the *Creole,* an American ship carrying slaves from Norfolk to New Orleans. This took place in November 1841.

The British navy was there to stop the slave trade. To strengthen this effort, in December 1841, Great Britain negotiated the Quintuple Treaty with France, Austria, Russia, and Prussia. Aberdeen invited the United States to join but also stated that if she did not her ships would be subject to visitation to determine if they were really American ships and if they were slavers. Everett advised joining the signatory powers subject to the British surrendering impressment. This would, he thought, do much to still the waters at home.

As a commercial nation the United States was a strong advocate of freedom of the seas. Interference with ships suspected of being slavers resulted in provoking and costly delays, and sometimes the ships were seized and brought into port, some of them free of guilt. These were sufficiently frequent to be a source of constant irritation and a reminder of the earlier days of impressment.

The British drew a line between the right of search and the right of visit. The right of search was limited to times of war. The right of visit was held to be no more than to board a ship to examine its papers for the purpose of determining its nationality. Because slavers frequently flew false colors, usually the American flag, the British looked on exercising the right to visit as a legitimate way to stop the slave trade. To the British public it appeared that to give up the asserted right of visit was tantamount to giving consent to the inhuman trade. No British statesman could have survived yielding this right.

Secretary of State Webster prepared a lengthy despatch for Everett for presentation to Aberdeen. The right of visit, he held, was no more than another name for the right of search. Inspection of a ship's papers offered no proof of nationality for as everyone knew slavers made a practice of carrying false papers. Therefore exercise of the right to visit often led to inspection of cargo and resulted in long delays.[43] No American secretary of state could have taken a different position, especially if he hoped to gain a two-thirds vote of approval in the Senate for a treaty being negotiated.

Aberdeen, in discussing Webster's dispatch with Everett, said it was an excellent document and that "he did not know that he should wish to alter a word." He agreed with Webster that there was no distinction between the right of search and the right of visit, but Sir Robert Peel held the contrary opinion, and he must abide by that. Faced with this situation Everett proposed that a public confrontation be avoided and that opinion be confined in notes.[44] This useful suggestion assured no more than a temporary remission of the aroused public feelings, and Webster was already considering another solution, one that had been discussed during earlier crises. This was to set up a joint naval squadron to police the African waters. It soon evolved into a proposal to station an American naval squadron off Africa, one that would act independently. Webster's proposal did call for joint action of the two governments.[45]

This won British approval, but the wording of Webster's draft underwent close scrutiny by President Tyler and his cabinet. The proposal that committed both nations to consult edged in the direction of a departure from the tradition of no entangling alliances. Tyler insisted on several changes. According to Hugh Legaré, the original language was not only very much softened but materially altered at the cabinet meeting.[46] In its final form the treaty did state "that the Parties to this Treaty agree that they will unite in all becoming representations and remonstrances, with any and all Powers within whose dominions such markets are allowed to exist." In Webster's draft the word "ernest" was used rather than "becoming," a change proposed by Hugh Legaré.[47] Article IX was later a subject of discussion in the secret sessions of the Senate. Legaré explained to Everett, "We had no mind at all to wound the susceptibility still less to invade the independence of Nations for the sake of a possible good and to set a precedent which in this case was sure to be well received, but which might be turned to the worst account in the future, on subjects very different from the slave trade and for ends anything but philanthropical."[48]

Aberdeen adhered to insisting on the right to visit, but he had informed Everett that no American ship would be subject to search. This appeased critics of the British. Ashburton reported from Washington that this had "done great good."[49]

A way had been found to confine the dispute to diplomatic channels. This was made possible by the good will and faith created by the Ashburton mission and by the success of Everett in London in assuring the Peel government that the United States wanted peace. The controversy was put to rest by the actions of Aberdeen and Webster. The strong antislavery feelings in Great Britain were appeased by Webster announcing that an American naval squadron would be stationed off the coast of Africa to assist in putting down the slave trade.

The *Creole* case posed equal danger of a breakdown of negotiations. The happenings that had occurred involving frightful tragedy touched deep feelings on both sides of the Atlantic. It remained for Webster and Everett on the American side, and Lord Aberdeen and the British Foreign Office to seek a settlement.

The *Creole,* enroute from Norfolk to New Orleans carrying slaves, was taken over by nineteen mutinous slaves who killed the captain and ordered the crew to take the ship into Nassau, a British port. The colonial authorities released the 135 slaves who were not engaged in the mutiny at once and the 19 alleged to be guilty after it was determined that as the crime was not committed within British jurisdiction the British courts ruled against hearing the case. The incident raised loud protests throughout the South. Secretary of State Webster first consulted Justice Story as to his views. Story advised that it was common for a nation to remit the pirate to the country to which the ship belonged, but this practice had "always been understood to be a matter to comity and discretion and not of national duty." The fact that under American law the slaves were property did not alter the case.[50]

Webster wrote a cautious but firm protest to the British Foreign Office, but he did not demand that the mutineers be returned, a concession that Aberdeen failed to acknowledge. He did ask for compensation. Webster could do no more than appeal to consideration of comity because there was no basis for appeal under international law and there was no extradition treaty.[51] The British, after consulting the law officers of the crown, replied that the British government had no legal authority to try the mutinous slaves or to hold those that had been set free. President Tyler promptly and in a high spirit declared that the British decision was nothing less than a subterfuge, that they would have returned the usual forms of property, but they were motivated by their disapproval of slavery.[52] Ashburton, who read Tyler's letter, termed it querulous and foolish.[53]

The refusal of the British to return the mutineers caused Everett to write a lengthy letter to Lord Aberdeen placing his protest on other than legal grounds. Everett's long epistle embraced three major points that he hoped would cause the British to reconsider. First, to set the mutineers free after the murder and taking over of the ship set up a direct temptation to further acts of murder and mutiny on the high seas. Second, to impose British views on slavery on an American ship was to interfere in the internal affairs of another country. Finally, he stressed that the *Creole* had not reached its destination; the stop in Nassau was a result of a tragic mishap, and the ship was still on voyage to another American port.[54]

Aberdeen's reply, delayed for several weeks, exhibited impatience. Although he did not state so bluntly, his response implied he could not understand why Everett should trouble him with the case. Everett knew well that the law officers of the Crown had ruled that the government lacked legal authority to act. Then stretching Everett's protest into an appeal on humanitarian grounds, Aberdeem quoted the Declaration of Independence. All men were created equal. For the British to acknowledge slavery as private property was to ask that they accept what they did not believe. Nor was it an act of intruding in the internal affairs of another country.[55] Given the strong antislavery feelings in England he could not have agreed to American demands, and he was fortunate enough to have legal rulings on his side.

Everett forwarded Aberdeen's reply to Webster with the comment that it appeared to him that the reply was irrelevant to the presentation he had made to Aberdeen. Webster, on receiving Aberdeen's response, expressed surprise. He defended what Everett had said and then expressed disgust. He was, he said, disappointed with its controversial spirit. He was surprised by what he called Aberdeen's misapprehensions. Webster had not demanded the surrender of the fugitives from justice. Nor had the legal ruling of the Crown officials as discussed in the House of Lords "had anything to do with the points raised by us." To Webster, far worse than the misapprehensions was the light in which Aberdeen seemed inclined to regard the murderers and mutineers. It appeared that Aberdeen viewed them as innocent. Webster held that they should have been brought to court as murderers and pirates.[56]

The *Creole* case posed great danger that the negotiations would end in failure, and it was so viewed by Ashburton, Webster, and Hugh Legaré. Legaré wrote to Webster in late July that it was time to put an end "to the odious questions that seem too likely to spring out of the course of conduct lately adopted & approved in the British colonies." The public clamor would be greater if nothing were done. The majority of Southern men "will make a terrible pother if there be nothing forthcoming under hand and seal."[57]

On 1 August, Webster sent Ashburton an appeal repeating once again the argument that the stand taken by the British Foreign Office was offensive. At the close of this note, softened by the tone of appeal in contrast to demand, he asked that if Ashburton lacked authority to negotiate on the *Creole* case, could he "engage that instructions shall be given to local authorities in the islands which shall lead them to regulate their conduct in conformity with the rights of citizens in the United States, and the just expectations of their Government, and in such a manner as shall, in future take away all reasonable ground for complaint."[58]

Ashburton replied that he wished that the controversy could be settled in London. He feared any settlement he might reach would be disallowed in London. Ashburton could not agree with some of Webster's points, although he respected his views. Ashburton added that he could engage that instructions be given to the governors of the British colonies to execute their laws "with careful attention to the wish of their Government to maintain good neighborhood."[59] Webster then was successful in calming critics. Finally, eleven years later, the Anglo-American Mixed Claims Commission awarded the United States $110,330 for the slave property lost.

Late in the negotiations after conclusion of the debate on the *Creole* case, Webster proposed that the prospective treaty should provide for extradition. This proposal arose out of the recent difficulties along the Canadian border where violators of the law of both the United States and Canada found escape by crossing the border. Ashburton readily agreed, but ruled out extradition of fugitive slaves. The British, he said, were not going to be placed in the role of slave catchers. The treaty as finally drafted provided for extradition of men charged with murder, arson, forgery, and other nonpolitical offenses.[60]

The final treaty satisfied prospective opponents of the treaty, and it was approved by the Senate by a vote of thirty-nine to nine. The treaty was welcomed on both sides of the Atlantic, although the strident voices of Lewis Cass, Senator from Michigan, and Lord Palmerston, the former British foreign secretary, both criticized the treaty as blots on national honor.

* * * * *

The *Creole* case went unsettled until 1855, but other cases of British naval interference continued under discussion. The United States as a leading commercial nation had a vital interest in freedom of trade and in the security of merchant vessels. In early 1842 Aberdeen assured Everett that orders had been issued to navy commanders not to interfere in any way or for any reason with American ships, but five cases still remained to be settled. These related to five ships, the *Douglas,* the *Tigris,* the *Jones,* the *Sea Mew,* and the *William & Francis.*

There were long delays as Aberdeen collected the reports from the naval officers off the cost of Africa. The *Jones* case had been in dispute for sixteen months at the time Everett assumed his post in London, and many more months elapsed before a settlement. That some of the actions of British naval officers were high-handed is illustrated in the case of the *Jones.* The ship was seized at St. Helena and then taken to Sierra Leone for trial. There it was left to rot. Eventually the British sold the cargo and turned over the receipts to the American owners.

Unlike his predecessor Everett was careful not to assume guilt until all the facts were in; he presented careful and detailed statements and persisted in pushing Aberdeen on each case. By 1843 each case had been settled, but there were to be others.

* * * * *

On the conclusions of the negotiation of the Webster-Ashburton treaty Aberdeen expressed regret that the treaty did not include a settlement of the Oregon question, and he told Everett that his instruction had called for settling that question.[61] Early in their negotiations Webster and Ashburton did discuss it briefly, but set it aside as the instructions stated that the boundary was to be at the Columbia River and allowed no room for full discussion.[62] Aberdeen hastened to correct what he judged had been a mistake. He informed Everett he had directed the British minister in Washington "to make known to the President the strong desire of Her Majesty's Government to engage, without delay, in a negotiation for a settlement of the boundary between the two countries on the Pacific Ocean and his wish that instructions should be sent me for that purpose."[63] The response was slow in coming.

Webster gave thought to a scheme calling for Mexico's cession of Upper California in return for an unspecified sum. The bounty paid to Mexico was to be used to pay American claimants and what remained of it to pay British claimants. As part of the proposed agreement the United States would agree on a boundary for Oregon. Webster did not contemplate simply relinquishing the territory north of the Columbia River, however.

Well before that Tyler's annual message to Congress aroused Aberdeen's distrust. The president spoke of Oregon as the territory of the United States "to a portion of which Great Britain laid claim," insinuating that it was the British who were delaying a settlement and raising the thorny question of the "right to visit" on which there was no prospect of agreement.[64]

Not until the middle of February 1843 was there a direct American response to the urging of Aberdeen. Webster now proposed a special mission—to Everett he confided that supposedly it would be headed by himself. He also instructed Everett to place the tripartite scheme before the British. The response was cold. Sir Robert Peel discouraged sending a special mission on two grounds: A special mission was only to be authorized under extraordinary circumstances, and should a special mission fail the situation would be worse than before. As to the fanciful tripartite scheme, Aberdeen did not wish to be a party to it.[65] That the special mission proposal was rejected was just as well because the House of Representatives voted down a bill authorizing a special mission at the time that Everett was discussing it with Aberdeen.[66]

In these first exchanges on the Oregon question Aberdeen urged that Everett be authorized to conduct negotiations on Oregon. Webster, at this promising juncture, declined.

Out of the apparently unproductive exchange emerged a proposal that gave promise of a solution. In reference to that part of the tripartite project that related to Oregon, Webster instructed Everett

Everett's Debut in Diplomacy

to be guided by what they had discussed earlier. In an earlier private letter to Everett, Webster had ruled out the Columbia River as a dividing line, because the mouth of that river made it unsuitable for a port. Then, in what might be described as in an offhand manner, Webster recalled an earlier proposal of 1826 by the British. It had been suggested, he wrote, "that the line of the boundary might begin on the sea, or the entrance of the Straits of St. Juan de Fuca—follow up those straits, give us a harbor at the southwest corner of these inland waters, and then continue South, striking the River to its intersection with the 49th Lat. North."[67]

Everett was not yet ready to pursue this offhand observation of Webster, and it is now clear that Webster mentioned it without intending that Everett should introduce it.

Why, then, did not Webster give Everett instructions to negotiate a treaty in London? At this point one is left to resort to what has sometimes been called impressionistic history. In February 1843, as Robert Winthrop described it, there was "a most furious war upon Webster." Part of this was due to his remaining in Tyler's cabinet, but Winthrop, a loyal support of Webster, believed that the Whigs would tolerate that "if only he will not use it as a vantage ground for battering down his own friends." Winthrop added, "His hatred of Clay will be his ruin, unless he restrains it."[68]

The strife among the Whigs had its counterpart in the divided Democratic party. The Van Buren faction had the support of the West, where Thomas Hart Benton was a leader. Benton, in turn, attacked John C. Calhoun at every opportunity.

It was in the midst of this intraparty rivalry that the Oregon question came to the fore in Congress early in 1843. Linn of Missouri introduced a bill providing for the extension of criminal jurisdiction to Oregon and set up rules for sale of land there. The bill was a clear violation of the existing treaty, and Calhoun and his supporters were successful in defeating the bill on those grounds. Webster dismissed the Linn bill as nothing more than a move by the Van Buren forces to rally.[69]

Politics did not stop at the water's edge. Webster explained why he did not send new instructions to Everett at a time when Aberdeen had held such great hope for a settlement and had urged that Everett be authorized to negotiate. Webster professed to Everett, "The truth is, if we negotiate about Oregon alone, I hardly know what instructions to give you, because I cannot tell what sort of a treaty two-thirds of the Senate would be sure to agree to. Here is the difficulty."[70] At the close of his stay in London, however, Everett wrote to Robert C. Winthrop:

I am filled with regret that Mr. Webster did not comply with Lord Aberdeen's request as he promised he would do and send me instructions. I have not the least doubt I should have been able to make an agreement on the basis of the 49th degree. Why I was not so instructed you need not be told.[71]

To the dismay of Everett, Tyler had, in late 1841, appointed Duff Green, the flamboyant editor, friend of Calhoun, and ardent defender of slavery to go to Europe and to sound out the possibilities for a loan.[72] Green was also intent on finding support for his own private ventures. Tyler, who hoped for a new commercial treaty, looked to Green to open the way. Green soon became involved in abetting General Cass, the U.S. minister to France, in an effort to block French approval of the Quadruple Treaty Great Britain had promoted to gain support in suppression of slave trade. As this treaty accorded to Great Britain the right of visit for the purpose of detecting offenders both Cass and Green saw in the treaty a surrender to the British and granting to the British a monopoly of world trade. Green so stated in blunt language in an article for the *Paris Journal of Commerce,* and he predicted a war between the United States and Great Britain.

Green's activity in England embarrassed Everett. Green hoped to promote a commercial treaty on free-trade principles, and to lay the basis for political cooperation between the North and South. He sent home reports, based on conversations with members of the Anti Corn Law League that the British were anxious for a commercial treaty. At the same time, Everett, after consultations with Sir Robert Peel and Lord Aberdeen, reported the contrary. The British were only interested in a new commercial treaty if they received preferential treatment, and this ran counter to American policy. Webster had also proposed a relaxation of British trade restrictions in the West Indies. Aberdeen curtly closed the door to that with the comment that England was free to regulate trade with her own colonies as she pleased.

The bumptious Green assumed "a lofty tone of remonstrance" with Everett threatening to urge Tyler to dismiss him if he did not cooperate. Green asked that Everett open the door for him to meet Sir Robert Peel as this would help him in improving his own private pecuniary speculations. In addition he sought Everett's help in setting up a commission of three Britishers who were to go to the United States and meet with an American commission composed of Webster, Calhoun, and an unnamed person. Together they would draw up a commercial treaty to be presented to Sir Robert Peel.

Everett's Debut in Diplomacy

Everett found this project inconsistent with the instructions he had received. After Green called on him at midnight to present his demands and posed a threat of writing to the president, Everett wrote private letters to both Tyler and Webster asking for an explanation.[73] Nothing came of Green's efforts.

Everett's complaint reached Washington after Webster had resigned as secretary of state and was replaced by Hugh Legaré, and Legaré took up the case with President Tyler. The president stated that Green had gone far beyond his instructions and that he had full faith in Everett. Legaré conveyed Tyler's views to Everett including the advice that Everett should inform Green of Tyler's rebuke if this became necessary.[74]

* * * * *

As early as the autumn of 1842 Everett had become uneasy about his relations with Webster. He made no specific complaints, but Webster's failure to delegate to him negotiations for a settlement of the Oregon question was disappointing. He confided to his close friend Robert C. Winthrop that Webster's reasons for so treating him were wrapped in mystery, but he suspected that Webster wished to escape from the bitter political struggle within the Whig party and would like to come to London.[75] Probably hoping to get at Webster's intentions Everett wrote a dispatch to Webster stating that though the British showed no enthusiasm for a special mission it would be honorably received and "that, if as I trust, you are to be the Minister, nothing would afford me greater pleasure."[76] He also complained to Caleb Cushing that Webster treated him coolly and that Webster probably planned to take his place. He confided that he objected to being replaced before he was "warm in his seat" and if some deal was underway "I must lose all self-respect before I could myself agree to it."[77] A month later he wrote to his father-in-law commenting on Webster and said, "Our great men are terribly selfish." It seemed to Everett that Webster sought to discredit him.[78]

In late February 1843 Everett received word that he had been named to a special mission to China. The news came as a shock, and for days Everett, believing he was being pushed out of the way to make room for Webster, wrote a series of letters to close friends telling of what had occurred. To accept the position meant that he would be separated from his wife and five children for an indefinite period at a time when he was much needed by his family. He also viewed the appointment as a demotion. The same thoughts were stirring in Boston, and Nathan Hale, editor of the *Advertiser,* criticized the move in the columns of his paper. In a letter to Everett, Webster tried to silence the distrust. He wrote:

> I believe the President thinks that there might be some advantage from an undertaking by me to settle the remaining difficulties with England. I suppose this led him to entertain the idea now abandoned (at least for the present of an extra mission). But in the present state of things I have no such wish to go to England—not the slightest.[79]

Although he acknowledged he had no wish to go on a more permanent basis and be saddled with the more routine duties of the legation, he qualified his statement. He would be interested if he could look forward to a brief stay and negotiate a major settlement.

Everett wrote to his old friend, Christopher Hughes, veteran diplomat:

> You see me gazetted for a mission to China. This intelligence came upon me unexpected and unwelcome, by the *Great Western*. My wife and children cry out against it and you know too well what family government is in New England not to feel the gravity of their opposition.[80]

To his brother-in-law, Sydney Brooks, he confided that he had been told that he had been appointed on the ground of fitness and "All view to other arrangements is disclaimed." He added: "On that point I have nothing to say."[81]

Webster's motives are certainly suspect; however, it should also be noted that in a letter to Everett explaining why he had been appointed, Webster stressed the importance of gaining information from the British as to their experience in negotiating with the Chinese as possible and determining what their future course would be. Webster explained that it was Everett's close relations with the British that had led to his being named. If this was the major consideration, it was undoubtedly inspired by Everett's dispatches in which he gave detailed reports on what he had learned from the British as to their adventure in China, and these dispatches emphasized the future importance of China trade and expressed the hope that the United States would seek to negotiate with China.

John Quincy Adams was pleased with the appointment and assured Everett it was an assignment of great importance. He could trust Adams, but he was not ready to trust Webster. He protested to Webster that he had received no warning, that the nomination contrasted with the policy of European powers who had reserved missions to China to diplomats of low rank or no rank, that the mission was most unlikely to be received in Peking, and therefore it would be of short duration. "Were I a young man, at the bottom of my class, without a family, there is so much in the appointment to arouse my ambition and excite my faculties. But I shall be past 49 when you get this letter and I have a wife and five children of ages to stand in the greatest need of a father's care."[82] Everett declined the nomination to China explaining his refusal as made necessary by family considerations. Everett's pride was hurt, and once again he was reminded that a public official never knew when his career would be cut off.

Webster arranged for the nomination of Caleb Cushing to head the mission to China. Everett, an associate of Cushing in his student days at Harvard was pleased, and throughout the mission he made every effort to be of assistance by giving him whatever useful information he could gather in London about the experience of the recent British mission to China.

* * * * *

Webster's resignation as secretary of state in May 1843 should have caused no surprise. Webster was in disrepute with the Whigs for sticking with Tyler after all the Whig members resigned from the cabinet in September 1841. Webster's political fortunes neared bankruptcy by late 1842, and that Webster all throughout late 1842 and early 1843 was contemplating resigning Everett knew well before the resignation occurred. The event marked a turn in Everett's position as minister of the United States to Great Britain.

Webster's successors were able, but they were also ardent Southerners, and their eyes were focused on Texas. Hugh Swinton Legaré, an able statesman, a champion of state rights, and an opponent of protectionism replaced Webster but died of ill health within a month. Tyler then appointed Abel Parker Upshur, a brilliant lawyer, a political theorist of sorts who argued that liberty was based on law and that democracy would destroy liberty. He served until 28 February 1844 when he was killed in an explosion on the warship *Princeton*. Then, the morning after that fatal accident, Tyler found himself with John C. Calhoun as secretary of state. His close adviser, Henry A. Wise of Virginia, precipitately asked South Carolina Senator George McDuffie if Calhoun would accept the post. Assuming that the inquiry was a firm offer McDuffie forwarded the offer to Calhoun who accepted. For his trouble Wise was compensated with heated indignation. Tyler shouted, "You are the most extraordinary man I ever saw, the most willful and wayward, the most incorrigible."[83]

Calhoun, a spirited advocate of the annexation of Texas, contended that it was a safety valve for slavery. Only if Texas were annexed and remained slave could slavery survive in the older states. Tyler had been determined to avoid tying the question of annexation to the slave question.[84] The president was obsessed with a fear of British encirclement. With the British to the North and West, should Texas become a client state of the British, the republic would be reduced to the equivalent of a robust young man reduced to immobility by confinement in irons.

Everett would miss his associations with Webster, but he did have the comfort of good relations with the president. Immediately after Tyler's annual message in 1842 Everett congratulated him and assured him that the message was well received. The message, on the contrary, aroused resentment.

There were good reasons for the friendly relationship. Tyler's difficulties with the Whigs stemmed from his vetoes of their national bank bills and his stand on the tariff. Everett's views on both these questions had changed. He now believed that party warfare made a national bank impractical.[85] The bank would be under constant attack from the opposition party and be a destructive divisive factor. Everett was no longer the ardent protectionist. He told Tyler, "As far as revision of our tariff is concerned, I am, and have long been, persuaded, that it would be better for our manufacturers to agree to almost any scale of duties which would give them a reasonable incidental protection and which being acquiesced in by the South, would be permanent, than by aiming at what is commonly called protectionism."[86] It was the passionate party warfare that he disliked. As he read reports of the Whigs deserting Tyler, of the bitter struggle among both the Whigs and Democrats, he decried the "political jungle."

One factor creating concern about Texas was the distrust of British intentions. The British interest in Texas stemmed from the advantage to be gained by freeing herself from dependence on the United States as a source of cotton and that an independent Texas with low tariffs would provide a market for British manufactures. The sharp increase in tariff duties in 1842 with the enactment of the Walker tariff sharpened British concern. At this same time the strong antislavery movement in England fixed its attention on Texas avowing that if Texas remained independent and if slavery could be abolished there, slavery in the United States would soon meet its doom. A third factor triggering interest in Texas was Aberdeen's concern about a recent decline of good relations with France. Aberdeen entertained the notion that this might be reversed if England and France made a common cause of the Texas question by uniting in support of Texas independence and in opposition to annexation by the United States. This was to take the form of inducing Mexico to recognize Texas as independent. If Mexico could be brought to do so, then the people of Texas would lose interest in annexation.[87]

It was in this setting that Lord Brougham gave a speech in Parliament that alarmed proslavery members of the Tyler administration. Secretary of State Abel P. Upshur, after reading the speech, sent a dispatch to Everett contending that the government in London "was now determined to abolish slavery throughout the American continent. . . . If this is the aim the duty we owe, not only to our interests but to our independence and dignity demands a prompt and decided counteraction on our part." He cited Lord Brougham's speech stating that Texas, suitable for free and slave labor, was desired by the United States to remain slave because it provided a market for the surplus of slaves in the older southern states. Brougham had stated that if slavery were abolished in Texas it would put a stop to "breeding slaves for the Texas market." He had urged that the Mexican government should be encouraged to acknowledge the independence of Texas for this might terminate in the abolition of slavery in Texas. Upshur noted that Aberdeen had made statements of a similar vein and that he was anxious for the abolition of slavery in Texas.[88]

Secretary of State Upshur and John C. Calhoun jumped to a defense of slavery. Both men had come to believe in the safety-valve theory. The older states with a surplus of slaves must be free to sell them to Texas. Should slavery be abolished in Texas, it would soon become a black republic and an asylum for fugitive slaves. The United States, said Upshur, "would have good reasons to apprehend the worst consequences, from the establishment of a foreign non-slave holding State upon their immediate border." Upshur held that the remarks of Brougham and Aberdeen represented British government policy.

When Everett met with Aberdeen in October 1843 to discuss Texas, the foreign secretary said he had read in a newspaper that the United States was being pushed to annex Texas because of Great Britain's intention to abolish slavery there, and he wished to state "if this measure were undertaken on any such grounds, it would be wholly without provocation." England had and would continue to treat Texas as an independent power, was pledged to encourage the abolition of slavery "as far as her influence extended, and in every proper way, but had no wish to interfere in the internal course of foreign governments."[89]

Duff Green had reported that Aberdeen was prepared to extend a loan to Texas for the purpose of abolishing slavery and that he had met with a group of American abolitionists. This report came up in the interview between Everett and Aberdeen, and Aberdeen acknowledged that he had first favored a loan but promptly dropped the proposal when his colleagues opposed it, and that the loan was not for the purpose of abolishing slavery. Everett, alert to the fact that the issue could easily lead to a crisis, took careful notes during the interview, and after writing his dispatch asked Aberdeen to check it for accuracy, which Aberdeen did. In a private letter to Upshur, Everett explained that the British public favored abolition, but there were great variations in how far they would go to achieve this goal. No British government could avoid subscribing to this general sentiment, but this did not mean that the government was prepared to act.[90]

In December Aberdeen sent a note to Richard Pakenham, who had recently been appointed minister to the United States, with expectations of negotiating on the Oregon question. Everett explained the British position on slavery, and he followed this with a second note in February. John C. Calhoun, who took over as secretary of state in March 1844, chose to see in these notes a devious cover-up of Aberdeen's intention, and on 18 April 1844, he wrote an eight-page peremptory letter portraying the virtues of slavery, charged Aberdeen with intentions to intervene, and held that an independent Texas, unable to resist indirect control by Great Britain, "would endanger both the safety and prosperity of the Union."

The coming to the fore of the Texas question, accompanied as it was by the expansion of slavery, so disgusted Everett that he thought of resigning. He confided in Winthrop that he supposed "nothing better could happen to me than to be recalled," and he supposed that some of his friends, seeing the instructions he had received, probably thought he ought not to wait to be recalled.[91]

Everett, always fearful of the arousing of public passions, saw that the Texas and Oregon questions would become ones of national honor and would lend themselves to exaggerations in political party warfare. He flattered himself that it was better for the public that he remain than give way to anyone the administration was likely to appoint in his place.[92]

Everett saw his situation differently from some of his friends in Boston who thought he should resign in protest. He felt he could possibly help stem the tide toward war, and he was willing to stay even though he was making a personal sacrifice. Time and again he

Everett's Debut in Diplomacy   117

cited the fact that his expenses exceeded his salary by nine thousand dollars annually, that he found it necessary to economize even on trifling matters, and that the work was laborious. He wrote to a friend, "My reward is in the consciousness that I am serving my country faithfully and in an honorable and arduous trust, and that shutting my eyes and my mind on every other consideration, and especially on all party views, I have been, and while I am here shall be, actuated by a sense of duty alone. These are I know stereotyped phrases of public men, but in my case, those who know most of the way in which my duties are discharged, are best able to vouch for me."[93]

Everett entertained no hopes of influencing decisions on the Texas question. He could do no more than act as a communications center between the two governments, but Oregon was a different matter. He continued to devote himself to a peaceful solution to that question. Aberdeen had favored a negotiation in London and assured Everett he would be delighted if Everett were granted full powers to negotiate. By the summer of 1843 Everett, in a dispatch to Secretary of State Upshur, revealed that he did not think it would be wise to carry on the negotiations there. He told Upshur that it seemed to him "out of the question to carry on such a negotiation anywhere but at Washington."[94] He did not explain his reasons, but a treaty negotiated under the eyes of Congress might have had a better chance of being approved or, perhaps, now that there was a new secretary of state he may have had doubts as to whether there was a sufficient meeting of minds so that he could negotiate with the confidence that he understood the feelings of his superior.

A promising turnabout on the Oregon question soon occurred. On 9 October, disregarding what Everett had stated, Upshur sent a dispatch granting Everett full powers to negotiate.[95] On informing Aberdeen he learned that it was too late. Aberdeen professed that he would have been delighted, but the present minister to the United States, Henry S. Fox, was being recalled because it was thought he was not the man for the assignment, and a new minister would soon be appointed. Everett thereon told Aberdeen that the instructions he had received from Upshur were masterful, exhausting both facts and arguments.[96]

Two weeks later in another interview Everett sought to persuade Aberdeen that a settlement along the forty-ninth parallel was reasonable from all viewpoints. On reporting this interview to Upshur he cautiously suggested that the president may wish to consider "whether we would agree to give up the southern extremity of Quadra and Vancouver island on condition that the entrance of the

Straits of Juan de Fuca be left open at all times and free to the United States with her navigation between that island and the mainland, and a free outlet to the north."[97] He assured Upshur that he said nothing about this to Lord Aberdeen.

These cautious soundings broke forth into a constructive dialogue on 29 November. Both men were equally eager for a peaceful solution, both trusted each other, and the discussion that afternoon approached what could have been an agreement satisfactory to both sides and thus avoided the tensions that came to dominate the immediate future.

It was Everett who took the initiative with a lengthy exposition of the reasonableness of the United States in having offered to settle by extending the boundary from the Rocky Mountains to the Pacific. This was to divide the area into approximately equal parts. He elaborated on the fact that France, Spain, and Russia had never surrendered their claims. Given the fact that Oregon was open to all countries and neither the United States nor Great Britain exercised sovereignty there was the possibility that France in her present expansionist course in the Pacific might decide to have her navy launch a settlement in the unoccupied area and then claim a share when Oregon was divided.[98]

Aberdeen did not challenge Everett's arguments, but he said it would be difficult to agree to stipulations that their opponents at home had twice rejected. This gave Everett his opportunity to make a proposal that would circumvent that difficulty. In his report to the secretary of state, Everett stated, "I regarded this observation now made to me for the first time . . . as very important." He then told Aberdeen that it would be difficult for the United States to make any modification of the former proposal except on one point, which he did certainly regard as very important to England, if she entertained any views to the future settlement of the country.[99]

The president, he continued, might be induced to leave the whole of Quadra and Vancouver Island to England. He had no doubt that there would be a large settlement in that area, and what he proposed would be a great advantage to England and would not involve a great sacrifice on the part of the United States. He observed that he was not authorized to say that this would be agreed to, but he thought it would and wished it would. Aberdeen agreed to take the proposal into consideration.[100]

In the course of the conversation Everett had cited the fact that the opposing party in England, in 1826, had gone so far as to offer the United States an enclave in the area they were discussing.

Aberdeen now asked if Everett was certain of this, to which he replied that he was, but he would be glad to check the facts.[101]

Two days later Everett sent Aberdeen a note stating that he had ascertained that the proposal had been made by Mr. Huskison and Mr. Addington to Mr. Gallatin on 1 December 1826.[102]

Everett was elated, and he assured Secretary of State Upshur that the "present Government are really willing to agree to reasonable terms of settlement." Of course, he added, they feel great difficulty in accepting what was then refused.[103]

The long conversation with Aberdeen occurred in the home of the foreign secretary. On returning to note this in his diary Everett wrote, "He said if we could keep down ill-natured agitation on both sides he thought there would not be much difficulty."[104] Unfortunately this was not to be.

The feelings in Great Britain were far from friendly. In part this was due to the private losses of investors when Pennsylvania declared itself unable to redeem its bonds. The strong antislavery feelings contributed to distrust. There was, said Everett, a general willingness to put everything American in the worst light.[105] Americans were no less prone to see sinister designs in British actions.

In April 1844, two months after the death of Upshur, Everett requested an interview with Aberdeen, and again they met in Aberdeen's home. His purpose in arranging the meeting was to inform the foreign secretary of the tragic death of Upshur. That a solution was within reach was a conviction with Everett, and he seized the opportunity to seek to persuade Aberdeen. The terms the United States had offered, the forty-ninth parallel, was, he said, wholly reasonable. Once again Aberdeen complained that it would be difficult to accept what had been thrice turned down, and once again Everett returned to the real possibility that this line could be modified so that Great Britain would retain Quandra and Vancouver, and thereby the fine ports of those islands.[106]

To the acting Secretary of State John Nelson, he stated that he thought that the British would eventually accept this, but it would be good to remember that the chief obstacle appeared to be their dislike of giving their public the impression that they were making concessions. Given this, he thought, that it did not displease Peel and Aberdeen that a cry had burst forth in the United States for 54°40'. "Such a course on our part," he said "will make it easier for them to stop at 49." Therefore it would be good policy on the part of the United States to emphasize the American claim to the territory to the north of the 49th parallel, although that claim was not without weaknesses. He added, however, that it would not be good to emphasize our claims to 54°40' to the extent that it would be difficult to recede.[107]

At this time the Texas question gave new momentum to the antislavery movement in England. Everett already found himself instructed to make protests against British actions growing out of the feelings that now dominated British thinking. Everett was opposed to slavery and termed it an anomaly.

When Calhoun took over as secretary of state, Everett was hopeful that a settlement could be achieved. Calhoun was in no rush to reach an accord, but he too was of the opinion that an agreement was in sight.

Other questions that were creating an adversarial relationship between the two nations contributed to the delay. The right of search question had not been resolved. It had been hoped that the stationing of an American squadron to support the British effort to put down the slave trade would set that question aside, but this did not materialize. Ships built in the United States as slavers carried produce from Brazil to Africa where the American crew left the ship, and it was taken over by Portuguese or Spaniards who then loaded the ship with the miserable human cargo. This, in turn, led to new incidents in which the British patrols stopped and sometimes detained American vessels. As a result Everett was burdened with scores of claims, while the British protested that the United States was not living up to its obligations. That the British were engaged in a humanitarian effort in seeking to stop the trade had a hollow ring for Calhoun who pointed out that the British, when they captured a slave ship, did not set the slaves free in Africa but sent them to the British West Indies where they were enchained in the apprenticeship system.

There were other points of sharp conflict. The British continued to hold fast to their rulings in the *Creole* case, and when fugitive slaves found their way to British territories, they were firm in their refusal to surrender them. In one instance some slaves held guilty of murder in Florida fled to the British islands where they were set free. In the eyes of the fervent antislavery people in England, slaves who rebelled against their masters should be pardoned for any incidental crimes. Everett was under obligation to do his best to have the British change their policy, and he devoted days to preparing statements of protest.

Calhoun's firm belief that the British would do everything possible to block the annexation of Texas was strengthened by the measures the British were pursuing in foreign trade. Imports from

Everett's Debut in Diplomacy

countries that tolerated slavery were made to pay heavier duties than those from territories free of slavery. There were loud protests from exporters of American tobacco that their goods were being burdened with excessive duties.

Calhoun had his first conference with the new British minister, Richard Pakenham, on the Oregon question on 29 August 1844, in the midst of the election campaign. Pakenham soon reported to Aberdeen that there was a disinclination in Washington to move forward with the Oregon question. Pakenham did inform Calhoun of his instructions. He was prepared to offer the United States an enclave on the Olympic river, but the Columbia river was to be the boundary.[108]

The election of James K. Polk to the presidency in November 1844 left it almost certain that Everett would be recalled when Polk took office. Both nations, it appeared in the summer of 1844, were in a position where political considerations at home made a compromise almost impossible. Aberdeen repeatedly responded to Everett's appeals stating that this was so. Faced with this situation Aberdeen proposed that the question be submitted to arbitration. He strongly favored arbitration because it would circumvent the point of national honor. Everett saw difficulties in determining what issues could be set before an arbitrator because unlike the dispute of the Maine boundary this was not a question of deciding between two lines. In reply Aberdeen said there was a twofold question, first "whether the United States had an exclusive right to the whole" and if this were decided in favor of England the question would be what would be a fair compromise. Everett now saw advantages in arbitration, but the administration rejected it. The difficulty in the United States agreeing to the proposal lay in the fact it would have little public support and the arbitrator might set a line below the forty-ninth parallel.[109]

There was the "eternal letter mill," as he called it, to keep Everett busy. Lengthy briefs on this or that routine question continued to take his time. In his diary he complained that he was burdened with hard work, and enjoyed no appreciation. He wrote, "I cannot divest my self [*sic*] of the feeling that I am sadly wasting my time in this eternal drudgery and that my recall will be the best thing that can happen to me." His strenuous efforts to promote peace appeared to have been in vain.

The election campaign of 1844 began with the Democratic Convention in Baltimore. Leaders from the states of Michigan, Ohio, and Indiana were successful in inserting into the party platform a call for the annexation of all of Oregon extending north to 54°40′.

Polk was committed to the platform. He won the election by a narrow margin over Henry Clay, in all probability because Clay lost votes to the Liberty Party candidate in the key state of New York. The Democratic party was the party of expansion, and it was tied to the annexation of Texas and Oregon. Polk was in full accord with his supporters, and he had his eyes on California, acquisition of territory that would permit a transcontinental railroad along a southern route, and Oregon. In this he was not alone. Caleb Cushing, now a Democrat, held that the British threatened to encircle the republic, and that the British should be left free to expand in the rest of the world without American interference; in turn, the British must not stand in the way of the United States in North America. Cushing was an advocate of the annexation of all of Oregon. It was the faction of midwestern Democrats, however, that Polk had to be most responsive to for fear he might find himself president of a divided party. His victory in the election not only meant that Everett would be replaced, but that the Oregon question would be immersed in heated party strife and probably be reduced to a question of national honor.

Party strife in England posed a similar problem. Peel's Tory party was under fire from the Whigs who, it appeared, would exploit any apparent conciliatory move. The Tories did not soon forget Palmerston's charge that the Webster-Ashburton Treaty was sheer capitulation.

* * * * *

Everett, given the atmosphere in London, feared that no American proposal would get a fair hearing in the press. This was on his mind when on 29 March 1845, shortly after Polk took office, he met the well-known and highly respected journalist Nassau Senior. Everett was asked to give him a general idea of the Oregon controversy. Everett went over the points of dispute and explained why he thought the offer of the forty-ninth parallel was a reasonable offer. Senior agreed and said he would write an article if Everett would furnish him the means of doing it. On his return home a week later he found Senior waiting for him. After further study and consideration of the modification that would leave Quadra and Vancouver to the British, an amendment that Everett apparently included in his explanation a week earlier, Senior had completely fallen into line with Everett's thinking. He was ready to write an article for the *London Examiner* and "perhaps in the *Edinburgh Review*." Everett, very pleased, noted in his diary that this was an important step.

Two days later Thomas Macaulay, famous as literary personage and a member of the Parliament, entertained a group of eminent leaders at breakfast. Everett and Senior were among the guests. Senior had now read the pamphlet by William Sturgis of Boston, a merchant, in which he proposed a compromise almost identical with that discussed by Everett and Aberdeen. He was so impressed with the article by Sturgis that he urged Everett to have it reprinted. Sturgis had sent his article to Joshua Bates, the American employee of the Baring Bank.

Nine days later, on 18 April, Everett and Senior met again, and he now had a draft of an article from the *Examiner*. Everett thought it had been written with great candor and temper. He now furnished Senior with volumes containing the negotiations of 1824 and 1826 and a copy of a report written by Caleb Cushing in 1839; Senior was now ready to write the article for the *Edinburgh Review*. Both Everett and Aberdeen read it and gave their approval before it was published. The article appeared in the July issue.[110] The Whigs in Great Britain denounced it.

In the spring of 1845 President Polk and the new Secretary of State James Buchanan tilted uneasily toward the compromise that Everett held coincided with the interests of both countries and would give the politically beleaguered administrations of both Sir Robert Peel and President Polk an acceptable passageway to peace. After offering the post to four choices only to be turned down, Polk appointed Louis McLane in Everett's place. McLane, a strong-willed man who was critical of the extremists in Congress, was reported to have told Polk that he favored compromise.

Buchanan was at this time preparing a proposal, and the thought was that it would serve as a first step toward negotiation and bargaining.[111] The proposal he made and the language in which it was phrased, however, deprived it of any spirit of compromise. It called for drawing the line at the forty-ninth parallel and did no more than offer the British use of the ports south of that line. Both the written and the oral communications put it in terms of a concession, and held that the United States had full claim to all of Oregon. The claim to the area north of the forty-ninth parallel was based on the transfer of Spanish claims to the United States in the treaty of 1819. These claims had been exposed to close examination in London and found to be weak.

Outright rejection of the proposal by Parkenham brought an end to the negotiations. Polk now took on the forbidding countenance of a great stone face, dismissed the fears expressed by Buchanan, and took refuge in his illusion that the British could not be kicked into a war. Here the matter rested at the time of Everett's return to the

United States. Aberdeen in London felt Pakenham was guilty of a serious error, for his instructions had left him leeway to bargain, and if necessary to accept the line he and Everett had discussed.[112] Polk soon withdrew his offer of a settlement along the forty-ninth parallel.

Everett's compromise proposal was soon swamped and almost lost to sight by news that served to promote suspicion and hostility on both sides. French talk about creating a balance of power in the new world, reports of British and French designs to protect California from seizure, speculations about an approaching famine in England and higher duties on imports of American wheat, and the rapidly approaching crisis in relations with Mexico created unrest. The details of these happenings are only peripheral to this narrative.[113]

In his message to Congress Polk was in large part self-congratualtory, but he was not belligerent. He called for a termination of the treaty of joint occupation, a proposal that was shortly approved by the House. It stirred up a long and heated debate in the Senate. Webster and Calhoun led the opposition. The debates focused on what Polk might do once the treaty was terminated. To this question Polk gave no answer. Belligerent talk ebbed in London thanks to Aberdeen. The London *Times*, usually unfriendly to the United States, published an editorial, inspired by Aberdeen, advocating a settlement along the lines so often discussed.[114] Everett was delighted, and informed George Bancroft, now a member of Polk's cabinet, and Daniel Webster that it was the work of Aberdeen and should be viewed as the official position of the British.[115] The same trend appeared in Washington including the White House where Polk, who disliked nothing more than to give the appearance of weakness, gradually agreed to assuring the British that a proposal from London would be submitted to the Senate. It was this move that finally broke the log jam and opened the sluice gate to constructive steps. Almost a year had passed since Polk took office. The delay owed much to the hesitance of Sir Robert Peel and President Polk, both of whom felt it necessary not to weaken their political flanks in the home country. In the meantime, representatives in Congress had indulged themselves in bold and nonsensical rhetoric.

The final moves were made quickly once the Peel ministry received word that the Senate had passed the bill terminating the treaty that provided for the joint occupation of Oregon. Thanks to Albert Gallatin, the notice drafted in the Senate was conciliatory and assured the Foreign Office that British settlers would be secure.

The new British proposal, drafted by Aberdeen while working in close cooperation with the American minister Louis McLane, followed the line that Aberdeen and Everett had first discussed three years earlier.

On his return to the United States in September 1845 Everett was something more than an observer of events. He carried on an important correspondence with Lord Aberdeen. In November he advised the British Foreign Secretary that even the Whigs would go no further than the modification of the line of the forty-ninth parallel.[116] He confided he was convinced that the only prospect of an amicable adjustment rested on the willingness of the two governments to settle it on this basis. Again in December, full of anxiety of the consequences if there should be a repetition of what Pakenham had done, he pleaded if an overture was rejected on the supposition that a boundary more favorable to England could be obtained it was at once an idea that was delusive. Before "the gates of Hell are unbarred" he hoped that Polk would renew his offer, but given the uncertainty of that, he felt "a mortification and sorrow . . . that you have not felt yourself able to accept a basis of settlement, which I am sure is the most favorable that can be had."[117]

By December Everett was ready to blame England for the near breakdown of negotiations, and he wrote to his old friend Robert Walsh that Polk's uncompromising posture was "not a bad tone in diplomacy when England is the other party" if it were accompanied "by moderation of pretension."[118]

He was no less anxious that the administration might not recognize that the Peel ministry faced an opposition that would welcome a war. In a letter to George Bancroft, now secretary of navy, he warned that there were several great interests in favor of war, and "the army and the navy pant for service." Moreover, "No small portion of the people of England have got to think that a war with the United States affords the best hope of putting an end to slavery, an object paramount with them to all others." There was the prospect, too, that the Whig minority in England might seek political advantage by goading and taunting the Tories for their alleged lack of spirit.[119]

Everett had enjoyed his life in London, more especially the friendships he had made, and working with Aberdeen was always comforting and reassuring. Everett was a realist, however, who never closed his eyes to the fact that those holding office must give the highest priority to national interest, and that those charged with the conduct of foreign affairs could not fail to consider public opinion whether that opinion was right or wrong. Looking back over the Oregon controversy during his final weeks in London he had reached the conclusion that "Taking the conduct of the two Governments from the beginning, I think ours has been the more reasonable and moderate in its pretensions."

The solution finally adopted did grow out of Everett's persistent efforts to demonstrate its reasonableness, but there were more weighty forces at work that made that solution acceptable to both sides.

* * * * *

Many factors contributed to the settlement of the Oregon controversy. Britain's readiness to agree to a compromise owed much to the importance of the American market, dislike of war with the United States at a time when relations with France were disintegrating, the declining importance of the fur trade of the Hudson Bay Company in the area between the Columbia River and the forty-ninth parallel, and the peaceful disposition of the British foreign secretary, Lord Aberdeen. America's willingness to compromise owed much to economic considerations such as the importance of British credit and the British market. The market, with the repeal of the corn laws at the time, lifted the hopes of the farmers of the Middle West who had been hard pressed.

It also was clear to the British that there was a strong strain of moderation among Americans. Everett represented sober thinking at its best, and so did the success of the Whigs in Congress who exploited the recklessness of the expansionists. Joshua Bates and Thomas Wren Ward, New Englanders in the employ of Baring Brothers in London, had direct access to British leaderss and contributed to quieting the alarm promoted by the expansionists.

Another factor contributing to the peace was the work of the aging Albert Gallatin, one-time secretary of the treasury diplomat and a New York banker, who had been deeply involved in negotiations on Oregon and who knew the intricacies of the question probably better than anyone else. Everett recognized the contribution that Gallatin made and thanked him, adding that what he had done surpassed in importance all of the great contributions he had made to the republic. Gallatin published, at his own expense, the argument in pamphlet form explaining both the just and unjust claims. Most important, in late February 1846 as the Senate was ready to approve termination of the treaty of joint occupation, Gallatin was successful in having the notice phrased in very conciliatory terms and, equally important, he pointed out that the major concern of the British was the security of British subjects residing in Oregon. The Senate met his wishes.[120]

5
Harvard Presidency

To move from the busy legation in London where questions of peace and war hung in the balance and where social life offered exciting conversation with leaders in the intellectual community posed a transition of difficult dimensions. When the first soundings came as to his willingness to accept the presidency at Harvard, Everett had doubts. There were those, among them Nathan Hale, his brother-in-law, who warned him that it would leave no time for either leisure or scholarly pursuits.[1] He accepted the presidency, but he did so partly because at the moment no more attractive opportunity presented itself and partly because of the urging of his many friends.

To the local community and especially the faculty Everett appeared the ideal choice. Harvard presidents were always Harvard graduates, and Everett was one of the most illustrious of the alumni. The faculty expressed their delight in a letter to the new president citing his dedication to learning and his success as a public figure.[2] Daniel Webster spoke more cautiously. He thought Everett's decision to accept was a great gain for the college, but he added, "I should rejoice on your account also, if there were not so much detail duty and small work, attached to your office. The Corporation ought to throw this off."[3]

Certainly all outward appearances made it appear that Everett was the ideal choice. The new president entered on duties with a dead seriousness and a complete dedication to the college. He anticipated that if all went well he could spend his remaining years there. His aim was to transform his alma mater into a university along German lines. It was to become a center of learning offering a broad program including science, a true university enriched with professional schools staffed by men dedicated to research, and it was to become the gateway through which young men acquired a reverence for learning and a sense of duty rooted in Christian principles.

These goals were set forth in his inaugural address. The university, he said, consisted of two parts, the academic and the professional. There was "the acquisition of knowledge in the various branches of science and literature, as a general preparation for the learned professions and the other liberal pursuits of life"; "the exercise and development of the intellectual faculties," and "the formation of a pure and manly character, exhibiting that union of moral and intellectual qualities which most commands confidence, respect, and love."[4]

The address was an invitation to learning. The acquisition of knowledge included acquiring language skills, discovering the art of communication, and learning how and where to go for knowledge. It was the preparation to study further and to acquaint the student with the great human achievements of the past.

The development of faculties, distinct from the acquisition of knowledge, was in Everett's words, "the most momentous portion; it embraced the building of discipline and the development of such cardinal powers as attention, perception, memory, judgment, abstraction, and imagination. The "grand mystery of the mind," he said, called for twofold caution, but the more we meditate "the more we shall incline the faculties to the conclusion that the mental faculties are in some peculiar manner modified, strengthened, and perfected by discipline." The human intellect, he held, was open to "boundless capacity, susceptible of unlimited improvement in the individual, and of being carried, in the steady progress of generations, to a point of perfection hitherto undefined and probably indefinite. The object of a university was to train these faculties "to the highest attainable degree of methods, promptness, and vigor."[5]

Everett had acquired a familiarity with the recent developments in science, and during his recent residence in Europe made friends with some of the leading men in astronomy. His enthusiasm for the new findings found expression in his inaugural address. There were he said, "some departments of exact science which must be regarded as forming the grandest study of which the human mind is capable, and as eminently calculated, for this reason, to give it strength and elevation."[6] In words of reverence he spoke of the science of "the heavenly bodies which is as little to number and weigh as the humblest arithmetic." Astronomy, "the grandeur of the laws which it discloses and applies; the boundless distance which it spans, the periods, all but eternal, which it estimates, impart a solemnity to this branch of science, which lifts the soul to the heavens."[7] Thanks to Josiah Quincy's efforts, Everett's predecessor, Harvard was soon to acquire an observatory.

Everett's third aim of education was to instill "a pure and generous spirit, warmed by kind affection, governed by moral principles, and habitually influenced by motives and hopes that look forward to eternity." Scientific and literary culture would not suffice. Contemporary society was sliding into "a practical heathenism" and "we worship, in American and in Europe, in the city and the field, on the exchange and in the senate—and must I not add in the academy and the church?—some gods as bad as those of the Panehton."

To the secular mind of the next century Everett's occasional retreat into traditional religious language may appear as pure obscurantism. Everett's use of that language, however, was more in the nature of a metaphor than statements to be taken literally. In his formative yeaars of early unitarianism Everett had been so fully exposed to the teachings of moral philosophy that he never wholly escaped the moral emphasis and that implied that all things must be held subservient to the moral end, and this included education. He had long since been emancipated from theology and in its place had come the dedication to an ennobling life. That he resorted to language that carried meaning to people in a church-centered community was part of the price of having accepted the presidency of a college immersed in moral philosophy.

Harvard must be dedicated to the formation of character on Christian principles. How this objective was to be achieved was another matter, but Everett fell back on a hope that the daily devotional exercises and the two chapel services on Sunday might be transformed from the killing influence of routine and habit into exercises that would inspire a sense of duty and a seriousness of purpose serving as an ally of the educational program.[9]

Ralph Waldo Emerson was present that day to listen to the man who had once been the light of his intellectual life. He now listened to Everett with distrust, believing that Everett had put on blinders so as not to be troubled as he pursued success in the political world. Emerson thought Everett's "grace and propriety were admirable through the day." "Nature" he wrote, "finished this man." "He seems perfectly built, perfectly sound and whole; his eye, voice, hand exactly obey his thought." Emerson, however, found Everett's final appeal to moralism chilling and melancholy. Everett, he thought, had deliberately given himself over to the corpse—"cold Unitarianism and Immortality of Brattle Street and Boston."[10]

Emerson was of a far different philosophical persuasion than Everett. Emerson was committed to the intuitive philosophy and intent on dismissing the myths of the past and rediscovering fresh sources of truth. Everett, with his strong historical sense, accepted myths for what they were, useful in their time for enabling a generation to piece together a meaningful, overarching interpretation of the world as they knew it. For Everett change came slowly. It was better that it was so. History had demonstrated time and again, most recently in the French Revolution, that hops, skips, and jumps, based on blueprints that took no account of the resistance to innovation, ended in brute force and reaction.

Among the many factors that would affect his presidency was the structure of the college, its financial resources, and the willingness of the faculty to cooperate in instituting change.

Harvard had 277 students in 1847; of the freshmen class 54 came from the New England states, 9 from the South, 3 from New York, and 1 from Pennsylvania. In addition to Harvard College, the undergraduate college, the university had three professional schools; the Divinity School, the Law School, and the Medical School. Instruction for undergraduates was dominated by traditional classical studies. The treasurer of the college Samuel Eliot, in his report claimed that undergraduate studies included chemistry, mineralogy, anatomy, physiology, and elocution. This was to claim too much, however. As Everett stated, the sciences were barely touched on and only incidentally in the courses of the first two years. It was this that Everett sought to remedy.[11]

The government was lodged in two bodies, a board of seven members called "The President and Fellows of Harvard College." This was the real governing body. The president was no more than an ex officio member. He had one vote, but was wholly subordinate to this board more commonly known as the corporation. The corporation was subject to the visitorial powers of the overseers consisting of the governor, lieutenant governor, the governor's council, the state senate, and fifteen clerical and fifteen lay members chosen for life. The overseers were the final board of control, but they met ordinarily only once a year, and their actions were more often of the pro forma variety.

The financial resources of the university left no room for innovations or unforeseen expenses. So much was allocated to each division. The university had a general fund or endowment of $140,000. The total income amounted to $23,639 in an average year, whereas the annual expenses of the college exceeded $40,000. The deficiency was made up by what was then called a tax on students, in brief a fee, and these fees averaged from $76 to $80 for each student.[12]

On his arrival at Harvard, Everett discovered the harsh truth. His wealthy father-in-law, P. C. Brooks, offered to donate $10,000 for the construction of a new home for the president, but Everett informed him that he had heard so many complaints about the lack of unappropriated funds and so much of the necessity of reducing student fees that he held a great repugnance to take a considerable sum out of the common stock for a house. He suggested instead that if given to the college as a gift, it would enable him to approach other rich men for donations.[13]

The financial stringency imposed inadequate salaries on the teaching staff. The average salary of a professor after years of service was $1,800, but some received less. The librarian was paid $1,000 a year and his assistant $500. Only $800 was set aside for purchasing books and for binding those in need of repair. Their laboratories consisted of little more than what had been gradually acquired for use in classroom teaching.

The inadequate salaries of professors embarrassed Everett. He readily acknowledged that a professor could not support a family on what he was paid.

The distinguished Louis Agassiz was lured to Harvard by Everett and paid $1,500. Shortly after he came he complained that he was unable to live on that amount. Everett admitted that this was true, but that the college had no funds for correcting the situation.[14] He could only advise the distinguished scientist that he would be able to supplement his salary with lecture fees. The professor of Latin and Greek, who enjoyed the full confidence of Everett, found it necessary to resign because he could not support his family. Professors Charles Beck, Cornelius Conway Felton, and Joseph Levering presented a memorial for increases in salary, but this was turned down because the money was not to be had. Everett's salary was a modest $2,500 a year.

The prospects were chilling, but Everett was quick to point out the strengths of the institution. He was rightfully proud of Asa Gray, famous for his *Manual of the Botany of the Northern United States,* of Benjamin Pierce who did much to awaken the public to an interest in science and who drew up the plans for the School of Science before Everett's arrival, and George Bond director of the observatory. He pointed to Jeffries Wyman, whose field was physiology, to Joseph Levering in natural philosophy. During his first year as president he appointed Louis Agassiz, geologist and zoologist, who introduced the laboratory method of zoology and who did notable work in the field of glaciers. Agassiz and Everett became close friends, and he attended Agassiz's lectures.

To his intimate friend George Bancroft, the historian, he reported that standards had greatly improved since they were students, but he added the qualifying phrase "as high probably as the demands of the community will warrant."[15]

Students were selected with a great degree of rigor, and those from the two academies, Exeter and Andover, were well prepared. But the screen was not fine enough to sift out those whose youthful exuberance easily triumphed over weak motivation.

Everett considered the university a fine seat of learning, but it was weighted down with apathy that kept it out of step in responding to society's new needs. To change the nature of higher education was like tunneling through solid rock, not only at Harvard, but in colleges and universities throughout the country. The time for change had arrived, but recognition of this was to wait until after the Civil War.[16]

Of the existing schools that made up the university, Everett considered the Divinity School the weakest. Wholly dominated by the Unitarians, the Divinity School was in poor repute with other denominations. Because Harvard was considered a sectarian college the public at large viewed it askance. Everett saw this as one of the university's greatest liabilities, and he favored separating the Divinity School from the university both administratively and geographically. On this, as on other reforms he wished to institute, he was vetoed by the corporation.[17]

America had not yet come of age, and neither had Harvard. It was certainly not ready to accept Everett's plans to establish a university along German lines. In terms of pushing into the modern era his most significant success was in establishing the Lawrence School of Science. The most firm adherent of the past could scarcely reject a donation of $50,000. Abbott Lawrence, the giant entrepreneur of the New England textile industry had in mind an Engineering School.

Everett, president of the American Academy of Science, wanted something more than an Engineering School, however. He was successful in reshaping the plan of Lawrence, and here he had the support of Benjamin Pierce, the mathematician and astronomer. Everett saw in the establishment of the School of Science a way to inject new life, to "render the school as far as the very different circumstances of the country demand and permit, a kind of German university."[18] He had high hopes of incorporating in the new school studies in philology, but this was denied by the corporation.[19] Everett saw in philology an instrument that would be highly useful to the historian.

Given its later connotation the name of the new school was

misleading. To Everett it meant advanced studies, specialization, and research. Science incorporated more than the methodical examination of the physical and biologic world; it included advanced studies in antiquities, literature, and history. Science was set off from the introductory studies not by the nature of the subject matter but by the intensity with which it was approached. Everett could write: "Although we call it 'Scientific,' we have made provisions for students of classical learning."[20] In the unique amorphous development of advanced studies the terms used had not yet acquired the more rigid connotations they have today. Everett's idea of a true university originated in his experiences at the University of Göttingen where rapid advances in the study of antiquities and a series of other fields created the degree of excitement that only discovery can kindle. He would have preferred to include professors of Greek and Latin; what mattered was not the professors' field but that the professors were feverish with the spirit of inquiry. The corporation's decision ruling out philology put an end to that dream, and, as Everett acknowledged, the new school was little more than a drawing on paper. At the time Charles Beck, the professor of classics, regretted that the new school should be named the School of Science for it should include the liberal arts.[21]

Everett greatly regretted that he was unsuccessful in incorporating philology. To a friend he confided that he had held out for it as long as there was any prospect of carrying his views.[22] He was neither the first nor the last college president to be defeated on the issue, but deprived of success his stay at Harvard seemed to serve no purpose although he could write in a philosophic strain to his dear friend, the queen's physician, Dr. Holland, that reform almost always encounters resistance "by virtue of a salutary principle of our nature, which provides a check upon the license of innovation."[23]

Amid the darkness of defeat and the monotonous duties of attending to the innumerabale menial duties, there was the glimmer of light of the academic community he dreamed of Harvard becoming. On the lonely island of Nantucket there was the maker of chronometers for the whalers, William Mitchell, who built his own telescope and who observed the stars. His only kindred souls lived in Boston and were members of the Academy of Science. There was also his daughter, Marie, who studied mathematics while tending the library in a small town and who, like her father, was an observer. On 1 October 1847, Marie discovered a new comet. Her father told Everett of the discovery, and Everett, the well-informed reader of the journal of the Royal Astronomical Society, became convinced that she was entitled to the gold medal award of the king of Denmark to the astronomical observer who had made the most significant discovery of the year. Amid his pedestrian duties at Harvard, Everett corresponded with friends in England, instructed the American consul in Copenhagen to inform the Crown of the recent discovery, and when his petitions were drowned in the mill of petty correspondence, prepared a detailed verification of Maria Mitchell's discovery. Her discovery was no accident. She became the first professor of astronomy at Vassar, the newly established college for women, and there she carried on her research and established a reputation of high repute.

At Harvard there was young George Bond who worked with his father as director of the new observatory. Their close participation in their work has defied determining who of the two was responsible for particular findings. On his father's death George took over as director. He immediately won the president's admiration, and rightfully so for George Bond soon achieved a reputation as one of the most brilliant astronomers in the new and exciting field. Everett shared in Bond's excitement. At the early age of twenty-three, while Everett was president, Bond, in the course of his observations of Saturn, discovered the satellite Hyperion, and two years later he found Saturn's crepe ring. This was only the beginning of Bond's work. His illustrated monograph on Donate's comet of 1858 won him the gold medal of the Royal Astronomical Society. His enduring fame rests on his being the first to use photography in the study of the stars.

For all the disappointments of Everett he experienced the excitement of being associated with a small circle of distinguished scholars, but he had undertaken a mission for which neither the corporation nor the overseers were ready. Perhaps the boldness of Charles Eliot could have won his way, but Everett was a reformer of great sensitivity. He first consulted the faculty on every important measure only to find that they gave first thought to their own self-interest. When the elective system was discussed, opinions hinged not on accommodating differences in individuals but on the effect of their own enrollments.[24] When the School of Science came into being, the major concern of many faculty was the conflict in schedules that would affect them.[25] To replace limited horizons with a broader vision in an institution deeply rooted in the past proved beyond Everett's capacity. He attributed his deficiency on failing health and strength, and protested that it was not a matter of courage.

Given the ponderous load of detailed and menial duties that

lesser men could have performed, the presidency was not designed to be a position of leadership. He was buried in the details of keeping the records, dealing with discipline, counseling students who were in difficulty because of poor performance, admonishing students declared guilty of infractions, investigating serious violations of the college laws, meeting with parents and visitors, answering the queries of parents, and sitting on all major college committees. Approximately three hours of each day were taken up with students judged guilty by the faculty of infractions or indecorum.[26]

Whispering during chapel services or leaving the service in a rush were deemed offenses. In the early period of his tenure students placed a bale of hay outside of his office and set fire to it; another time they set fire to the college chapel. In the latter instance Everett left it to the city authorities to take action.

The beleaguered president complained: "Nominally the head of a great literary institution, I find my self [sic] in reality the justice of a police court, without any time I can call my own to read, write, or think."[27] Record keeping alone took much of his time. Every week each faculty member filed a report stating the student's grade and describing any incident of improper behavior. These were carefully filed, and at the end of the month the president and his one assistant were left to establish the student's ranking in his class. Deductions were made from the academic grade for any offenses.[28]

On entering the presidency Everett believed that there had been too great laxity. He could accept the exuberance of youth, but he thought it must be held in rein and not lead to an environment of levity that relegated studies to a low profile. Before being plunged into the abyss of discipline he entertained the opinion that the situation could be corrected by kindly and reasonable appeals.

Seeing Everett's dignity and sensitivity the students set out to make life hell for him. The president's punctilious manner lent himself to caricature, and the students made the most of it. In July 1846, after the first five months in office, six students were dismissed and told that they could not return.

Among the sympathetic observers of Everett as he sought to deal with the discipline problems was John Langdon Sibley, the assistant librarian. Sibley thought there were only a few students who were disposed to be mischievous and troublesome toward the president, but before Everett's first year had come to a close he concluded that Everett was unable to deal with the difficulties. Sibley wrote in his diary: "He will hardly be able to govern all of them by the high principles and motives he has adopted, which are too high to be fully appreciated by boys and young men who are only gentlemen when it suits their convenience. It is a pity that he is made of delicate nerves and feelings, though he never shrinks from duty when necessary to act."[29]

In March 1847 Everett was burned in effigy, and a few days later a fire was started in the entry hall to his office. Sibley thought the incident had its origin in Everett's effort to abolish the Navy Club and class suppers. Both, said Sibley, were disgraceful to the college. A few mischievous students took delight, he wrote, in torturing a man who was exceedingly sensitive.

The discipline problem diminished before he decided to resign, however. The final year was a quiet one. Students ceased to make disturbances, and only one student was dismissed.

Edward Everett, during his years at Harvard, was deeply unhappy. Men who present an outward appearance of success sometimes are a host to a deep inner distrust and insecurity that belie their standing in the community. Everett was not lacking in courage and he had great strength of character, but the presidency placed him in a position of compromising. What ought to be done could not be done. To represent Harvard meant to approve of what it was, and that was to be placed in a false position. He confessed to his devoted friend Robert C. Winthrop that for the sake of peace and harmony he was in danger of sacrificing his sense of duty and conscience.[30] The position, he was convinced, had a palsying effect.

Everett's mental health was threatened. He had come from a prominent position and one of prestige. The legation in London was likewise a position suited to his talents. As minister he faced disappointments, but the mistakes and failures were not his mistakes and failures. At Harvard he was blamed for all that went wrong. He was publicly humiliated, and he was spending his days on menial tasks.

He complained constantly of ill health, but his complaints appear to have been less a result of his physical condition than of his unhappiness with the presidency.

He attributed his ill health to prostate problems, and when he learned that his brother Alexander had died in an illness brought on by an infection of the prostate, he decided that he too would soon die of the same ailment. Everett had scarcely passed the meridian of life; he was fifty-four years of age when he descended into gloom over his physical condition.

Assurances from his private physician, Dr. Warren, that there was no reason why he should not attain the normal life-span, failed to comfort him. In a spell of despondence he wrote a lengthy letter to his friend Dr. Holland in London, the queen's physician, describing in detail his condition. This factual account included the difficulties resulting from the need of urinating frequently. If he took tea at six o'clock in the evening, he awakened in the middle of the night and could not go back to sleep. He felt no pain in urinating, but he did have a feeling of discomfort in the whole urinary region though he could not say it was pain. He also suffered a general stiffness in the lumbar region. These symptoms, he stated, whenever they preyed on his mind, became more discomforting than he could wish. He added a second grievance in Latin: "The passio aphrodisentis valde debilio est. Unus ejus sine dolore sed die poetra mina supradute symotomata aggravantur."[31]

The depression experienced as the president at Harvard had unforeseen effects on Everett's physical condition. Everett was ill suited for dealing with the problems he faced; he was too sensitive and easily wrought up. There was an element of fragility that forced him to retreat when the going became rough. Everett recovered, but he was to suffer illness once again when political storms raged.

The letter he wrote to Dr. Holland preceded by one month his report to Charles G. Loring explaining the many duties of the president. The crucial test had not yet arrived, but he was already determined to resign. He was then at work on drafting a new set of laws for the university. He explained to Loring that he had planned other changes than those he was finally incorporating in the new statutes. In the revision he recommended the revival of the practice of class tutors who would work closely with the students.[32] This, he thought, would relieve the president of a small portion of duties but not in instances where students faced serious anxieties over prospective dismissal.

Everett had gone further and proposed a more basic change, however, the appointment of a dean of the faculty who would be charged with the administration of discipline. This would leave the president free to devote his time to the general supervision of the institution. A senior professor, Everett assumed, would be appointed, and it would become necessary to relieve him of some of his teaching duties. Therefore an additional tutor would have to be named, and Everett intended that he should be paid out of the president's salary. Whoever became dean would consult with the president on serious discipline cases so that Everett did not foresee any great relief, because it was these problems that had taken so much of his time.

Had this proposal been made earlier and carried through, Everett might have been able to weather the storm. It was now too late.

Everett had already decided to resign, although he had not set a time. He informed Loring that the discipline had greatly improved, but that in the course of two years of the presidency he had changed from a reasonably healthy person into a feeble and ailing old man.

During those two years Everett had wasted some of his capital on trivial questions. Less than two months after his inauguration, he proposed that officers of the college be required to attend all chapel services, two each day of the week including Sunday. He entertained the opinion that their attendance would cause the students to be more reverent. Prayers for blessing in their labors would be helpful. In his letter to the faculty, Everett explained that he did not forbear to dwell on the subject because it was a matter of individual conscience; he disclaimed the right to act the part of monitor toward any of his respected associates. At the meeting of a faculty committee to consider the proposal Dr. James Walker, a clergyman, wisely moved that attendance should be recommended but not required and that this recommendation should only apply to Sunday services. Everett accepted this in good grace, but he himself never missed a service during his almost three years of tenure.

He was more spirited in his advocacy of two other changes. He made an important issue of returning to the use of the original college seal and to the use of the name "The University of Cambridge," this on the ground that the name so appeared in the state constitution. In both instances he met with strong opposition from Samuel A. Eliot, the treasurer of the college, a powerful figure in his own right. Everett had foolishly convinced himself that defeat on these two proposals was tantamount to a vote of no confidence.

Publicly Everett announced that his reason for leaving was his health, but to Robert C. Winthrop he confided that this was not his real reason. He was leaving because of difficulties in his relations with the faculty and the corporation, a fact he chose not to publicize because it would do injury to the college. He had found that "he could not depart from the tradition of his [Quincy's] administration of 16 years, without conflicts and struggles, for which I do not want courage but strength and health." To his brother-in-law Sydney Brooks he wrote that "my position is certainly not to my liking inasmuch as I have all the care and anxiety incident to Public Life without the satisfaction of working in a larger field." In his letter to the corporation he reminded them that the office of president "is one mainly of executive detail clothed with no power but that which proceeds from his individual vote in the different academical boards of which he is an *ex officio* member."

The day of his resignation his distinguished historian friend, William Gardiner Prescott wrote: "Mr. Everett goes out in the odour of sanctity—that is, in much better odour than he has lived in there, for the scholars have just begun to appreciate his good qualities." Everett's fetishes, his too great faith that rational religion would create an environment conducive to learning, and his too great sensitivity had stood in the way of his implementing a great ideal, the ideal of the German university.

6
Voice of Moderation amid Reckless Adventurism

Victory in the Mexican War left in its wake restless and opportunistic politicians ready to serve special interests and embark on adventurous projects. This was the period when bustling America caught its first glimpses of world power. Amazingly rapid developments of the railroad system, steamboat transportation, and domestic industry inspired confidence in the nation's strength and in the opinion that the republic had a role to play in international affairs. The Young America movement found its home in the Democratic party and its strongest support in the Midwest, where Stephen Douglas of Illinois, Lewis Cass of Michigan, I. P. Walker of Wisconsin, and Edward Hannegan of Indiana expounded on the duty of Republican America to support the revolutionary movements of 1848 in Europe. The Young America movement had a short life, but the assertive spirit it embodied lived on through the 1850s. With the election of Franklin Pierce in 1852, special interests concentrated on ventures in Central America, Cuba, and northern Mexico. Roy F. Nichols, biographer of Pierce, wrote with good reason that Pierce and his secretary of state, William L. Marcy, "may have wondered sometimes whether they were managers of foreign policy or errand boys of business. Looking at the situation in 1848 Everett warned, "There is nothing novel in our present embarrassments: they belong to a career of conquest. Each step forward creates the necessity of taking another. Such was the history of Rome and Napoleon: such had been the history of the British government in India. Let us retrace our steps before we add another example to the list."[1]

* * * * *

Everett's interest in foreign affairs was as sharp as ever. The revolutions of 1848 caused him to fear that a large-scale war was imminent. As the revolutions spread to eastern Europe it appeared to him that if Austria intervened in Tuscany or if the fighting in Austria was prolonged, then Russia would intervene, and France would be tempted to move.[2] As the revolutions gave way to peace, and Louis Napoleon came to power in France, he apprehended further strife. The government of Louis Napoleon, Everett believed, did not have the power, if it did have the will, to stay quietly at home. He wrote, "the army impatient for action—soldiers want adventure and plunder; the non-commissioned officers want promotion; the Colonels and Generals want Marshalls' batons, and all want glory."[3] Louis Napoleon, he thought, was not the man "to hold these fiery elements in check as he owes his name to his uncle."[4]

Everett shared his insights with the newly elected president, Zachary Taylor, half hoping that the new executive would appoint him to a foreign post. He did not hesitate to remind the president of his successes in London, but he accepted the fact that during his presidency at Harvard he had rendered no service to the Whig party and had no claim to reward.

* * * * *

In the midst of the great debates of 1850 that led to the compromise of that year, Zachary Taylor died and Vice President Millard Fillmore took his place. He promptly appointed Daniel Webster secretary of state. Once again, because the appointment entailed greater personal expense, wealthy friends raised money so that Webster could accept.

In the autumn of 1850 Webster turned to Everett for assistance. During the early days of the Hungarian revolt led by Louis Kossuth, President Taylor sent an envoy to Hungary, Dudley Mann, with instructions to be "the first to congratulate her" should Hungary be able to maintain independence. By the time Mann reached Hungary the revolution had collapsed. Some time later, after President Taylor learned that the Austrian minister to Washington, George Hülsemann, had surreptitiously obtained a copy of the instructions to Mann, he reacted by including an expression of sympathy for the Hungarians and of the Mann mission in a message to Congress, and he subsequently sent the documents relating to the mission to the Senate. It was not until Webster had become secretary of state that the Austrian minister officially protested these claims.

Distraught by the recent eruption of sectional feelings, during the debates on the Compromise of 1850, Webster saw in Hülsemann's letter an opportunity to rally national feelings, and domestic political considerations took command. In October, while stopping in

Boston en route to his ancestral home in Franklin, New Hampshire, he asked Everett to draft a letter to Hülsemann. It required a master's hand, said Webster, and he instructed Everett that it was necessary to uphold the late President Taylor's action to defend the right of the American government and people to express their sentiments, and "yet show the cautious and conscientious abstinence of the Government of the United States from everything which should look like real intermeddling with the politics of other countries." Webster said he would prepare a draft of his own, and they could compare the two.

Everett completed his draft in four days and adhered to Webster's instructions. Though not belligerent in tone, Everett's letter was an expansive exposition of American rights and devotion to liberty. He held that the action of the United States conformed to the law of nations and that Austria had provided a precedent when that government, during the American Revolution, received a representative of the American rebels. That Americans, who cherished their own liberal tradition, should sympathize with a people fighting for freedom was only natural and within their rights.[5]

Once in Washington Everett's original draft went through several revisions that added insults to the already long homily. Webster wrote to Everett stating the letter "has been revised, a little enlarged, copied and dispatched."[6] Everett did not read the final note until it appeared in the *National Intelligencer* a week later. His eyes fixed on the assertion that compared with the United States the possessions of "the House of Hapsburg are but a patch on the earth's surface."[7] He wrote in his diary, "some of the changes made by Mr. W. in the draft prepared by me, in the way of additions are improvements, others decidedly the reverse, . . . it is addressed to the American appetite for highly spiced statements."[8]

In a letter to Robert C. Winthrop he expressed disgust with the entire transaction. A mistake had been made in making the letter to Hülsemann public before it was delivered to Vienna. He observed, "it is in fact wholly an operation for the domestic market." Moreover, said Everett, there was no need of sending Dudley Mann in the first place for all needed information could have been obtained from Mr. Stiles, the American Minister in Vienna. Had Webster been secretary of state earlier, Everett thought, he would not have sent a special mission. He considered it a great error to permit popular sympathy with the Hungarians to dictate an overt move to promote a revolution in the heart of Europe to which the United States did not have access and where it could not exert any influence.[9]

* * * * *

Everett felt the need for a change—preferably a government position. He was restless, "afloat" without a position. He had often complained about life in politics, but the fact was he loved it. The change came early in 1852 when his daughter, Charlie, now married to a Naval officer, invited him to come to Washington. He stopped in New York where he delivered an address that brought him compliments. In Washington he enjoyed himself to the fullest. He had dinner at the White House with President Fillmore, visited with him at length at another time, had dinner at the residence of the British minister, and met with other foreign diplomats. As his spirits rose he felt better and could write to his wife that for the first time in months he was able to sleep without sniffing ether or chloroform.[10] He wrote daily letters to his wife telling in detail of his experiences. He visited Mount Vernon, admired the scenery, but deplored the neglect that was bringing decay.[11] He noted in his diary, "If I mistake not they [the days spent in Washington] are destined to exert a powerful influence over the coming years of my life."[12] Not long after his return to Boston he reported that Webster had urged the president to appoint Everett secretary of state if he resigned.[13]

On 24 October 1852, Daniel Webster died. The passing of Webster, so often reviled in his home state ever since the 7 March speech, turned the nation into mourning. Thousands passed by his burial place, and many newspapers ran biographical sketches applauding the "God-like Daniel."

During the preceding year, with both Fillmore and Webster as candidates for president in the next election, Everett had done his best not to alienate the president. He was quietly supporting Webster and sooner or later Fillmore would learn of this. He informed Fillmore that he held him in high respect, but Webster had been his friend for many years, and he was promoting his nomination. He assured the president that should he be nominated he would gladly support him.

Everett and President Fillmore were in complete agreement on foreign affairs. On 27 October, just prior to a meeting honoring the late secretary of state, Fillmore offered him the position that Webster had held. He asked for a few days to consider the invitation explaining that he must make arrangements for the care of his ill wife. Having made arrangements he accepted and departed immediately for Washington.

The most immediate question facing him was the dispute with Peru concerning the Lobos Islands. The islands were rich in guano, deposits of bird droppings accumulating over centuries of time. These deposits had value as fertilizer, and by the 1830s ships in great numbers from England, France, and the United States carried on a highly profitable trade. American ships engaged in the trade circumvented Peruvian authorities, thereby lowering the costs of the guano.

In March and again in May 1852, Peru issued decrees stating that all ships that should approach or anchor at the islands or places containting guano would be liable to seizure or confiscation unless they first had permission from the government of Peru. Important shipping interests in New York and Boston immediately protested to Secretary of State Webster and contended that the islands were not offshore and therefore were not subject to Peru's jurisdiction. Webster, now humiliated by his disappointing showing in the Whig national convention and in a sullen mood, hastily accepted this argument, and on 8 June, Secretary of Navy William Alexander Graham ordered naval ships to protect the American merchant vessels engaged in the trade.[14] With this assurance some twenty-five ships set sail for the Lobos.

A crisis followed. The Peruvian minister in Washington, in a carefully prepared statement, showed in convincing fashion that Peru had exercised jurisdiction over the islands ever since Peru became independent and that the United States had recognized Peruvian jurisdiction. A mistake had been made, but Webster, although he recognized this privately, took the position that he must wait until he had a report from the U.S. minister in Lima. Time would not wait, however. Reports reached Peru that American ships were on the way, and the prospect of a naval encounter aroused the wrath of the local citizenry. J. Randolph Clay, the U.S. minister, who was convinced that Webster had made a serious mistake and so warned, now sent a dispatch stating that if force were used, it was doubtful that American lives and property could be protected.[15]

Webster arranged for countermanding the order to the navy ships in the Pacific, but there was concern that these orders would not reach the ships in time. Therefore Webster sent a message in a pleading tone asking that the Peruvian authorities permit merchant vessels already at sea free access without conforming to Peruvian regulations. He did not retreat from his refusal to recognize Peru's sovereignty in the islands.[16] Thanks to the discretion of J. Randolph Clay, who did his best to assure Peru's foreign minister that Webster would change course, Peru agreed not to interfere with ships that sailed between 8 June and 25 August.

This was the situation when Everett entered his duties as secretary of state. He immediately took up the question with Peru's minister in Washington, J. G. Osma. His conciliatory approach opened the door to an agreement. On 16 November, he delivered a letter to Osma acknowledging Peru's sovereignty over the islands, withdrew all objections of the late secretary of state, and conveyed his thanks to Osma for the generous terms Peru had agreed to in relation to the trade.[17] To Clay, the U.S. minister to Lima, he sent his compliments on his conduct "during the somewhat embarrassing scenes of last summer and autumn." He praised Clay for his discretion and good judgment at a time of crisis.[18] Clay, in turn, was happy to report that the terms laid down by Peru would permit "what is called in mercantile language, a handsome voyage."

Everett faced a zealous and powerful group of interests who fixed their attention on Cuba, Central America, and Mexico. The victory in the Mexican War added to the entrepreneurial lust for territory and profits. In both New York and New Oleans there were shipping interests who looked to government as an instrument to be used. Shipping interests would profit by annexation of Cuba, a port of call for ships going from New York to New Orleans.

New Orleans, in dread of new railroads from Chicago and St. Louis to California, saw itself being left far from the main lines going across the continent. To save New Orleans it would be necessary to build a canal through northern Mexico. The Tehauntepec route would establish the city as the main terminus between the Pacific and the Atlantic Coast. The gains would be even greater for the company holding the Garay grant. That dubious grant called for a transfer of 5 million acres of Mexican territory to the company, land reputed to be rich in minerals.

Cuba had long been viewed as a highly strategic point given its location across the routes to Central America, but from the days of Jefferson it was agreed that if it did not fall into the hands of Great Britain or France, Cuba posed no danger. After the victory in the Mexican War, however, Cuba took on new significance. To the slaveholding states there appeared to be a prospect of the slaves in Cuba being set free, and the slaves contituted roughly 30 percent of the island's population. Visions of a black state revived memories of Haiti. In addition, cruel Spanish rule in Cuba led to the beginning of a revolutionary movement. American expansionists charged that the British were anxious to take over Cuba and set the slaves free. High duties on imports into Cuba added fire to the enthusiasm. A Cuba annexed to the United States would make the island an important market for American goods.[19]

Fillmore turned a deaf ear to the new brand of imperialists within the Democratic party. Everett agreed with the president. His record as secretary of state repudiated the adventurous politicians who paraded under the banner of Young America.

The election campaign of 1852 whipped up a cry for red-blooded Americans to replace the timid foreign policy of the Whigs with a display of self-assertion. Any would-be concessions to the British were equated with an absence of honor. England served as the whipping boy and quiescent Whigs as the symbol of weakness. Steven Douglas, Lewis Cass, and Pierre Soulé were the front line of the offensive, and in back of them were George Law, Romulus Sanders, and yet-to-be recruited Judah Benjamin, still a Whig and president of the Tehuantepec Company. They exploited public prejudices and appealed to emotions.

In the Thirty-Second Congress, representatives of Young America summoned the nation to uphold national honor. Their foremost aim was the annexation of Cuba, but little was said about that until President Fillmore in his annual message warned that the acquisition of Cuba would be a hazardous adventure. Before that they found it more useful to concentrate on the Clayton-Bulwer Treaty with England and the latest efforts of the British to limit American fishing rights in the Bay of Fundy.

The debates offered Young America the opportunity to vilify the British. During a debate on the Central American treaty Steven Douglas of Illinois, a member of the Senate, warned his audience that "nearly every English book contains lurking and insidious slanders and libels upon the character of our people and the institutions and polcy of our government." British abolitionists, he charged, threatened American security. And, said Douglas, "she keeps her missionaries perambulating the country, delivering lectures, and scattering broadcast publications designed to incite prejudice, hate, and strife between the different sections of the Union."[20] When the question of fishing rights came before the Senate, Lewis Cass of Michigan called for a rigid stand affirming the nation's honor. "We did not get the right to fish on the ocean from England, nor from any other power," he said in a decisive tone. "We got it from Almighty God, and we mean to hold on to it, through the whole extent of the great deep, now in the days of our strength, as our fathers held on to it in the days of our weaknesses."[21] Fishing rights suddenly became the great cause of men from Louisiana and Arkansas, depriving the New Englanders of their former monopoly of that cause. Pierre Soulté led the way, attacking Daniel Webster for his leniency in responding to the latest British orders. The British navy squadrons sent to the Bay of Fundy to police the area should have been driven out by the American navy. William Seward arose to say that he found it comical that these two senators from the Southwest should have suddenly acquired such a deep interest in fishing rights and that they should attack Webster who more than any other had distinguished himself as the New England fisherman's best friend. As far as pushing out the British naval squadron, the difficulty was that there was no squadron there.[22]

The question came to the fore because of the Canadians' desire to gain freer access to the American market. The British minister in Washington had proposed a reciprocal trade treaty, but this awakened no interest in the Fillmore administration. Then on 12 July 1852, Secretary of State Webster received notification that the British were now instituting new patrols in the Bay of Fundy and would strictly enforce the provisions of the Convention of 1818. The note made clear that American fishermen were to be barred from fishing not only from three miles off the coast, but the prohibition would apply from headland to headland, a ruling that prohibited Americans from fishing in the bays including the Bay of Fundy.

Again Webster hastily drafted a note to John F. T. Crampton, the British minister, a note couched in bellicose language, pleasing to the American audience, that he promptly delivered to the press.

In his haste he made what has been rightfully called a serious blunder.[23] He did not speak of American rights under the Convention of 1818 but of the privileges the British had extended during the past thirty years to American fisherman. As to rights, he only spoke of defending the property rights of Americans, not of the rights that Edward Everett had vigorously asserted while minister to Great Britain as being inherent in the Convention of 1818. By failing to place his protest on the ground that the rights were a matter of treaty, Webster in effect abandoned these rights.

Everett saw the error at once. When the London *Times* retrieved from the files the notes Everett had given to Lord Aberdeen in 1845 contending that the Convention of 1818 assured the American fishermen rights to fish in the bays and dismissed Everett's argument as of no consequence, Everett wrote a twenty-two page letter to the editor tracing the issue from the time of the negotiations in 1818 to the present. It was a sober and factual account aimed at enlightening the influential London *Times* that the United States had a strong case.

Everett's letter read like a dispatch from the Department of State. The purpose of the negotiators in 1818 was to remedy the evils perpetrated by Americans on the coast and on the shore, and at the same time to reserve to Americans "as large as liberty of fishing as was consistent with this purpose." The American negotiators held that the bays in which they had renounced the right to take fish and dry were the "shore bays along the coast and not the large outer bays like the Bay of Fundy." It could not have been the purpose to prohibit Americans from fishing in the Bay of Fundy, which is from fifty to sixty miles wide at its mouth. When, in 1815, a British commander warned an American vessel off the coast some forty-five miles from Cape Sable, his act was disavowed by the British government. Lord Bathurst wrote, "It is not of fair competition that his Majesty's government [has] reason to complain, but of the preoccupation of British harbors and creeks in North America by the fishing vessels from places where the fishing might be most advantageously conducted." On the day the convention was signed, an American note read that it was hoped that with the renunciation of inshore fishing a considerable portion of "the actual fisheries will . . . be preserved."[24]

Up to 1839 neither colonial nor British cruisers made any seizures other than of fishing vessels that entered the small bays within three miles of shore. Everett cited other British acts to support his interpretation of the treaty.

Everett recalled that when he was minister to Great Britian, lengthy discussions occurred between him and Aberdeen. It appeared that although Sir Robert Peel adhered to the British construction of the Convention of 1818, he and Aberdeen were prepared to make concessions and did agree to open the Bay of Fundy. Aberdeen saw as one obstacle to further relaxations the high duties on fish imported into the United States. In 1846, however, duties had been lowered to 20 percent, and imports of colonial caught fish increased nearly tenfold. Everett then asked, given the generous treatment accorded these imports, if this was a time to increase the vigor with which American fishermen were treated.[25]

Everett's letter held firmly to the contention that the Convention of 1818 preserved the rights of Americans to fish in all except the smaller bays along the shore and outside the three-mile limit. This interpretation differed from that of Webster who made fishing not a matter of treaty rights but of comity between the two nations. Both Webster and Everett saw in the dispute a question that could be resolved by negotiation, and Webster retreated from his initially bold position as the weeks passed.[26]

Everett's argument left the United States in a stronger position, but Webster's view of the Convention of 1818 may have been correct. Indeed, Everett was not as persuaded as he appeared to be in the letter to the London *Times*. At this time he was corresponding with W. H. Trescott who was writing a book on American foreign relations and who asked Everett to read his manuscript. Trescott raised questions concerning the negotiations of 1818, and was critical of Rush and Gallatin for agreeing to the paragraph renouncing American rights to the extent they had. Everett did not wish to criticize his old friend Rush, and stated that after all he had the approval of John Quincy Adams, a man of great authority. He then added: "But that all these clear headed and vigilant statesmen should have agreed to renounce the 'bays' and take no pains to guard against the extension of that term to the outer bays, especially such as the Bay of Fundy and Chaleurs, is to me a great mystery."[27] Everett made no such acknowledgment to the British minister, John F. T. Crampton, when they began negotiating.

In their negotiations they dealt not only with fishing rights but with the broader question of trade between the Canadian provinces and the United States. Everett and Crampton drafted a treaty, but the new administration of Franklin Pierce delayed taking action.

Then occurred the affair of the *Crescent City,* a ship that stopped in Havana en route to and from New York to New Orleans. Enthusiasm for the annexation of Cuba had been kindled by incidents involving American ships entering Havana. On 2 September 1852, the Cuban authorities refused to admit the *Crescent City,* which belonged to the U.S. Mail Steamship Company headed by George Law, an entrepreneur of unsavory reputation and an active member of the Democratic party. Law not only welcomed the incident but sought to promote further ones in the hope of starting a war. The Cuban authorities refused entry because the purser of the ship, M. Smith, had supposedly written scurrilous attacks on the Cuban government.[28]

The incident gave rise to sharp outcries especially in New Orleans. At a mass meeting in New Orleans Judge Larue, in tune with his audience, commented: "It is said that we have been endeavoring to raise an issue with Spain in order that we might take possession of Cuba. Well, suppose we had, Cuba naturally belongs to us geographically." The possession of Cuba, he said, was "absolutely necessary to the safety of the United States." Judah Benjamin added that the island would have long since been freed had not the federal government looked upon the filibustering expeditions with a hostile eye.[29]

This ominous development in the midst of the election campaign was of grave concern to Fillmore, and it was decided to send the newly appointed minister to Mexico, Judge Conkling, to his new post by way of Cuba. Conkling bore a note from the president to the captain general of Cuba, Canedo, explaining that the action taken regarding the *Crescent City* was causing him great difficulties. Included with the note was an affidavit from Purser Smith clearing him of the charge of having written sharp attacks on the government in Cuba. Canedo was to protest later that he had been assured that both Purser Smith and Admiral David Porter would be removed from the ship. The admiral's speeches attacking Cuba while he was being feted in New Orleans as a hero had been offensive. Faced with a dangerous situation the captain general rescinded the ban on the *Crescent City* entering Havana.[30]

At the same time President Fillmore sent a public letter to the Collector of Customs at the port of New York ordering him to curb the activities of George Law. The letter boldly stated that if Law pursued his course his ships would be denied protection, that the question of peace or war was not for Law to decide, and the difficulty was one for negotiation between the governments of the United States and Spain.[31]

Thus matters stood when Everett arrived to serve as secretary of state. Still to be acted on was a joint note from England and France that had been received in April. The note proposed that the United States join with those two powers in disclaiming "both for now and hereafter, all intention to obtain possession of the Island of Cuba, and that they respectively bind themselves to discountenance all attempts to that effect on the part of any powers or individuals whatsoever."

An answer to this note had been delayed, as Fillmore had explained, because an election campaign was not the appropriate time to respond. It now fell to Everett to prepare an answer.

Everett stated three major reasons for declining the proposal of England and France. To join would be a departure from the traditional policy of not becoming involved in the internal affairs of Europe, a policy established by George Washington and Thomas Jefferson, and adhered to since their day. Second, to join in the proposed self-denial agreement was to equate the interests of the United States in Cuba with the two European powers. The proximity of Cuba to the United States gave it a greater interest. Third, the United States had no present intention or interest in acquiring Cuba, but it could not bind itself for circumstances could arise when self-interest would require it to adopt measures not now demanded.[32]

The charge by the foreign offices abroad that the United States was guilty of land grabbing was met with the retort that some European nations had engaged in far more land grabbing and with far less justification than the United States whose acquisitions had been of contiguous territory. The United States had never chosen to protest the aggrandizements of Great Britain and France. What the United States had acquired was fully in accord with the law of political existence. Everett made no apology for the annexation of Texas; the internal divisions it had provoked, he asserted, had no place in a communication with a foreign power. Everett reaffirmed the American policy of no entangling alliances. He expressed the hope that they would certainly understand that for the United States to join with the powers of Europe in such a self-denial would only serve to give a powerful impulse to those feelings for adventure the administration had held in firm restraint. No administration, he explained, "could stand a day under the odium of having stipulated that with the great powers of Europe, that in no future time, under a change of circumstances, by no amicable arrangement with Spain, by no act of lawful war, . . . by no consent of the inhabitants of the island, should they, like the possessions of Spain on the American continent, succeed by rendering themselves independent."[33] In the event of an overriding necessity of self-preservation, the United States should have free hands. This left open the option of annexation, leaving the door open to future imperialism, but in Fillmore's annual message to Congress, a month earlier, Everett had already warned that annexation of Cuba would be a hazardous adventure. Everett described the situation in a long and bold letter. The *New York Times,* after confessing that it had not always held the author in high regard, pronounced it "one of the most admirable papers ever issued from the Department of State." Letters flowed in complimenting him.

* * * * *

Everett was busy at his post as secretary of state when two of his political associates from Massachusetts called on him. One of the two sought to ascertain whether he wished to be elected to the Senate. Everett did not record his answer, but on 16 January he received word that he had been nominated by the Whig caucus. The state legislature elected him. He was still secretary of state on 3 March and took his seat in the Senate the following day.

He was named at once to the Committee on Foreign Affairs and the Committee on Territories. On 21 March 1853 he delivered a speech on Central America, a subject then beclouded by acrimonious charges against Great Britain and alleged violations of the Clayton-Bulwer Treaty of 1850.[34]

The speech began with an explanation of why the Clayton-Bulwer Treaty was necessary if a canal was to be built through Nicaragua. Nicaragua and Costa Rica both claimed control of the banks of the San Juan River, the stream leading to the point where the canal was to originate. The channel for ships followed the Nicaragua side on some stretches and at other points the Costa Rica side, making necessary agreements by both of these countries. Another barrier was the unstable condition of affairs between Nicaragua and the British protectorate known as the Mosquito along the coast, including the port of Greytown at the mouth of the San Juan River. Everett held that the weak and unstable Central American republics could not resolve these problems and therefore it was necessary for the United States and Great Britain to arrange a settlement.[35]

This brought Everett to the crucial question as to whether the current fashion of ascribing to England devious circumventions of the treaty were justified. He chose to accept British assertions that her protectorate over the Mosquitos was not a creation since the treaty, but that it had two hundred years standing and came into being when Spain in her days of glory sought to monopolize trade in the area. As for Greytown, it was populated almost wholly by Americans. Honest efforts were underway to bring peace between Nicaragua and the Mosquitos. The ancient rivalry between these two regions made settlement difficult, but the British were acting in good faith. Everett strengthened his case by citing a recent diplomatic note from London demonstrating a sincere effort to resolve the difficulty. As to the uneasiness created by the recent British establishment of a colony over Belize and the Bay Islands, her action was injudicious, but that area did not fall within the sphere to which the treaty was directed.[36]

Seeking to discount the distrust of the British, Everett cited the good faith of the British in withdrawing from the Hawaiian Islands in 1842 after a British naval captain had raised the British flag, how they had negotiated the northeastern boundary dispute in good faith, and of their reasonableness in settling the Oregon question.

Turning to the broader question of what the American posture should be in the Caribbean area, he held that greatness in size was not synonymous with true greatness. He, too, like Stephen Douglas, believed in the glorious future of the United States, but Douglas made it dependent on future expansion and assumed that future greatness was to depend on following a policy of hostility toward

Europe. Developments in the friendly states of Europe, said Everett, gave promise of a glorious future for those countries. "I wish I could persuade him [Stephen Douglas] that the glorious future of America is not inconsistent with an equally auspicious future for the friendly powers of Europe."[37]

The danger, said Everett, was that "we are apt to regard geographical extension as the measure and the index of our country's progress." To be sure, greatness did not develop within the bounds of a petty state, and extension of territory was not invariably bad; expansion need not carry with it conflict with other powers; "we shall in the natural progress of things have as much of it, and as rapidly as the best interests of the country require." Greatness, he said, "if we wish a real, solid, substantial growth" will come by the simple increase of our population "not by the geographical accession of dead acres, not by the purchase of Cuba, or by the partition of Mexico."[38]

Knowing that his remarks could be distorted, he explained that he did not countenance "a pusillanimous doctrine of nonresistance. . . . American commerce spread over every sea and the immense island frontier must be protected." He warned, however, "while we act on the maxim 'in peace prepare for war,' let us remember that the best preparation for war is peace."

Everett declared there was no place for either love or hate in international affairs. He agreed, he said with Senator Douglas, that "England does not love us." This was beside the point. He proceeded: "In the relations of countries which are governed by Constitutions, by Parliaments, and by Congresses, there is no room for love or hate, or for any sentimental influence; enlightened regard to the public interest is the only rule of action. . . . Between us and England, and the rest of the constitutional Powers of Europe, there is room only for the influence of the dictates of an enlightened regard to the public weal." As to relations with England he was persuaded that all parties in that country desired a mutually beneficial and peaceful intercourse, which, he said, should be considered "a cardinal principle of our policy."[39]

Everett was now experiencing the exhilaration of success. He won wide acclaim and was prominently mentioned for the presidency. He put aside the suggestion probably because he knew too well that it was premature to entertain such hopes but also because he recognized that the Whig party was on the point of dissolution. In the election of 1852 the party had carried only Massachusetts and Vermont. New party alignments were being discussed. In the meantime the Democrats were in control.

7
To the Point of No Return: The Kansas-Nebraska Act

Throughout the years Everett was hounded by the opposition who persisted in recalling the blunder of his first speech in Congress when he said that if a slave revolt occurred in the South he would join in suppressing it. By 1835 the antislavery movement gained adherents. On 28 October 1837, he issued a statement. It read: "I regard slavery a social, political and moral evil of the first magnitude; whose removal, as soon as it can be constitutionally done and peacefully effected, ought to be, and I believe is ardently desired by every good citizen and every good man in this country. Its proposed indefinite extension, by the annexation of Texas, I should regard as the greatest evil that could befall the Union." Passionate abolitionists could not wait until it could be done constitutionally and peacefully, and Everett appeared, as the years passed, as timid in the face of evil. The fiery abolitionist, Wendell Phillips, was to say of Everett that he had muscle but no heart.

The antislavery movement was an integral part of the broad changes occurring in American society. Regionalism, nationalism, immigration, and industrialization catapulted the North and the South into confrontation. Slavery was only one of the causes of confrontation and the Civil War. Each section approached the other with suspicion. The South became intent on containing the rapidly growing North with its rapidly increasing population, growing industry, urbanization, and expanding agriculture. The North was equally determined to put an end to the extension of slavery and Southern dominance of the federal government.

The rapid changes taking place in the population of the northern cities, the breakdown of the two national parties—the Whigs and the Democrats, the revolution in transportation that came with the development of a national railroad system and steamships, created both optimism and feelings of uncertainty as to traditional values and ushered in a new age. In the words of one distinguished historian, Roy Nichols, these changes unsettled people when they needed balance.

In no place did these changes make themselves felt more keenly than in Boston, where thirty years before the Boston Associates had launched the textile industry. The early philanthropic hopes of the founders to avoid the miserable conditions that had developed in England had not been realized. From the beginning the girls at work in the mills were better paid than those in England, and the provisions made to house them were superior to those in British mill towns. The girls were supervised, and close attention was paid to any lurking moral deficiencies.[1] The girls worked a twelve-hour day and a six-day week. By carefully husbanding their resources most of them were able to accumulate some savings and return to their farm homes and after a few years establish homes.

By 1850 the farm girls had been replaced by immigrants. No longer was provision made for adequate housing or their general welfare. What had occurred in the textile industry extended to the now large urban center in general. By 1849 there were 24,892 paupers in Massachusetts. Forty-one percent of the population were foreigners. In Boston there were 1,500 vagabond children who did not attend school and had no means of support.[2] "Between 1815 and 1860," a historian has concluded, "the economy of Massachusetts underwent a transformation fully as dramatic as the one that swept across England in the half century prior to 1815."[3]

There were compensations for the upper classes. The theater, the opera, and the concert hall in Boston provided a distinguished fare including some of the finest European performers. The Boston Athenaeum, founded in 1807, provided the best in literature for business leaders and intellectuals. Harvard had scarcely earned the right to call itself a university, but it had some distinguished scholars. Philanthropy was alive and had made possible the Massachusetts General Hospital. The imaginative and distinguished Samuel Gridley Howe had built the Perkins School for the Blind and developed methods for the blind to read. In addition he and Dorothea Dix led the movement to have the legislature provide for the establishment of the first state mental hospital in Worcester. The two dynamos, Howe and Horace Mann, crusaded for the development of the first colleges for training teachers.

Boston and New England at large inspired a reverence for learning. At midcentury it was the home of the first generation of American historians Jared Sparks, George Bancroft, William Prescott, John Motley, and George Ticknor. Nathaniel Hawthorne, Ralph Waldo Emerson, and Henry Thoreau established the city's literary reputation. Joseph Story, professor of law at Harvard and associate justice of the United States Supreme Court, enriched the New England heritage with his famous *Commentaries.*

A close-knit circle of public figures dominated Massachusetts politics. Daniel Webster was the most able of the politicians, and his vision of a strong Union was expressed in some of the most famous speeches in our history. The Whig party held control. Among its leaders were Everett, Rufus Choate, Abbot Lawrence, and George Ashmun. The party earned distinction as the foe of Andrew Jackson and the Democrats, but to the disgust of men like Charles Francis Adams and other young men such as Henry Wilson, Horace Mann, Richard Henry Dana, and Charles Sumner, the Whigs failed to come to terms with the new problems that faced the nation. The old line Whig leaders spent much of their time warning the country that Jacksonianism was akin to French Jacobinism. Whigs were committed to the check-and-balance system, because it stood as protection against the momentary passions of the masses.

Conformity reigned supreme in Boston among the elite who prized propriety in manners and gentlemanly virtues. Richard Henry Dana broke through the crust when he aligned himself with the new antislavery element. His old friend George Hilliard, a prominent Whig, deplored Dana's irreverent behavior. When Dana met him and asked what Hilliard meant by a critical statement, Hilliard replied: "I mean that if a man lives in Boston and feels about his position and her action as you do, if a man disapproves of her characteristics and interest and conduct, he ought either to keep quiet or leave the city." Dana retorted: "I told him that the principle would do in a Club or in a Society, but not in a community of equal rights." It was just this about Boston and the Whigs that the fiercely independent Charles Francis Adams resented, and while he despised Jacksonian Democracy, he denounced the Whig party as dominated by people with closed minds who adhered to no principles.

Charles Francis Adams, Everett's brother-in-law, held Everett guilty of conniving with Webster to deprive hs father of a seat in the Senate. As the years passed hostility was replaced by mutual understanding, and Everett was to inform his son that Charles Francis was the most able of the Adams family. Adams looked on Webster with contempt. In 1839, when the wealthy of Boston once again raised a large sum of money to enable Webster to go to England, Adams took him to task: "His career is entirely unexampled in our history. And it is much to be desired that it should never be

The Kansas-Nebraska Act

emulated." At the close of the legislative session in 1842 he expressed what he felt: "It is pretty plain to see that the fate of the Whig party is sealed beyond redemption. A party held together by no principles and led on by political gambles can have no other fate. But what the next thing is to be is involved in a perfect nest of darkness."[4]

* * * * *

Even before the war, the annexation of Texas had been condemned in the Massachusetts press. In January 1845 a contributor to the *Massachusetts Spy* in Worcester warned: "The slave power of the South, already begins to lift up its tyrannical head, ready to grasp its open jaws, the freedom of the North." From this time forth the *Massachusetts Spy* was a radical promoter of antislavery views and denounced the South.[5] Before the war a small band headed by John Quincy Adams and including his son, Samuel Howe, Charles Sumner, Henry Wilson, and Horace Mann met to protest against the annexation and the extension of slavery.[6]

Thanks to the Mexican War and the acquisition of almost half of Mexico the slavery question could no longer be sidestepped. The war, said Everett, was a war of conquest, and nations that embarked down this path were headed for creating an empire. It had happened to Rome, and it was likely to happen to the republic. More timely was his observation that while states had originally entered a contract assuring no interference with slavery where it existed, the Constitution did not allow for the extension of slavery. Everett consistently adhered to this position. What he feared was the dissolution of the Union if a purely sectional party emerged that would turn its back on compromise.

In August 1848 that danger was clearly visible. A new party, the Free Soilers, met in Buffalo. Immediately before the meeting Everett was approached by Charles Francis Adams with an offer of the nomination for vice-president, an offer he rejected. At Buffalo the Free Soilers nominated Martin Van Buren in the hope of gaining the support of New York. It was then decided that the western delegation should name the candidate for vice-president. Richard Henry Dana, who entered politics for the first time, described the scene in his diary as Charles Francis Adams was placed in nomination.

> Never, since my ears first admitted sound, have I heard such an acclamation. Men sprang on top of their seats, threw their hats in the air, and even to the ceiling. The cheering was repeated, news, spread to the tent, and in a moment we heard it given back, with interest.[7]

Antislavery not only enlisted the consciences of men, it shook their political loyalties. The enthusiasts were in fact divided between men like Adams and Dana who would dedicate the new party wholly to antislavery and those who blended political ambition with an interest in pushing forward some of the Jacksonian program.

Everett, both an antislavery man and a dedicated friend of the Union, saw danger ahead. He wrote in his diary that this was the first time in which "a party organized with express reference to Slavery has appeared in our election. Should it become permanent and possess itself of the power in the Northern States it would necessarily produce the separation of the Union."[8]

Pressed on all sides on the territorial question, Congress, throughout 1850, sought a compromise. The introduction of the Wilmot Provision in 1846, although it was defeated, alarmed the South. It would have barred slavery in all the newly acquired territory. The North, looking on the Mexican War as a slave-power conspiracy, was determined to prevent its extension. The compromise finally adopted provided for the admission of California as a free state, the organization of New Mexico and Utah as territories without explicit provisions as to slavery, an end to the slave trade in the District of Columbia, and the Fugitive Slave Law. Daniel Webster and Henry Clay were hopeful that the compromise would preserve peace and bring an end to the controversy over slavery. This hope was doomed by the Fugitive Slave Law, a measure that left the fugitives to be hunted and deprived them of jury trial. Federal commissioners would be the sole arbiters of whether the apprehended black was a fugitive. Commissioners, who decided against the fugitive, were paid a larger fee than if they set him free. The law provided heavy penalties for anyone harboring a slave. Aimed at protecting the interests of the southern slave owner, it brought home to northerners firsthand observation of cruelty of the slave system.

The Compromise of 1850 was not really a compromise, and it did not settle the territorial question. Everett never doubted that the breakup of parties and the rise of a sectional party inevitably meant dissolution of the Union. The breakup of the parties was inevitable given the violent feelings that had arisen. Yet, that was the concession Clay and Webster made to the South, and short of that concession it is most likely that there would have been no Compromise of 1850. Either dissolution of the Union or war or both would probably have taken place in 1850. "In my opinion" wrote David Potter, eminent historian "the evidence on balance, indicates that by 1850 southern resistance to the free soil position was so strong and widespread that if the Union were to be preserved, the South had either to be conciliated or to be coerced. It is true that the disunionists in the South began to lose ground before the Compromise was enacted, but I believe that this was because compromise was confidently expected and the South distinctly preferred compromise to disunion."[9]

Extremism on both sides, North and South, exaggerated the difference between sections and generated feverish feelings. Everett thought that feelings rather than differences of material interests were the cause of the upheaval.

The events that had occurred in 1848 and after had already placed the sections in a posture of confrontation. The Free Soil party, though unsuccessful in the election of that year, had been successful in promoting antislavery views and by 1850, as Salmon Chase said, "it was hard to find in the free states an opponent of slavery prohibition."[10] Moreover, the spectacle of Van Buren, former president, running on the Free Soil ticket, must have made it easier to dismiss the sanctity of party regularity. In the campaign the stress was on antislavery and the domination of the Democratic party by the slaveocracy. Van Buren confided to John A. Dix, fellow New Yorker: 1848 had "produced impressions which neither you nor I will live to see eradicated."[11] Unionism remained strong, but there were limits to Southern unionism. The Georgia Platform praised the Union but also stated that if conditions that they had laid down should be violated, they would resist it even to the disruption of every tie binding Georgia to the Union."[12] Everett recognized the importance of feelings. The South feared the dominance of the North because it had long been clear that the North was rapidly emerging as the center of industrial and financial growth. It had reason to fear that northern dominance would reduce it to an inferior partner. Honor was at stake.

This was no less true of the North but in reverse. The antislavery movement was propelled in part by the northern conviction that the South had an undue influence and stood in the way of enlightenment, progress, and humanitarian values. Charles Francis Adams, the epitome of realism, deplored the lack of moral principle in politics. "It is slavery that is at the bottom of this," he wrote in his diary. "I am more satisfied of the fact every day that I live. And nothing can save this country from entire perversion morally and politically but the predominance of the Abolitionist principle. Whether this will ever take place is very doubtful. I have not much hope."[13]

A more inflammable piece of legislation than the Fugitive Slave Law could scarcely be imagined. Former slaves who had lived in the North for years could now be taken by "slave catchers" and returned to their former masters. Daniel Webster, hoping that the slavery question had been set aside and that the Union had been saved, defended the law. To his longtime admirers, he had fallen from grace. His earlier protestations against slavery now had a hollow ring. Webster defended the law as nothing more than an extension of the earlier Fugitive Slave Act that made more secure property in slaves. The burst of protest and outrage in New England reduced Webster, the God-like figure, to, as Whittier put it, a fallen angel.[14]

* * * * *

Evertt differed from Webster on the obnoxious law. From the beginning of the debates in Congress in early 1850 he believed that the South must exhibit a willingness to make concessions. Unless Southern men of influence, he wrote, had the courage "to take ground against the extension of slavery and in favor of its abolition in the jurisdictions of the United States, we shall infallibly separate; not perhaps immediately but before long."[15]

* * * * *

Everett viewed the contemporary scene with dismay. Political groupings increasingly moved toward positions that were in diametric opposition. Calhoun had already helped to foster a regional Southern nationalism that was unbending. The Whig party was falling asunder because of the pressure for change. More and more it appeared that the sections bordered on taking positions that were beyond compromise. Everett held fast to his old convictions that the interests of the people as a whole were best served by a more encompassing central government, that the Constitution transcended in importance the current political fashions, that the check-and-balance system offered the best assurance of justice and freedom, and that calm, dispassionate political deliberations offered the only hope of moving forward. This was what he represented. What he saw and feared was the dissolutin of the Union.

He believed in compromise but he could not accept the Compromise of 1850 with its Fugitive Slave Law. As early as February 1850, Everett declared, "The passage of more stringent state laws for the arrest of fugitives is impossible." Everett refused to defend the bill in a speech when asked to do so. When friends of Webster circulatd a memorial defending Webster's 7 March speech, he refused to sign it. Any attempt to enforce a Fugitive Slave Law, he said, would revolutionize politics. He confided in Winthrop that if he were in Congress he could not vote for it "nor as a citizen would I perform the duty which it devolves on all good citizens."[16] He soon learned from George Ticknor Curtis, who had asked him to sign a memorial praising Webster, that this memorial was initiated at the suggestion of Webster himself. Everett noted in his diary, "It is hardly worthwhile to be great on these terms."[17]

Everett viewed the Southern extremists with alarm, blaming the South as much as the ultras of the North for promoting disunion. He was not able to align himself with the Free Soilers, the new political party, because, although they did not boldly call for disunion, their position would lead straight to that result. He asked how destroying the Union would help the slaves. Should the South secede, he predicted, it would probably result in the creation of a huge slave confederacy incorporating Cuba and parts of Mexico. Everett grasped at the hope that if the slave question were left for time to resolve, slavery would disappear. Slavery was already on the way to extinction in Delaware and on decline in the border states.

As the controversy intensified, Everett warned that heated passions would not permit time to run its course. After attending a meeting in Fanueil Hall, where G. T. Curtis and Refus Choate upheld the constitutionality of the Fugitive Slave Law and appealed to national feelings, Everett dismissed their efforts as futile. To Dr. Holland in London he confided, "but I scarcely need to say, that it is out of the question to awaken any *feeling* in favor of such a law. It is a great folly on the part of the South to ask for it, for the moment it is strongly enforced, it becomes inoperative. . . . In a word, unless the South has the sense and grace to yield to the general conscience of mankind on this subject, the Union is gone, a deplorable catastrophe for us, but incalculably more so for them."[18] He had little hope that either sense or grace would triumph in the South. Viewing the scene from Boston he was convinced that antislavery feelings were nourished by nothing more than the ultraism of the slaveholding states.

In March 1851 Everett embarked on another futile campaign to promote Webster's nomination for president.[19] To disagree with Webster on the Fugitive Slave Law proved to be no barrier. His only options, he thought, were to support Webster or to support the Young Whigs and the Free Soil movement, and that was to head the country toward disunion.

This delicate situation, where he had friends on both sides, led him to remain behind the scenes. The Whigs scheduled a convention to be held in Springfield on 10 September, and the state central committee invited Everett to chair the sessions and to write the address stating the party's position. He wrote the address but with the understanding that his authorship should remain secret. He soon learned that the convention would pass resolves condemning the Fugitive Slave Law and refuse to endorse the nomination of Webster. He refused to attend because it would identify him with the radicals.

Everett was now caught in the cross fires of heated factionalism. Complicating the situation his friend of long standing, Robert C. Winthrop, was a candidate for governor, and Winthrop's success depended not only on a moderate course but also his opposition to the Fugitive Slave Law. Webster was committed to supporting the Compromise of 1850 without reservations. Everett had to make a choice. To go to the convention where resolutions would be passed that contravened the heart of Webster's program would alienate not only Webster but the other members of the committee Everett had organized for support of Webster's nomination.

Everett was at a loss about what to do. On 2 September he wrote to Webster asking him if he should go to Springfield and assured him, "I have no wish in the matter but to gratify and serve you."[20] That same day, however, he wrote to a leading Whig friend that it was certain that his presiding at the convention would be taken unkindly by Mr. Webster's friends "and that consideration is decisive with me."[21] He did not wait for Webster's answer to the letter of that day. He informed him the next day that he would not attend it.[22] The situation was embarrassing. Joseph E. Sprague, a friend and a prominent Whig, urged him to attend and warned him that not to attend would hurt him politically. Everett replied that he had given no thought to the effect on his personal position, and that could not influence him. He was, he said, a proscribed man and "no person suspected of being a friend of Mr. Webster has anything to hope for while the commonwealth continues to be governed by Col. Schouler."[23]

He was convinced that the Union could not stand except on the general platform indicated by Webster. The Union, he said, "must go to wreck if the North pursues a course against which the whole South revolts." His having taken the lead in seeking Webster's nomination made it difficult to retreat. As opposed as he was to the Fugitive Slave Act, he allied himself to Webster believing that only his program could save the Union.

The Free Soil Party in Massachusetts was at the crossroads

where a decision must be reached as to whether the party was to concentrate all its energy on antislavery or to fuse with the Democrats and broaden its reform program. Free Soilers of the Henry Wilson wing were determined to destroy the Whig party in the state. Charles Francis Adams had many times despaired of the Whig party, but the Democrats wholly disgusted him as ignorant and representing the lowest elements in society. He was alert to the political ambitions of men like Wilson who were ready to exploit the popular antislavery issue to further their own advancement.

When the Free Soil Committee met in August 1850, a proposal passed that a commitee be named to meet with the Democrats and work out a plan of union. Adams opposed the plan with such vigor that he was not invited to the next meeting of the Free Soil State Committee.[24] This did not deter other Free Soilers, including Charles Sumner, who had never been a strong supporter of the Whigs. That a fusion of some kind appeared reasonable is not surprising. While the Democratic party nationally was under the control of men like Stephen Douglas and Southerners, there were also many northern Democrats with strong antislavery sentiments. A working accord offered the only hope for Free Soilers and these dissident Democrats of gaining power.[25] By joining hands they would control the state legislature.

It was soon agreed that they should work together to elect George Boutwell governor and Charles Sumner to the U.S. Senate. This would remove Robert Winthrop, who had been the favorite whipping boy ever since he voted for war against Mexico, from the Senate. Winthrop was opposed to the war, but the Polk administration had coupled the decision on war to the bill providing support for troops on the Southwest frontier, and he did not see his way clear not to vote support. The attacks on Winthrop were inspired by hope of destroying the Whig party in Massachusetts.

The bipartisan political deal faced difficulties. What was occurring was clear to everyone. To Everett it was as corrupt as buying votes with money, and it only convinced him further that society was suffering from a laxity of morals and that the Free Soilers were not pure do-gooders undefiled by selfish ambitions. At this stage Everett and Charles Francis Adams shared the same healthy realism. Carrying through the deal in the legislature provoked a political fight, and the struggle went on from January to April. Sumner was not named to the Senate until the 26 April. A group of stiff-necked Democrats led by Caleb Cushing refused to support him.[26]

Everett witnessed the fall of the old order with dismay. He confided to his diary in October 1850 that he had never known the political horizon so dark. Developments in Boston showed that the fugive slave law could not be enforced, and "the indications from the South are that in this event measures will be taken to dissolve the Union."[27] In July 1851 the aggressiveness of the South frightened him. He wrote: "If it is the wish of the South to increase the agitation of the slavery question, to paralyze every person entertaining conservative principles, and to make every man, woman, and child in the Free States ready for separation, they have only to enforce these demands."[28]

At the same time that Everett opposed the extension of slavery he deplored the rise of the Free Soilers. He was convinced that many of them seized hold of the antislavery movement to further their political interests. What he feared even more was the appeal to mass feelings, the passions aroused, and the vilification by the reformers of anyone who differed with them, but he had long been a friend of Charles Sumner; despite their conflicting views they were to continue a cordial, if not a close, association. In October of 1851 Sumner came to call on Everett, and they spent the evening together. On Sumner's leaving Everett wrote: "A man of great and various accomplishments and no ordinary talent but playing I fear a dangerous game of ambition for himself and the country."[29]

There had occurred a deep split among the Free Soilers. Early in the autumn of 1853 Charles Francis Adams warned Dana that Henry Wilson was a mere demagogue.[30] When the Massachusetts Constitutional Convention met, the Wilson faction was aggressive in pushing for reforms. Adams and Dana went along with the Whigs on most issues, and the split of the Free Soilers led to sharp and hostile exchanges. Adams and Dana had no use for the Democratic party with whom Wilson and Sumner were ready to share programs. Neither Adams or Dana, however, were ready to surrender to the Old Whigs, the Cotton Whigs, who still supported the Compromise of 1850. When Wilson was nominated for governor in 1853, Adams held the Free Soil party guilty of lacking principles. The Free Soilers, he wrote, were "a party of dirty, negotiating, trading politics . . . ultimately to be traded over into the democracy, if there is a decent chance to effect it."[31] Dana summed up the positions of the parties in early 1854: "The Whig Party had lost its tone, the Democratic Party never had any, and the Free Soil Party has been lowered by the coalitions and managements of [Henry] Wilson and others, until it has lost or essentially impaired its power of doing good."[32]

* * * * *

The Kansas-Nebraska Act

Historians inform us that what was occurring in the years between the introduction of the Wilmot Proviso in 1846 and 1854 had far-reaching results, and that antislavery was only one of several factors leading to the breakdown of the two-party system. The rise of nativism, anti-Catholicism, and the temperance movement represented causes that appeared at least, and often more, important to voters than the cause of antislavery. These popular causes came at a time when the two major parties were breaking down. As the questions of a central bank and protective tariff were no longer central, the two parties approached a consensus without a direct confrontation on issues that was meaningful to the average voter. Both the parties and politicians were viewed increasingly as mere time servers interested only in the personal rewards of office holding. Michael Holt, author of *The Political Crisis of the 1850s,* concluded that what destroyed the old two-party system, "was the loss of the ability to provide interparty competition on any important issue." "What destroyed the Second Party System was consensus, not conflict," Holt states. Parties became unable to sustain voters' loyalties. Voters turned to third parties or to promotion of their causes by nonpolitical associations. It was this collapse of the old order that was a major element in the causes of the Civil War.[33]

These developments explain much about the election of 1852. The Whig candidate, Winfield Scott, in an effort to mobilize the immigrant vote, made an awkward effort to appear as the friend of the Catholics and that had as its chief result the antagonizing of the strong nativist element in the Whig party. The Democrats, seeking to still the dissension in their ranks, nominated Franklin Pierce, who had taken no stand on the issues dividing the party. The results were the death of the Whig party, and before the close of the Pierce administration, the Democratic party was hopelessly weakened. Historians point out the way was open for a new party alignment well before the Kansas-Nebraska Act in 1854.

* * * * *

The Mexican War brought with it deep schisms in both major parties culminating in the fight over the Kansas-Nebraska bill. The Barn Burners in New York supported the Wilmot Proviso that would have excluded slavery from the territories acquired from Mexico. Throughout the North there were Democrats who took sides against slavery. In 1847, Martin Van Buren was asked, "Did you ever see a Party so completely at sixes and sevens as the Democratic Party now is?"[34]

In the aftermath of the divisive Compromise of 1850, in 1852, the

Democrats, failing to muster a two-thirds majority for any of the leading candidates, nominated Franklin Pierce. He was elected by a margin of only 200,000 popular votes. The genial and pleasant Mr. Pierce, not a man suited to manage in a time of crisis, proved a disaster. He promptly lost all respect and support as he sought to please all factions. Democratic schisms widened into irreconcilable divisions. At the same time the divisions that divided the Whigs during the election campaign brought the demise of the Whig party. The party had campaigned throughout its existence on the issues of the National Bank and the protective tariff. Well before 1850 these were dead issues, and the Whigs offered nothing in their place.

The aspiring and energetic politician in Illinois, Steven Douglas, was appalled by the Wilmot Proviso because it cut across party lines. As the divisions widened in the party he concluded that his role was to steer a middle course. He was at the same time dedicated to rapid development of the West and especially to the extension of railroad lines across the continent. He was, says his able biographer, sincere in his concern for his party and the future of the nation.[35] As a politician he was, by 1853, equally concerned about building a broad base of support throughout the Middle West. Given these hopes he sought for a middle-of-the-road plan that could be accepted by both sides. This led him to become the champion of popular sovereignty with its democratic ring, "Let the people decide," but popular sovereignty was also ambiguous. Were the early settlers in a territory to decide or was the question of slavery to be decided at the time of achieving statehood.

In February 1853, William Richardson of Illinois introduced a bill providing for the organization of the Nebraska territory. In discussion of the bill the question was raised as to whether it affected the Missouri Compromise. Joshua Giddings of Ohio said it in no way affected the compromise. This led to questioning by southern representatives who feared the formation of an important territory in the heart of the nation as a free state. Given their fear of a future in which the rapidly growing North would dominate the Union, southerners from the deep south opposed the bill. The bill passed the House, but when it came to the Senate it was laid on the table. Douglas, a man in a hurry, faced frustration. Unless he could win southern support for the bill it was doomed. As early as November 1853, Douglas confided privately that his intention was to bring forward a bill that would repeal the Missouri Compromise.[36]

Douglas knew well that the compromise had acquired a sanctity in the public mind and that it could not easily be set aside. Since its enactment in 1820, it had come to connote a standing agreement between the sections that assured peace. To overcome this obstacle Douglas introduced a bill the following January that simply ignored the compromise while at the same time providing for popular sovereignty.[37] Early in the session he confided to Everett that no one would be so unwise as to present a bill that called for outright repeal, but Southerners were not prepared to let the bill go forward with its ambiguous phrasing. Archibald Dixon of Kentucky introduced an amendment that in effect would repeal the compromise. On 23 January, Douglas brought forth an entirely new bill that enabled a territorial legislature to decide the slavery question. The effect was that no new territory would be bound by the historic compromise.

Douglas commanded the important Illinois delegation. Southerners had immediately made support of the bill a test of party loyalty.[38] Douglas himself maintained that support of the bill provided a test of party loyalty. The Pierce administration took the lead in making it a party test. The Southerners and many northern Democrats went along.

Everett, now in the Senate, recognized that the bill was sure to pass. Herein lay a major development leading to the Civil War. The time had come for him to deliver a speech; he wrote in his diary that he was now about to give the most important speech in his life. Ever conciliatory in his disposition, even in time of political storms, he confined himself to use of calm language.

He concentrated his speech on Douglas's contention that the Compromise of 1850 had already repealed the Missouri Compromise and passed over all the pro and con arguments that had come forth in the controversy over slavery. He objected to the obscure language of the bill. If the Missouri Compromise was to be repealed, the bill should say so. The legislation of 1850, he contended, referred specifically to New Mexico and Utah, and did not lay down a general principle to be applied in all new territory. The report of the committee that had drafted the compromise in 1850 had nothing in it to even suggest that a principle of general application had been discussed. The act was specific as to where it was to apply. In the acts of 1850, the boundaries of both territories were carefully stated. Everett had read the debates in Congress. "I do not find a single word from which it appears that any member of the Senate or the House of Representatives, at that time, believed that the territorial enactments of 1850, either as principle, or rule, or precedent, or by analogy, or in any other way, were to act retrospectively or prospectively upon any other Territory."

What then was the Compromise of 1850? The compromise, said

Everett, consisted in not inserting the words of the Wilmot Proviso. In voting against the Wilmot Proviso, Webster "used these remarkable words: Be it remembered, sir, that I now speak of Utah and New Mexico, *and of them alone.*" Douglas had contended that the Compromise of 1820 had been rescinded in that portion of Texas below 36°30' that had been ceded to New Mexico and a limited piece of Louisiana territory had been transferred. To this Everett responded:

> In the first place, it was a very small portion of territory, very small, indeed, compared with the vast residuum; and can we suppose that the few hundred, or it may be a few thousand, square miles taken off in this way from Texas and the old Louisiana Purchase, and thrown into New Mexico and Utah, can, by way of principle or rule, or in any other way, qualify or modify, or repeal a positive enactment covering the remaining space, which is as large as all the British Islands, France, Prussia, the Austrian Empire, and smaller Germanic states put together?[39]

There was, said Everett, no great material interest at stake. Slavery would not make its way into the territory now in dispute. "The climate, the soil, the staple production are not such as to invite the planter of the neighboring states, who is disposed to remove from the cotton regions of the South, and establish himself in Kansas, or Nebraska."[40] Why then repeal this time honored and conciliatory statute? It is said that it is derogatory to the South. Everett could find no reason to believe it was derogatory, and the South had viewed it as a blessing when enacted.

A few days later Charles Sumner took the floor. Tall, handsome, learned in literature, a more magisterial figure had not appeared before Congress. In his difficult pilgrimage between a dwindling legal practice and disappointment in not receiving an appointment to the faculty of the Harvard Law School, he had stumbled into politics. No man was more certain of his own rectitude, no one a greater moralist, and no one surpassed him in vilifying an opponent.[41]

Sumner focused on two points. The South was guilty of depravity in seeking the repeal of the Missouri Compromise. It was turning its back on a commitment that both sections had honored for decades. The bill did so for the sake of slavery, "the forcible subjection of one human being, in person, labor, and property, to the will of another." The conscience of the world was now awakened to the evils of slavery, and, in contrast, we are about "to open a new

The Kansas-Nebraska Act

market for the traffickers in flesh, that haunt the shambles of the South."[42]

Sumner took issue with Everett's contention that slavery would never find its way into Nebraska because of climate, soil, and the staple productions were such as to stand in the way of slavery. Sumner contended to the contrary. Missouri, the close neighbor of the new territory, had more than eighty-seven thousand slaves. In the heat of controversy Sumner held that the repeal of the Missouri Compromise would lead to the extension of slavery throughout the Middle West, in violation of the sacred principles of the nation, principles the South had once approved.[43]

Everett commented on Sumner's speech. It was, he said, a speech of great force and eloquence, but those portions dealing with "the question of slavery in the abstract was calculated to give great offense and embitter the sectional animosities which threaten the permanence of the Union. But the other portions, bearing upon the immediate question at issue & particularly arguing against the repeal of the Missouri Compromise were extremely pertinent and conclusive." At this point Everett expressed a view: "The difference, not of interest, but of opinion and feeling are irreconcilable; the extension of our territory and settlements require that the question should be met and when met in the present temper of the two sections it admits of no amicable solution."[44] This astute affirmation proved only too true.

The South and party regulars responded with contempt and disgust. Who was Sumner? By what right did he assume to speak for the entire North? By what right did he assume the right to castigate men with the charge that they were guilty of treachery? "This is the member," said Moses Norris of New Hampshire "who now assumes to teach the Senate of the United States the ethics of a purer political morality, and in the purer doctrine of the Fathers." Sumner's speech strengthened the southerners belief that the fanatical abolitionists, who had been no more than a sect, were gaining control.

The "Appeal of the Independent Democrats," an explosive bundle of bombastic rhetoric in which Salmon P. Chase appealed to the reverence in which many northerners held the Missouri Compromise. The appeal had been presented to the public in January. As Allan Nevins wrote: "His appeal was charged with a voltage of emotion which gave its language searing intensity."[45] The appeal, largely the work of Chase, charged the South with a monstrous plot. It invoked the condemnation that it was the work of the "slave power," that the South and the nation had been reduced to mere puppets in the hands of the master slaveholding class and Southern "depotism" aimed at reducing the entire nation to bondage. Douglas was, of course, denigrated.

The appeal was full of historical inaccuracies, but its insulting language helped mobilize southern senators on the side of Douglas. It also had a great impact on the politics of the North. Eric Foner, author of *Free Soil, Free Labor, Free Men,* considers it "one of the most effective pieces of political propaganda in our history."[46] The idea of "slave power," partially myth, solidified antislavery opinion.

Here was the danger that Everett feared above all else. Wide acceptance of the appeal confirmed Everett's horror of mass thinking, slogans, myths, and generalizations. Everett could not accept the political world where real stakes almost inevitably set aside reason in the name of moral righteousness and security. That history was replete with such instances, Everett, as an inveterate and careful reader of history, knew only too well, but there was nothing he despised more than rule of the passions.

Far into the night on 3 March the bill was up for a vote in the Senate. Everett noted the number of members who were fortifying themselves with liquor. The scene, with angry diatribes echoing through the hall, provided a test not of serious debate but of endurance. At half past three in the morning, ill with fatigue, Everett withdrew. At five in the morning the vote was taken. The issue was never in doubt. The bill passed by a vote of thirty-seven to fourteen.

Everett, who left the Senate chamber at three in the morning, and other members, who had been absent, sought to have their votes recorded the next morning, but they were denied. Everett's enemies accused him of deliberately avoiding to vote. Some of his friends, including Seward, offered to sign a letter testifying that he had been ill, but it was deemed wiser not to seek to convince editors who would not be convinced. Everett, opposed to the Kansas-Nebraska bill from the beginning, was charged with the failure to vote. His enemies contended that his speech was below the tone of public opinion in Massachusetts.

Everett justified the moderate tone of his speech, citing the fact that if the bill was to be defeated it was necessary to win southern support and the support of northern moderates. At the time he gave his speech there was hope that many Southerners would vote against it, but they rallied to defend the measure. Chase's emotional antislavery circular, the "Appeal," and Sumner's attack on the bill as opening the door to the extension of slavery made Southern opposition a matter of honor. Everett, the man in the vulnerable middle, was surprised and grieved "at the readiness that exists to think evil of me."

Everett, greatly troubled, explained his position to Abbott Lawrence and George Ticknor, the "Upshot of which is that if the disaffection to my course and the disposition to cavil at all I do continues, I will resign my seat in the Senate." Charles Francis Adams was to comment that Everett did well enough in fair weather but succumbed when the going got rough. At the close of the month Everett wrote in his diary: "And so ends the month of March, which all things considered has been one of the least joyous of my life."[47] In May, he resigned his seat in the Senate. Then and later, critics called his resigning ignominious.

Everett's withdrawal from politics coincided with the divisions already tearing parties apart and the storms following the Kansas-Nebraska Act. That act brought the sword and not peace. The entire North revolted against the law, and the events that followed in Kansas put in motion further changes in the political arena. The Whig party was already on the edge of extinction and with the many desertions from the Democratic party it became increasingly clear that the nation was headed for a drastic party realignment following sectional lines. Stephen A. Douglas faced a revolt, not only in his own state of Illinois, but in Ohio and Indiana. The Northwest, now the most rapidly growing area of the country, had already shifted the balance of power to the North and toward antislavery.

At a public meeting in Chicago, Douglas sought to explain to a crowd the virtues of the Kansas-Nebraska Act. From his opening remarks he was harassed by shouts of disapproval and charges that the act was no more than surrender to southern proslavery forces. The longer he spoke the greater the protestations. Finally, the hostile crowd burst into song:

We won't go home until morning,
We won't go home until morning!

The haughty senator, succumbing to fatigue, angrily declared that unless he was allowed to proceed he would go home. Finally, shouting that it was now Sunday morning, he said, "I'll go to church and you may go to hell!"[48]

At a dinner in Boston attended by Abbott Lawrence and other prominent citizens, Lawrence "expressed his firm belief that the states of Kansas and Nebraska would come in as slave states." Everett thought otherwise: "They will in all probability be settled by German and other foreign immigrants who are hostile to slavery; and it is not at all likely that Slave-holders will give the preferences to this new frontier wilderness (from whence it is easy to escape) over the cotton and sugar region of the South where slave labor is so much more profitable and the tenure of this property is so much safer."[49]

While he could, for the moment, view the prospects in Kansas and Nebraska with equanimity, Everett was ever more alarmed by what he saw as the headstrong determination of many southern leaders. He concluded that the South was moved by pride, by an obsession that "the grasping North has grown rich on Southern plunder, that it was moved by an uncontrolled spirit of adventure." The heresy, as he predicted three years earlier, "pervades the whole system of Southern States. The section has been wrought almost to madness by the nullifiers." "Given this situation," he wrote, "the anti-slavery agitation is a shower of sparks on a magazine."

The scene in Kansas played directly into the hands of the antislavery people. Missouri proslavery enthusiasts rushed into Kansas and were successful in establishing a proslavery legislature. The new legislature imposed severe penalties on anyone voicing antislavery views and established a proslavery test oath for officeholders.

Shortly immigrants arrived from the East. The New England Immigrant Aid Society raised funds to enable men with antislavery views to move. These new immigrants established a new territorial government in Lawrence. The legislature promptly prohibited slavery but also established a ban against free Negroes. Everett contributed funds to the New England Immigrant Aid Society. Before long journalists went to Kansas eager to seize on both facts and gossip that discredited the South. Everett eventually recognized that the representatives of antislavery papers were exaggerating the crisis in Kansas and that most settlers in Kansas were more interested in established land claims than they were in the slavery question.

Richard Henry Dana in Boston observed: "The change wrought by the Nebraska bill is astonishing." The moderate Whigs, he reported, who had distrusted Webster's course in 1850 were now "out clear and firm, and full of sympathy for us." "They felt," wrote Dana, "that they had been deceived by the South, and that they have misled others."[50]

8
Everett the Orator

Everett's fame in his own day rested on his oratory. In large part the oratory of that time was a theatrical art. Substance was overshadowed by the speaker's skill in appealing to love for the dramatic, patriotism, liking for the filiopietistic, and colorful language that brought to them feelings for beauty or the sharing of past tragedies. Tears and cheers alternated during Everett's performances.

A time would come when Everett would refer to his orations as ephemeral, but each oration was prepared with care, patient assembling of information, and careful selection of figures of speech, anecdotes, and appropriate citations from classical literature. What he wrote reflected his command of language, his care in choice of words, and his insistence on clarity. Before each oration he memorized the manuscript and practiced the gestures that would enhance his delivery.

Those who sat in his audience commented on the breadth of his learning; his strong mellow voice; the splendor and thought of his diction; and his abilities to hold the attention of his subject, inspire trust, never engage in vilification, and exemplify the propriety and restraint he prized.

His reputation extended to the country at large. Thousands came to hear him. The pleasure he gained in winning public acclaim compensated for the time he gave to preparation, and for the long and strenuous trips he endured. He was to comment more than once that for every engagement he accepted, he rejected two.

Judged by later standards, his orations were too ornate and filiopietistic. Critics called some of his portraits plaster cast productions that lacked substance. Critics such as Ralph Waldo Emerson and Charles Francis Adams found him exalting his skills as an orator at the expense of substance; critics thought he failed to confront the problems of the day and used language indulging in escapism.

Everett was well aware of the problems of the day and feared what the future might bring. His exaltation of the republic, liberty, and education were central to his orations. He avoided the paramount issues of a new day. The values he held dear were of prime importance, but others saw the present in a different light. The dictates of a changed society placed no emphasis on what Everett held most important: order, the virtues of the check-and-balance system, faith in education, and dispassionate politics.

* * * * *

Everett, in his early years, spoke to a generation mindful that the Revolution was the great turning point, the birth of their republic. It was inevitable that they take pride and glorify the War for Independence. Everett knew his audiences, and he nourished that pride. For all of his love of historical studies and his admiration for the British form of government, his mission was to kindle the public spirit and to strengthen support of the Union.

The talents of Everett raised patriotism to the highest of virtues. In his oration at Lexington in celebration of the sixtieth anniversary of the opening battle of the Revolution, a few survivors of that skirmish were present. He assured them that the mass of people who had gathered were there to pay them homage, they were there "discharging a filial, pious duty." Their "sacred" memories must be transmitted from father to son. It was a duty sanctioned by reason and justice. Everett anointed the occasion with hyperbole.[1]

The military events of that day sixty years before were part of his listeners' family history. He brought forth the names of almost every participant. He cited incidents that occurred, he cited how a victim of a gunshot waved to his wife in the window, struggled across the green to reach her, and then fell never to rise again.[2] He referred to the "vigorous growth of transatlantic liberty" that had been manifested. Samuel Adams, who had stood firm as their fellow citizens suffered the agony of death: "He saw the morning sun, whose first slanting beams were dancing on the tops of the hostile bayonets, would not more surely ascent the heavens, than the sun of independence would arise on the clouded fortunes of his country."[3] Among the heroes was Jedediah Morse, who after being wounded, marched on to Concord to fight another day. The battle scene, in all its gruesome reality, was reviewed. In concluding, Everett asked a rhetorical question about the consequences of that day. The men at Lexington had met the test with feelings like Luther when he denounced the sale of indulgences. Turning to the cemetery where the patriots lay buried, he said: "No voice but the arch angel shall penetrate your urns; but to the end of time, your remembrance shall be preserved! To the end of time, the soil whereon ye fell is holy, and shall be trodden with reverence, while America has a name among the nations."4

Commemorating Lafayette at another ceremony, Everett recited the major events of Lafayette's life stressing his love of liberty. What man in the audience, Everett asked, would rather share his fire with Napoleon rather than Lafayette? If there was such a man, Everett exclaimed, "that man has not an American heart in his bosom."5 In closing Everett bowed before the portraits of Washington and Lafayette that were hanging nearby and closed with the words: "Speak, speak, marble lips, teach us the love of liberty protected by law."6

* * * * *

It was inevitable that Everett should be called on to deliver the eulogies for the great statesmen he much admired. The dramatic deaths of Thomas Jefferson and John Adams only a few hours apart on 4 July 1826 marked the passing of an age. Everett overflowed with both sadness at their passing and with his admiration for the era they represented. The event recalled the days of 1776 and the sufferings that had been experienced while Boston was under siege. Everett chose to refresh the memories, praise both Jefferson and Adams for their achievements, and hoped that the memories of the two patriots would stir up feelings of admiration for "the men who were called to the helm, when the wisest and most sagacious were needed to steer the newly launched vessel through the broken waves of the unknown sea."7

It is not only the tones of high praise for the two men that stands forth, the personal feelings he expressed that day tells much of Everett's own devotion to the political tenets of an earlier period. These convictions were a major influence on Everett in the years ahead. Speaking of Adams and Jefferson, Everett said, "We are assembled, not to gaze with awe on the artifices and theatric images of their features, but to contemplate their venerated character, to call to mind their invaluable services, and to lay up the image of their virtue in our hearts."8 Herein lies the historical significance of those ceremonial orations.

* * * * *

Everetts' eyes were on the future as well as the past, and his vivid imagination reached to a far horizon. Speaking at Yale on "The Education of Mankind" he spoke of civilization in the process of extending itself throughout the world. It was not formal education that absorbed his attention. That was too often based on the assumption that it consisted of pouring information into an empty pot. In the past, "education had often been the training of a learned class which enabled them to isolate themselves from the community, and gave them the monopoly of rendering the services, in church and state, . . . and the honors and rewards which, by the political constitution of society, attached to the discharge of those services."[9] It was, said Everett, "the training of a privileged class; and was far too exclusively the instrument by which one of the favored orders of society was enabled to exercise tyrannical control of the millions which lay wrapped in ignorance and superstition." This has now changed. We are now making some moves toward an education of a community. The decline of one order and the accession of another is gradual. Change is inevitable, however, and it is coming with accelerating speed. Our duty is to prepare the next generation for the changes underway.[10]

How then are we to prepare the way for civilization where it has not yet penetrated? This is not a matter of trying to train one child at a time. It is, he said, education in a more comprehensive sense. The great inventions of the present, the useful arts and the knowledge of the speculative arts have been in the process of accummulation for thousands of years leading to change. It is society that is the teacher. This new society must be a good teacher.

Even in our relatively refined age large portions live in ignorance. There is a gigantic task before us. This points to the end for change. Everett confessed that it was difficult to own himself as an enthusiast. It was imperative that we study the past and learn more about how advancement occurred. It seemed now that political causes were in operation to bring into play the great modern instruments of national education—the press, free government, and the Christian faith. Asia and Africa must be civilized. He cited the vast changes that had occurred in their own community and asked that they not be discouraged.[11]

The hope of the world, and indeed of the republic, lay in education because education was favorable to liberty, morals, and courage. This address to the students at Amherst was a traditional appeal. It is significant that as early as 1835, however, he feared the developments at home. In a free government there was nothing "but the intelligence of the people who keep the people's peace."[12] Unfortunately, along with the great progress in learning and knowledge, have come the pretenders, "like the growth of rank weeds." "It is an age, I grant, of cheap fame."[13] It was this fear that caused Everett to be a promoter of education. Education would enable people to detect the frauds, to be suspicious of emotional appeals, and cause them to pursue knowledge. And knowledge "opens all the wonders of creation" and for the man of knowledge mysteries unfold.[14] These were the forebodings and the values of a learned man caught in a turmoil of politics.

* * * * *

Everett's departure from politics after the Kansas-Nebraska Act left him once again adrift, and again he embarked on a new enterprise, one that accorded with his fame as an orator. The opportunity presented itself when the Mercantile Association of Boston invited him to speak at their celebration of Washington's birthday. He set to work at once. When he began the preparation of his address he confided, "I find it difficult to give freshness and individuality to the sketch." He concluded that Washington's greatness did not lie in his being a genius, for he was not. He noted too that Washington had become a beau ideal in American life enshrouded in a tale of bravery, patience, and political leadership.[15]

It was Everett's fame as an orator that made him a national figure. His speeches were carefully prepared, delivered without the use of notes, and enhanced by a voice that carried to immense audiences. Charles Francis Adams wrote that as an orator, Everett had perfect poise and self-possession. "His modes of hitting the audience remain the same, brilliant contrasts, happy allusions, striking anecdotes," but Adams added, "there is no depth or maturity of thought, no greatness of view, no ingredients that make the Statesman or the Philosopher."[16] Adams's evaluation of Everett's speeches was valid but not of Everett's private thoughts.

The Washington he protrayed embodied the virtues that Everett held most dear. Washington's greatness lay in his devotion to the Union. He was, said Everett, "less powerful in the prerogatives of office than in the love and veneration of his fellow citizens." In the midst of sectional controversy Everett accented Washington's loyalty to the republic. "Oh, that his pure example, his potent influence, his parting Counsels could bring us back the blessings of national harmony! Oh that those benign lips could break the silence of the canvas, and teach us to unite again in one bond of fraternal love, as we are united in one precious remembrance of the past, in glorious vision of the future one bond of Constitutional Union."[17]

He won the respect of his audience for his learning by the vast panorama he drew of the world's history from the time of the American Revolution through to the final collapse of Napoleon. He described the scene, "Among all the wise in counsel, the valiant in battle, the firm and prudent in government, the pure in life—I find not one of any nation, in any part of this remarkable period of history, who has left so deep an impression of himself in the public opinion of mankind; not one, the sum total of whose qualities, and the aggregate of whose character, can be measured with that of our Washington."[18] More important than the revolutions by which old dynasties were overturned was the transfer of power from the aristocracies to the people. A long line of worthies, chieftains, thinkers, philanthropists, had passed over the stage, the greatest in any period of history. "So rich in character, so crowded with events, so productive of institutions and reforms, and prolific and so prodigal of life, so auspicious in anticipation" and amid all the great names a shining star, it was not conceded that the star of Washington shines brightest and shines alone.[19]

What then was at the heart of Washington's greatness? There was, he said, an absence of the brilliant qualities so often associated with greatness. Possession of those traits would have marred his greatness. Greatness lay in moderation. He represented the golden mean, equally removed from excess in either direction and all in due proportion.

Four days after his first delivery of the lecture he was invited to give the same lecture in Providence. Two weeks later he gave the address before an audience of eight thousand in the Music Hall in New York City. From there he went to Philadelphia, where he called on Ann Pamela Cunningham, an invalid, who had organized the Mount Vernon Association among the women of Virginia with the purpose of persuading the Virginia legislature to purchase the estate and rescue it from decay. They met again a week later in Richmond, where she first heard Everett's address. At this point, Everett offered all future proceeds from the address to the Mount Vernon Association.

The restoration of Washington's home now became central to all of his activities. He traveled thousands of miles through the South and West. Audiences in Augusta, Charleston, Richmond, Charlottesville, and Baltimore, as well as other southern cities, gave him enthusiastic receptions. On his trips to the West he visited the cities of upper New York, Detroit, Ann Arbor, Chicago, St. Louis, Cincinnati, Louisville, and Lexington. Scarcely a New England town of any size did not have the opportunity to hear him. By the close of 1859 he had given the "My Washington" address 136 times and, including the interest that had accumulated from the fund he had established, Everett had raised $90,000.[20] He maintained an exhausting schedule, traveling by train during the day to meet his engagement the next evening; only occasionally were sleeping cars available, and the food available at depots, if the train stopped long enough to permit seating, was scarcely edible. Sometimes there were disappointments, among them having his gold watch stolen in Toledo while he changed trains.

Everett found his speaking tours exhilarating. The receptions were friendly, and funds flowed in for the saving of Mount Vernon. He loved travel, praised the new sleeping cars, and only fretted over the absence of rest rooms on the trains. The speed with which he could tour the country led him to pleasant contemplation of the changes that had occurred. His first trip to Washington in 1814 consumed a week. Now the same trip to took less than twenty-four hours. His audiences were usually warmly apprciative, and their approval gave him great satisfaction. He regretted the occasional twenty-five-cent admission fee, because it yielded little in the way of proceeds and was humiliating. Some children, he observed, attended out of curiosity and had no interest in the subject, and some young people, he noted, "resort to public places to do their courting." In a moment of disillusion with the atmosphere surrounding his appearances he observed, "As far as the attraction of my address goes I cannot prevent the public if they please from putting it on a level with a travelling circus, a menagerie, or a Sophomore delivering his first Lyceum lecture in the winter vacation."[21]

The fame of Everett and his address caused Robert Bonner, editor and owner of the New York *Ledger,* a newspaper with a large circulation, to invite him to contribute a weekly article for one year for $10,000. Everett specified that his remuneration should go to the Mount Vernon Association. The fifty-three articles, published in book form as the Mt. Vernon Papers, dealt with a variety of subjects ranging from biographical sketches of William Prescott, the astronomer William Bond, Henry Hallam, and Alexander Von Humboldt to brief accounts and descriptions of European cities. The series was such a success that Bonner invited Everett to extend the series for another year. Everett continued to write frequent columns throughout the Civil War.[22]

* * * * *

In the fall of 1857, the country was hit by the second of its great depressions. The cause, wrote Everett, was the private and business debt entered into during the years of rapid expansion. The unemployment of masses of workers in the industries in the new urban centers, led Everett to propose to Robert C. Winthrop, president of the Boston President Association, that he give an address and that the proceeds go to help the needy, and this was arranged. Everett entitled his speech "Address on Charity and Charitable Institutions."

Only recently poverty had been generally attributed to individual delinquency, but a new view came to the fore as a result of the business cycle. Everett, who had formerly attributed much of the poverty to excessive drinking, had changed his opinion. Men, he now thought, were victims of forces beyond their control. "In the older and more thickly settled parts of the country, and in the large towns," he said, "the cheerful din of the factory and workshop were hushed, and those employed in them sorrowfully dismissed from their accustomed labors."[23] Now the poor, who had nothing in reserve, faced severe distress.

He held that the wealthy, who found excuses to refuse assistance, were people to be pitied, "pity for their barren and unblessed affluence."[24] Everett attacked Malthus, who wrote off the poor as so many surplus potatoes. Whatsoever studies might reveal they should not obscure the fact that while there had always been poverty and suffering it was also a law of nature "that suffering should be relieved."[25] To those who would say that charity merely adds to the number of mendicants or that poverty was the product of incompetence or indulgence, Everett declared that differences in ability and varieties of character "are strongly and inseparably mixed together in the great brotherhood of humanity . . . and that it is not the less privilege than the duty of the strong, the prosperous, and the well provided to assist those who falter by the way."[26] A mature civilization was only mature as long as it acted on this principle. He delivered the address in thirteen cities and the proceeds totaled $12,500.

9
Everett Confronts the New Age

Antislavery feelings and the political reverberations in 1854 in the years following constituted only one aspect of the troubled scene that was giving birth to a realignment of political parties. Students of the antebellum decade now have before them a new and imposing study by William E. Gienapp, entitled *The Origins of the Republican Party 1852–1856,* which brings new light on the overlap of nativism, anti-Catholicism, the temperance movement, and antislavery. Each of these commanded men's loyalties. All four were present in the Know Nothing movement. Many Free Soilers joined the Know Nothings. Seven of the Know Nothing congressmen elected in Massachusetts in 1854 were former Free Soilers. Know Nothings remained powerful well into the election of 1860.

Gienapp demonstrates that the breakdown of the two-party system began at the state level, and it was well underway before the Kansas-Nebraska act. The uneasiness amid the changing population led to fears that deeply rooted republican principles of government were in danger. The heart of nativism, anti-Catholicism, centered around the belief that Catholicism was centrally controlled and that the church hierarchy aimed at political control. Faced with public schools whose curricula included Protestant beliefs, the Catholic population aimed at first at changing the schools. When this failed, they turned to establishing their own schools and calling for public support of their schools.[1] This ran counter to the Constitutional principle of separation of church and state, and aroused crusades on behalf of protecting the republic from being undermined by a foreign institution. The feelings involved erupted, and for multitudes the supposed dangers had a higher priority than the question of slavery.

Closely allied to the nativist movement was the temperance movement. The greater laxity toward drinking among many immigrants furnished another basis for complaint of the nativists. The Protestant clergy decried drinking as the source of broken homes and pauperism. In the western states where the Methodists and

Presbyterians dominated, prohibition became a major political issue, and it influenced party alignments. Activists in the cause affirmed that prohibition should have the highest priority, and no political party could afford to offend them.[2]

This conglomerate of causes found a political home in the Know Nothings. Each of these issues were prominent at the local level. As Gienapp makes incontestably clear, to ignore these centers of political division at the local level and to give exclusive attention to national issues "seriously distorts the political perspective of the typical voter as well as the sources of mass behavior.[3] These forces continued at work from 1854 to 1860, and they created infinite difficulties for the antislavery people as they worked to establish a northern sectional party dedicated to the principle of no extension of slavery.

Know Nothingism provided a bridge from the Whig party to the Republican party.[4] The Whigs could no longer mobilize public support on the issues of the National Bank and protective tariffs. These issues were dead, and Everett was among the first to recognize this fact.

The sharp divisions in the Democratic party following the Kansas-Nebraska Act contributed to the sudden rise of the Know Nothing party. More important it led directly to the beginnings of the Republican party. A coalition of antislavery Democrats, Whigs, and Free Soilers met at Ripon, Wisconsin, in February 1855 and recommended the organization of a new party to be called Republican. At a party meeting in July, in Jackson, Michigan, the name Republican was officially adopted. Not until the election of 1856 did the party show its strength.

The Kansas-Nebraska Act cut off any possibility of useful negotiation of sectional differences.[5] It further weakened the democratic party. This was apparent in the elections of 1854 and 1855 when the party suffered defeats. The antislavery people kept the events in Kansas before the public. Newspaper accounts exaggerated the developments. Everett never believed that slavery would make its way into Kansas. He was correct in stating that it would be settled by immigrants who had no great interest in the slavery question. However, the act served the purposes of the antislavery movement. It testified to the aggressiveness of the South and enabled men like Chase and Sumner to conjure up an image of a South dominated by a slavocracy intent on extending slavery far beyond its existing limits.[6] At the same time it fostered a lurid picture among Southern extremists of a North intent on dominating their section and imposing on it the abolition of slavery in the District of Columbia, the slave trade in the southern states, closing off all new territories to slavery, and eventually abolishing slavery. It also enabled the North to embrace an ideology that allotted to its own section the aura of democracy, free labor, and free men, and to create an image of the South as dominated by slave owners, an area that was inferior in productivity and that aimed at turning the clock back.

All of these developments disgusted Everett. He had traveled in the South and enjoyed friends there, and minimized all the differences except slavery. He believed the two sections had a major interest in the survival of the Union that outweighed the differences.

* * * * *

Amid the kaleidoscopic changes such as the influx of immigrants, new currents in organized religion (including the sudden rise of the Mormons and the shift to Transcendentalist doctrines within Unitarianism), rise of urban centers, new and rapid means of transportation of both land and sea, and the breakdown of the two-party system, a transformation of political culture occurred. To Everett it was a disconsoling scene. He complained of the increasing laxity in morals, the new advertising profession with its deceptive claims, and the less than honest business practices. It was the breakdown of political parties that troubled him most. He was certain that the rise of a sectional party portended the breakup of the Union. This was an inherent part of Everett's political philosophy. In his student days in Paris everyone talked of the madness of the revolution. Like others Everett read Burke's *Reflections on the French Revolution* and became a dedicated admirer of Burke. He distrusted the role of passions, the role of the mob in social upheavals, the sudden prominence of generalities that were half-myths. After the Kansas-Nebraska Act he resolved to have no part in politics because as a moderate man he was out of step and could have no influence.

In the midst of these changes there suddenly emerged on the political scene the Know Nothing party. Probably no single development in the 1840s and 1850s contributed more to restlessness and alarm than the flood of immigrants. In the 1840s, 1,713,251 arrived. The number rose to 2,598,214 in the next decade. America was both the promising haven for Europe's poor, and the dumping ground for paupers and undesirables. Various European governments, both local and national, promoted immigration and often sought to relieve themselves even of criminals by encouraging and promoting immigration. The result was that a large percentage of paupers dependent on public support in the eastern cities were immigrants. Reports from American consular officials were often exaggerated, but the facts were sufficiently dreary without embellishment. In 1854 the New York Association for Improving the Condition of the Poor reported that during the months from December to November it had aided 15,500 families. It declared that no fewer than 617,000 immigrants had received help since 1847 at a cost of $2,250,000.[7]

These immigrants, who built America, differed, in most cases, from the natives in religion, in values, and in the daily habits of life. Only time could ameliorate the conflicts that arose. That a nativist movement came into being, however tragic and unjust, was perhaps inevitable. It did not suddenly burst forth in the 1850s, but not until then did it become a political question. Various nativist organizations, preponderantly anti-Catholic, combined in 1853 under the name "The Order of the Star-Spangled Banner." It began as a secret organization in which all members were instructed to deny any knowledge of the organization's existence. It was this that led Horace Greeley to dub them "Know Nothings," a name that stuck. The party quickly transformed itself into a major political party that in 1854 achieved unprecedented success. The phenomenal growth of the party sent tremors through the established political leadership. Fear of what the party might seek to do flourished. At the heart of the sudden success was the dissatisfaction with the old parties. Here was a party that offered a channel for the general demand for reform.

Everett explained the phenomenon as old-fashioned antipapacy and the fears of native workers, and he saw in it the further loosening of the bonds that held society together.[8] What could not be so easily dismissed was that in the election of 1854 the Know-Nothing party polled 63 percent of the vote in Massachusetts. "But what avails of educating people," Everett asked. "Massachusetts is already the best educated state and Boston the best educated city in the world and 81,000 of the voters have, this year, joined together by secret and illegal oaths." Among the many paradoxes of the day nothing appeared stranger than that the Know-Nothings were joined by a large majority of the Free Soilers. Perhaps they found a way to reconcile their antislavery feelings with sharp restrictions on the freedom of the aliens, but it seems more likely that they hoped to turn the new party into a vehicle for furthering their own cause. Everett observed: "It is now evident that this new organization is wholly opposed to Anti-Slavery agitation and yet the Free Soilers of this State, have been eager to rush into it. Our political history

Everett Confronts the New Age

contains no instance of a party so unprincipled as the Freesoil party."[9] When the new Know Nothing governor, Henry Joseph Gardener, delivered his inaugural address, he recommended stringent laws against aliens forbidding any one to be naturalized until they had lived in the country twenty-one years.[10]

Nativism did not die with the breakup of the Know Nothing party. It continued to be a subject of debate in Congress in June 1856. Nativism had support in the South. Stephen Adams, senator from Mississippi, contended that the South had as great an interest as the North because immigration was responsible for the North having a majority in the House of Representatives. He expressed widely held feelings in that section. The North had gained, in the last ten years, from 1840 to 1850, seven members. If the flood of immigrants continued the North would soon have a majority of two to one. Having warned of this danger, he informed his colleagues:

> What would be the consequence, Mr. President? Does any one doubt, if such political power existed, that the North would not at once change the Constitution so as to abolish the three-fifths representation for our blacks in the House? . . . I make no threats, for the reason that I think it unbecoming in any Senator to do so, and then if I should, it would alarm no one if I did. I may be permitted, however, claiming to be a conservative man, to express my opinion, founded upon a knowledge of the people of the South, and that opinion is, whenever you consummate, by passing into a law, any one of the aggressive measures now in contemplation by a portion of the northern people, namely: the refusal to receive a State into the Union for no other cause than that she tolerates slavery; abolish slavery in the District of Columbia; interdict the slave trade between the States; repeal the fugitive slave act, without adopting such a substitute as would be a fulfillment of the requirements of the Constitution; or change the Constitution without the consent of the South so as to change the rights of the South . . . before submitting to humiliation and disgrace, we would cast them to the winds forever.[11]

Whatever new development arose, it became involved in the antislavery controversy. Southerners were dominated by fear of an ever-stronger North that was embarked on a campaign of hostility to southern institutions. The fear was not wholly imaginary, but the genesis of the developments in the 1850s promoted the growth of myths, false generalities, and unlimited distrust. Everett, dismayed, found an escape in a return to oratory.

* * * * *

Everett never ceased to view the rise of the Free Soil party as a disaster. He took the same position when the Republican party came to the fore in the election of 1856. He did not vote in the elections of 1858 or 1860. On each occasion he explained in his diary that a sectional party, if elected, would result in the secession of the southern states. He was equally consistent in not voting for any Democratic candidate. He could not, he said, vote for the party that was responsible for the Kansas-Nebraska Act.

Given this public posture it was inevitable the antislavery leaders should accuse him of moral turpitude or timidity. The criticisms were understandable. A New York clergyman wrote to Everett that opposition to slavery was a question of right and humanity while the preservation of the Union was only of policy and expediency, and that if the two could not coexist the Union must give way.[12] This was precisely the dilemma Everett faced. He was opposed to slavery, and he was dedicated to the Union. This conflict paralyzed his public life. He could not cope with this new political fervor.

At the same time he was far removed from being a neutral in the conflict between the sections. He professed at times to being neutral, and he wrote to Thomas McCauley in 1855: "The South and North are equally wrong headed and impractical, the ultraism of the North being the most dangerous, inasmuch as it is founded on truth and justice. Neither party is willing to trust anything to time, conciliatory words or measures, and the certain progress and working of things together toward the disappearance of slavery." "The world," he wrote, "is ruled by a wisdom that cannot err, which in its own good time will deliver us from this dreadful scourge and conduct us to that glorious future but for this would seem beyond the reach of vicissitude and as certain as the march of time."[13]

In June 1856 Charles Sumner saw in the events in Kansas and in the speeches of his southern colleagues a demand that he expound the truth in blunt terms. The speech, "The Crime against Kansas," was not a product of a momentary frustration but of weeks of careful preparation. In print it ran to 112 pages. His able biographer wrote, "Like the rest of the senators, he was unaware that the Kansas struggle involved not merely freedom and slavery, but also land speculations, bitter rivalries over the location of the territorial capital and personal ambitions of would-be congressmen from the territory."[14] He failed to understand that there "was no ineradicable hostility between Southern pioneers in the region, virtually all of whom were non-slaveholders, and free state settlers, who wanted forever to ban free negroes from Kansas."

The day of the speech, 19 May, followed weeks of heated debate, but Sumner raised the crescendo by a portrayal adorned with literary allusions, graphic language, and a tone of judgment akin to

Everett Confronts the New Age

that of a biblical prophet. He leveled a severe indictment of several southern senators, in particular Andrew P. Butler of South Carolina, who was not present. The attack on Butler went so far as to ridicule Butler's phyiscal handicap, a labial paralysis that affected his speaking. Preston Brooks, a member of the House and Butler's cousin, decided on vengeance. On 22 May, after the Senate adjourned at noon, he assaulted Sumner at his desk with a cane. The attack was a determined one, and Sumner was severely beaten.

Everett was shocked and signed a testimonial in defense of Sumner. "The general views set forth on Mr. Sumner's speech on the Kansas question are those universally entertained here and are fully concurred in by me," he wrote.[15] A few days later he prefaced his delivery of the Washington address at Taunton with a condemnation of Brooks's attack. The speech is notable because at no other time did Everett burst forth into such a bold indictment:

> The civil war—for such as it is—with its horrid train of pillage, fire and slaughter—carried on, without the slightest provocation, against the infant settlement of our brethren on the frontier of the Union, and which has at length, by an act of lawless violence of which I know no parallel in history of Constitutional Government, stained the floor of the Senate Chamber with the blood of the unarmed, defenseless man, and a Senator from Massachusetts, ah, my friends, these are events, which for the cause of free institutions throughout the world, it is worth the gold of California to blot from the record of the past week.[16]

These were the boldest words Everett used. After a mass meeting in Fanuiel Hall held in protest and in which great excitement was expressed, Everett confided in his diary: "The occurrences unless controlled by very wise healing counsels at Washington (which it is not at all likely to be) will do more to strengthen the abolition party than anything that has yet occurred. In fact it is the beginning of the end."[17]

Two weeks later he wrote a letter of sympathy to Sumner stating, "With reference to the atrocious proceedings in Kansas we have been of one mind from the first." He added that had he read the testimonial first, however, he could not have signed it, but "I am sure you are too liberal to expect more than a general concurrence in your speech."[18] Sumner's abusive indictment of individuals did not meet with his approval. A few days later he contributed one hundred dollars to the victims of strife in Kansas.

What Everett thought privately his critics did not know, but they did know that he did not attend a mass meeting in Faneuil Hall in support of Sumner, and his absence was noted in the press. When he journeyed to Richmond, Virginia, to give his Washington address, his critics at home denounced him.[19]

By the summer of 1856 he speculated that the forthcoming election would be the last presidential election, for the North would not tolerate Buchanan with his pro-Kansas policy and the South would not accept a nominee of the sectional Republican party.[20] He warned that it would be a great mistake to think the impending conflict would be simply a war between the North and the South; "it will be carried with ten fold horrors within every state."[21] He predicted a reign of terror like that of the French Revolution. He voted for Fillmore, the nominee of the American party, in 1856. On election day in 1858 he wrote in his diary that he did not vote, for to have voted for Democrats would have been to endorse measures of the administration in favor of slavery "which I strongly condemn. . . . I am aware of all of the discomforts of the position of a man who had been at all in political life in assuming a neutral position, but it is in my case unavoidable."[22]

News of John Brown's raid at Harpers Ferry let loose an emotional outburst in Boston. Caleb Cushing, the ardent expansionist who had called for the annexation of all of Oregon and championed expansion in the Caribbean in the 1850s, viewed the entire antislavery movement as the work of loco focos. He ridiculed the outpouring of adulation for Brown. He declared "in these most extraordinary manifestations which have occurred in the State of Massachusetts and elsewhere—prayer meetings, public assemblies of rejoicing and of pretended subscriptions—in all these, it is said there is an extenuation (if there be no other suggestions) applicable to the case, that should change our appreciations of the character of the acts of John Brown."[23] Some likened Brown's execution to the crucifixion. Just as Christ died to save men from religious sins, John Brown died to save us from political sins. The more general response was condemnation of his act but admiration for his martyrdom.

Among Unionists the realization prevailed that the reaction in the South would be a decisive step toward seccession. A meeting was called for 9 December in Faneuil Hall for the purpose of calming the public mind and conveying to the public how the South would view Brown's acts. Everett and Cushing were scheduled to speak.

The leading antislavery newspaper in Boston the *Atlas and Bee,* on 5 December, called the meeting ludicrous. The editor focused his attention on Everett. Everett, he wrote, was a man of great talents and great fame and worthy of respect, but it was the Southern fire eaters in Congress who should be rebuked: "If you are to rebuke fanaticism and treason, strike it upon the head in Congress. Regale us with one sentence to which the heart of Massachusetts shall respond, and which will remind us of the days when yourself and Webster spoke from Plymouth Rock." Two days later the editor again assailed the meeting. The meeting was ridiculous, would amount to nothing, and if it were to have any significance it "would have to place Boston on its knees to Richmond and Charleston."[24]

The *Atlas,* however, reported that the speech was received with much applause, "and at its close, he was again honored with a round of cheers."

An editorial the following day subjected Everett to sharp criticism, and expressed how leaders of the antislavery crusade viewed Everett. The editor said nothing about the substance of Everett's speech, but criticized him for sitting on the sidelines beginning with the debate in the Senate on the Kansas-Nebraska Bill, held that he had been pro-Southern in his sympathies, found him guilty of failing to attend the meeting in Fanueuil Hall after the attack by Brooks on Sumner, and of not speaking publicly and not criticizing Brooks. "If ever there were two opportunities when even a man of the most extreme moderation might have spoken for New England, they were these." Everett's silence prompted the writer to charge that he was so forgetful of the North and so tolerant of the South "that it may almost be said, acquiescence constitutes his patriotism."[25]

This view was shared by other leaders in the antislavery controversy. John Gorham Palfrey described Everett as the "eloquent iceberg."[26] Privately Everett was not neutral, but his silence and retreat under the cloak of moderation at a time of heated agitation in which "conscience Whigs," convinced that slavery was a barbarous evil, inevitably stamped him as a timid man, a man unwilling to expose himself to agitation. There were many criticisms of Everett. Horace Greeley never missed an opportunity to place Everett in an unfavorable light. The attacks troubled Everett, but he invariably explained them to himself as rooted in the fanaticism of men who were leading the country to disunion and war. As Everett saw it, his critics were irresponsible men who chose to ignore the dreadful realities that were ahead.

In the winter of 1859-60 the Constitutional Union Party was organized by former Whigs in both sections of the country. Everett was discussed as the possible presidential nominee, but he was adamant in his refusal. He believed that at best the party could only throw the choice of president into the House of Representatives and, if successful there, it could only lead to a weak administration, for it would have little support in Congress. To his chagrin, after

John Bell was nominated for president, Everett was nominated for vice-president. He protested that it had never occurred to him that after withdrawing his name for the first position he would be considered for the second. He tried to withdraw, but urgent pleas from party leaders led him to give way. The pressure had been great. He noted, "Deputation after deputation from town and country, friends individually, serenades—in short a process of compulsion which I could not resist" took place. To his friend Robert Bonner he confided that the nomination could not succeed, "and that is the best thing about it."[27] To another he wrote that his nomination was of no consequence, "a mere ripple on the great wave of affairs."[28]

Though Union meetings in Massachusetts were well attended and the crowds exhibited enthusiasm, Everett never expected victory. Furthermore, he declined to campaign and made it a rule not to attend political meetings. The battle for the Union, as he saw it, had already been lost. Confronted with the election of either the Republican candidate, Abraham Lincoln, or one of the two Democratic nominees, he preferred the latter, but soon changed his views of Lincoln.

In the early fall before the election Everett entertained some hope that the Unionists would poll enough votes to block the election of Lincoln. It was not that he distrusted Lincoln, whom he described as a moderate and reasonable man. His fear was that if the election placed the wholly sectional antislavery Republican party in power, the South would secede. In early October he read reports that the Union party would sweep the South, and given his own hopes he found them easy to believe. He also thought that the Unionists would capture New York. He held out no hopes for a Unionist victory in Massachusetts. He predicted that in his own state the Republicans would win an overwhelming victory. Then came Lincoln's sweeping victory in Pennsylvania that killed all Unionist hopes.

Everett was equally disillusioned prior to the election by the Breckenridge press in the South that warned that Everett was a rank abolitionist. An anxious citizen in Alabama wrote to him concerning the widely circulated story that two of Everett's children attended schools in which there were Negro children. To this he replied that in Boston public law prohibited segregation, that his son who attended a public school did attend school with a Negro, that his daughter who attended a private school also had a classmate who was a Negro, and that it had never occurred to him that there could be any reason not to send his children to these schools.[29]

The Breckenridge attack on Everett was obviously inspired by hope of weakening the Union ticket in the South where for a time it appered to have some chance of making a strong showing. He wrote to both Breckenridge and Governor Wise of Virginia that the charge rested on his having signed resoutions of the Massachusetts state legislature as governor in 1837 condemning slavery. He had done so at a time when there was discussion in the South of emancipation.

After the election of Lincoln, the North had to face up to the possibility of secession. There were sharp divisions as to the course to be taken. Unionism was strong in Boston. Bell, the Unionist candidate for president, polled more than 5,000 votes; Lincoln carried Boston by a margin of more than 4,000 votes. In Worcester County, in the heart of that state, where antislavery had long been strong, Lincoln polled 16,105 votes and Bell only 1744. The leading newspaper in Worcester County, the *Masschusetts Spy,* hailed Lincoln's victory and, at first, envisioned no danger of secession. The editor dismissed the "Disunion Outcry" and gloried in the end of control of the country by southerners in the Democratic party. "For years," wrote the editor, "the Southern leaders of the democratic party have controlled the politics of the country by threatening periodically to destroy the Union. . . . But this villainous power is no longer available. It is a consolation to know we have at last reached the point where there must be an end to the rascally outcry of disunionism."[30] A week later the editor held that the South had nothing to fear, that Lincoln and the Republicans would not disturb slavery in states where it already existed.

There ensued a bitter fight between the antislavery people and the Unionists who favored concessions. The South, said the editor of the *Spy,* was not willing to compromise; it demanded concessions. He opposed the extension of the Missouri Compromise line to the Pacific because the South was bent on territorial acquisitions in Mexico and Central America, and these countries would be alarmed by acceptance of the proposal.[31]

The Boston *Atlas & Bee,* before the election, reflected the mild attempts of moderate Republicans to appeal to Southern Unionists. Henry Winter Davis, who had been elected to Congress by the Know Nothing party in the 1850s, who later became a Republican, and was considered for the nomination for vice-president in 1860, sought to assure the South. In an article for the Boston *Atlas & Bee* Davis of Maryland stated that should Lincoln be elected the South had nothing to fear. As to the territorial queston nothing had changed since 1850. The Republicans had never attempted more than to reestablish things as they existed before the repeal of the

Missouri Compromise. They had only opposed slavery where it should not go.[32] After the election this newspaper continued to oppose concessions. The editor of the *Atlas & Bee* opposed the Crittenden proposal that called for extending the Missouri Compromise line to the Pacific but approved of Charles Frances Adams offer to admit New Mexico as a slave state. Everett, the leading Unionist, gave his blessing to the Crittenden compromise, and so wrote to him.[33]

Early in February 1861 a meeting was called to meet in Faneuil Hall to consider the Crittenden Compromise. At this meeting the Unionist, Judge B. R. Curtis, supported extending the compromise line to the Pacific, but opposed applying it in any new acquisitions of territory. In assenting to this compromise Curtis explained that Unionists were moved by the conviction "that whether a given territory shall be ultimately slave holding or non-slave holding depends upon laws of soil and climate and cannot be affected by political combination or legislative action." Curtis called for the repeal of the Personal Liberty laws, a step that Everett also approved.[34]

In late January, a committee of Unionists called on Everett and asked him to carry a memorial to Congress. He sent a letter from Washington to the Unionist meeting in Boston advising the Unionists that there was no hope of reaching a compromise. "As it is," he wrote, "the people alone can avert the dire calamities that are impending. Political leaders are hampered by previous committals. The action of Congress is too much impeded by the forms of legislation and the tediousness of debate." In closing Everett advised, "To hold fifteen states in Union by force is a preposterous idea. If the border states must go, let them go in peace."[35]

This was a position supported repeatedly by Horace Greeley. The sudden realization that war was probable stunned the public at large, and had there been a popular referendum this position might well have won approval. In the months between Lincoln's election and his taking office the country was paralyzed by overwhelming despair and despondency.

In Washington, Everett and Robert Winthrop presented a memorial from the Unionists in Boston. The memorial was wrapped in an American flag. They met with Crittenden and Seward. Everett saw that there was no hope of achieving a compromise. He had a long walk with Charles Sumner who later called on Everett at the house where he was staying. Everett noted in his diary that Sumner was "under a state of morbid excitement approaching to insanity."

Sumner presented Everett with a project for the acquisition of Canada and a separation of the non-slaveholding states from the South, providing they would consent to live in the Union on the basis of the Republican platform.[36]

Some weeks after the election Everett wrote to his old confidant, C. A. Davis, stating what he believed to be the essential cause of the secession movement. Davis thought the repeal of the personal liberty laws would be a step in the right direction, and this was proposed because it was thought that these laws were the major complaint of the South. Everett warned that dealing with the real difficulty was deeper and more difficult. "It is," he wrote, "the organization and triumph of the Republicans in the non-slaveholding states of a party, with which the South never can nor never will cooperate and constituting in this way a permanent government of the South by the North. To such a state of things this South will never submit."[37] Everett was deeply aware that a kind of hysteria had taken possession of the deep South. He was also convinced that slavery was the central issue. He professed to be anxious to help the Southern Unionists, but he recognized that "the overwhelming weight of a triumphant majority" prevents "us from holding out any assurance to the South which would be of any value."

Recent studies of the antebellum South have been enriched by the work of cultural anthropologists and historians. They have sought for the distinctive characteristic that was central in the South. Some have concluded it was fear, others honor, others the institution of slavery. William Barbey states that fear of slave revolts reached a peak in 1860 and unified the South into a section that could not accept Republican rule. He concludes:

No matter how much Southerners disagreed as to how immediate or distinct a threat a Republican victory would present, they were united in the belief that racial integrity and control must be maintained. Since emancipation was unthinkable, the mere existence of antislavery federal administration pledged to restrict slavery was a menace to Southern civilization. In this crisis atmosphere, with emotions close to the surface, even conservatives were forced to insist on the South's right to resist a Republican victory.[38]

The question as to whether Everett was a timid man and moved by a lack of courage or an unrealistic and sentimental outlook is with us yet. In a study noted for both its careful scholarship and creative strengths George A. Forgie, in a book entitled *Patricide in the House Divided: A Psychological Interpretation of Lincoln and His Age,* sees two fashions or currents of thought that influenced events. He employs the word "sentiment" to describe one strand. By sentiment he means the long tradition of looking to the founding fathers as heroes. A transformation occurred in the middle of the nineteenth century as rapid change and an ever-increasing rush of contemporary problems turned attention to the present. There now appeared the phrase that "the dead cannot save the living." These two approaches, sentiment on the one hand and realistic ties to the Union on the other, existed side by side.

Everett, as Forgie correctly points out, resented the changes occurring all about him from theological and philosophical changes to laxity in business affairs. He was, as noted earlier, a prisoner of a bygone age. Forgie writes of Everett: "In a filiopietistic age it would be difficult to find a more filiopietistic man—toward his own father, the founders, and the past generally—than Edward Everett." As an orator Everett appealed to the past knowing that Americans cherished that past and they shared this sentiment, a feeling stronger than politics that could possibly bring them back from the great divide of politics. Everett sought escape from the political disunity he so despised.[39]

Forgie rules out an explanation in terms of Everett's basic beliefs and experiences. Richard Henry Dana, a contemporary of Everett, who had disagreed with Everett politically, chose to think otherwise. He dismissed Everett's Washington lectures as a pale sedative inadequate for the storms that led to the Civil War, but he explained that Everett could be best understood by looking at the larger picture. He had withdrawn from politics because to participate only served to make him a target of suspicion of timidity and "inadequate instincts and opinions." The value he placed on the Union was not mere patriotism or pride. It was, said Dana, "a solemn conviction that it was the one experiment, in the fullness of time, and under the most favorable circumstances possible, for the widest and highest moral and intellectual development or human nature." He did not share the faith of Emerson in the goodness of man, and should the Union fall it would open the way for destruction of great political principles, representative government, and government by laws. As to government, "He knew it was an institution of man; and he knew too much of the passions and weaknesses of human nature to be of the number of those who think that a vast people can make and unmake society and fundamental institutions, at their pleasure, without loss or peril."[40]

The proof of Everett's courage and boldness, when he saw an important cause at stake, came after the firing on Fort Sumter. In the words of Dana: "Whatever else the war emancipated, it had emancipated him [Everett]."

10
Role of the Orator in the Civil War

The temper of the country in 1860 was one of fear, distrust, and mutual recrimination. John Brown was being canonized in the North, not for his acts, but because of willingness to be a martyr. The South, in return, concluded that the zealots of the north condoned slave uprisings. As James M. McPherson writes: "Keyed up to the highest pitch of tension, many slaveholders and yeomen alike were ready for war to defend hearth and home against those Republican brigands."[1] The feeling prevailed that within the Union, Southerners could have no security.

Republicans were jubilant at the prospect of the northern sectional antislavery party achieving power. There was no general agreement as to what should be done and when. The Republicans, meeting in Chicago, set victory in the election as their highest priority. To achieve victory necessitated mobilizing support of many shades of opinion on the slavery question and avoiding antagonizing the many nativists and temperance people within the ranks.

Salmon Chase and William Henry Seward appeared to be the strongest possibilities for nomination, but Chase was too radical for many, and Seward had insulted the nativists. Both were set aside in favor of Abraham Lincoln, the western prairie lawyer. Lincoln had made clear his position on slavery, but always in moderate tones and without vindictiveness. His performance in the debates with Steven Douglas, in the course of which he took the position that the country must move forward toward freedom and not retreat into permitting the institution perpetuity and nationalization, strengthened his standing. He had driven Douglas into taking a stand that a territory could prohibit slavery. While it saved him from ruin in Illinois, this destroyed Douglas in the South.

The Republican campaign was a masterpiece in enlisting workers in local districts, arousing emotional support, and avoiding clashes between the sharply divided factions within the party. In the course of the campaign Southerners warned that the election of Lincoln meant secession. Republicans dismissed this as a worn-out threat and refused to believe it.[2] When Lincoln won, the first threats of secession were not taken seriously, and not until South Carolina seceded did the futile search for a compromise get underway.

It was no surprise to Everett. He had long since taken the southern threat seriously, and as secession progressed he, among hosts of others, hoped for compromise; if that failed, he proposed that the South be permitted to depart in peace.[3] Everett was ready to make concessions to the South. He supported the Crittenden Compromise, a proposal that was a virtual surrender of Republican principles. The amendments it proposed would have guaranteed slavery in the states below 36°30' for the future by stipulating that it was not subject to future amendment, demanded that there be no interference by Congress in any territory acquired in the future, would have prohibited the abolition of slavery in the District of Columbia except with the consent of the local inhabitants and unless slavery was abolished in Maryland and Virginia, and would have prohibited Congress from interfering with the interstate slave trade. The Crittenden Compromise was voted down in committee and later in the Senate.

The several efforts at compromise, inspired in part by the hope of keeping border states in the Union, won from time to time the reluctant support of individual Republicans, but they ran afoul the president-elect who stood firm, warning that concessions would disgrace the party and lose all the strength the party had won. Every compromise proposed offered concessions only to the South.

The time for compromise was past. The lines of conflict had become firmer during the election campaign. For Southerners the central issue was slavery, and they had reached the decision that the Republicans were determined to revolutionize the South and that it was necessary to take preemptive action "to forestall the dangers they conjured up. The South could not afford to wait for an 'overt act' by Lincoln against southern rights."[4]

* * * * *

The secession of six southern states by mid-January 1861 provided the most severe trial the Union was ever to face. The breakup of the Union, which had appeared remote, was now in process. Washington buzzed with the latest reports to find a compromise.

Everett wavered amid the general uncertainty and feelings of desperation. Now, as the Union was breaking into pieces, he could only say let the slave states go in peace. When an acquaintance pleaded with him to use his influence to have the troops removed from Fort Sumter before the Confederates launched an attack, Everett did not hesitate to lend a helping hand. He called on General Winfield Scott and found that the General agreed that the fort should be abandoned. Scott advised Everett to see the president, but Everett found the president occupied in a cabinet meeting. He soon was informed that Scott had conveyed his views to the president.[5]

At the moment Everett was ready to sacrifice all for peace, and he wrote that to hold fifteen states in the Union by force was an absurdity. "The idea of civil war accompanied as it would be by servile insurrection is too monstrous to be entertained for a moment. If our sister states are determined to separate from us let them go in peace."[6]

The same spell of uncertainty gripped the Lincoln administration as to whether it should give up Fort Sumter or strengthen the fortification. Seward, who was to become secretary of state did not have authority to act, but he sent word to the Confederates that Sumter would be abandoned. Lincoln's cabinet also advised him to give up the fort. Only Montgomery Blair advised to the contrary. Fort Sumter was of lesser importance from a military view, but it was of great importance from a political standpoint. Sending reinforcements to hold the fort was considered but set aside. The necessary forces were not available. Lincoln rejected Seward's advice. After thoughtfully weighing options, he decided that provisions only would be sent and so notified Governor Pickens. As James M. McPherson writes in his recent book, "Lincoln's new conception of the resupply undertaking was a stroke of genius."[7] This left the Confederates with the two unhappy choices, bowing weakly to permitting the supplies to pass or to stop it and thereby take the blame for firing the first shot. In Charleston the Confederates were tired of waiting, and the populace lined the shore ready to cheer an attack. On 12 April, the war began.

* * * * *

The Confederate attack brought an end to Everett's wavering. War signaled the end of watchful waiting and futile hopes. Everett shed his uncertainty and became at once an ardent defender of the Union.

The prompt decision of Everett was not singular. The entire North set aside divisions in sentiment and joined in defense of the Union. This included Democrats as well as Republicans. Stephen Douglas told a crowd in Chicago that there was no middle ground. Every man must be for the United States or against it.[8]

During the crisis Everett underestimated Lincoln. On 15 February, after reading in the press of Lincoln's trip across the country, he commented in his diary that Lincoln's speeches "have thus far been of the most ordinary kind, destitute of every thing not merely of felicity and grace but of common pertinence." Everett remarked, "He is evidently a person of very inferior cast of character, and wholly unequal to the crisis."[9]

This view of Lincoln was shared by both Seward and Charles Francis Adams. The two men met and discussed the failure of Lincoln to come to terms with the situation. Seward said the president had "no system, no relative ideas." Adams wrote in his diary that the country seemed to be drifting into war and added: "I see nothing but incompetency in the head. The man is not equal to the hour."

The criticisms of Lincoln were only in part justified. It is true that his speeches were full of ambiguity and clichés. The president, however, presided over a party that was little more than congeries of parts holding conflicting views. Directness or boldness could wreck his party at this time when it was crucial to promote party unity.

Everett, during the crisis, observed that conservatives remained quiet while the radicals were making all the noise. He attributed this to be conservatives' dislike of revolutionary disturbance; they felt estranged. Everett, himself a conservative, felt that he had nothing in common with either side. That he took the position he did was due in some part to his seeing the situation as hopeless, and it was just that as far as preserving the Union short of war. To face the tragedy, accept it, and resolve on a constructive course of action was for the moment beyond him.

Until the firing on Fort Sumter, Everett favored letting the Confederate states go in peace. It would, he thought be futile to hold them by military force.

* * * * *

He observed that the Confederates had been assured that the fort would not be furnished military supplies and that the guns at the fort could not reach the city of Charleston three miles away. He saw in the attack the launching of an offensive war by the South and that the Union must defend itself. In retrospect he observed that there had been no hope of compromise. He concluded that the South would have rejected a carte blanche offer to settle on whatever terms the South proposed. South Carolina based its action on the liberty laws in the North that protected fugitive slaves. Slavery, he believed, was the major cause of the war. He was determined to assist the Union in the only way he could, by devoting his oratorical talents to mobilizing public support for the Union cause.

> Disapproving as I did conscientiously of the course of policy pursued by the Republican party, I disapprove much more of the Secessionists, and in as much as it is now an alternative between supporting the government and allowing the country to fall into a state of anarchy and general confusion, I cannot hesitate as to the party of duty.[10]

Charles Francis Adams saw the change and was to write: "The progress of events had brought him to a point where his fears no longer checked him, for his interests . . . ran on all fours with his convictions." "To me" said Adams, "his four last years appear worth more than all the rest of his life, including the whole series of his rhetorical triumphs." He could now be the practicing Nationalist who did not need to live amid crippling compromise.

Now that his decision had been made he promptly made it his duty to support the Union cause. On 24 April, he urged Robert Bonner of the *Ledger* to support the government.[11] Early in May, in nearby Roxbury, he gave the first of his many speeches on the state of affairs. He sent a copy to Secretary of State Seward who thanked him and said it was "one of the most admirable and valuable of your efforts in support of the Union."[12] Charles Francis Adams, new United Minister in London, praised the speech and distributed copies where he thought it would do the most good.[13] On 4 July, Everett spoke in the Music Hall in New York. By early fall he was on tour again and spoke in Ogdensburg and Brooklyn.

Everett denied that the Constitution included the right to secede, and he took care to support this view with care. The Confederate charge that the North dominated the federal government he dismissed as contrary to facts. He told his listeners that for sixty-four of the nation's seventy-two years the presidency had been filled by Southerners or Northern men in whom the South had confided, and "for a still longer period, the controlling influences of the Legislature and judicial departments of the Government have centered in the same quarter." To refute the economic grievances set forth by the South, he cited the growth and prosperity of the South. Now, he said, because the North for the first time chose a president by her unaided electoral vote, the South resorted to war. It was not the North that had waged war; "it has been forced upon" it. Now the South was asking the North to surrender fifteen hundred miles of coastline, the navigation of the Gulf of Mexico, and the lower reaches of the Mississippi River. There could be no yielding to such demands.[14]

One of the severest critics, George Lunt, editor of the Boston *Courier,* later charged that Everett was wrong in holding the South guilty of rejecting the Crittenden Compromise. It was the radical Republicans, Lunt stated, who had defeated the compromise. Everett acknowledged that the Republicans had opposed the compromise, but that the Republicans rejected it was to the expected. It was in direct conflict with the program they had supported during the election campaign. Crittenden had never expected the Republicans to support his proposal. To blame the Republicans, said Everett, "is a pure piece of mystification." Undoubtedly, said Everett, "everyone would have been glad to have the Republicans support those resolutions, as we should be glad to have the Millennium set in tomorrow."

What Crittenden hoped, said Everett, was that the senators of the border states would be satisfied with his proposals and support them and then the conservatives of the North would support them. Eight border state senators voted against them, however, and six abstained from voting. Lunt had also stated that Jefferson Davis was ready to support the Crittenden Compromise. Everett, who had been in the company with the leaders of disunion while in Washington, testified that contrary to Lunt, Jefferson Davis had not once given any indication of support. Not only did Davis not support the Crittenden Compromise, he did not wish it to pass.[15] Everett, in his speech, held that had the South been presented with a carte blanche, they would have rejected it. Ambitious southern leaders, he charged, were ready to tear up the sacred union so as to gratify their own ambitions.

Believing that he would be more effective if he avoided identification with a political party he refused to speak at party gatherings. When the Union party, whose candidate for the vice-presidency he had been in 1860, called a meeting in September 1861, he not only refused to attend but advised the leadership to abstain from all political action and to support the government.[16]

By fall he was ready to resume his speeches in support of the Union. On 16 October, he delivered for the first time his address on the "Causes and Conduct of the War" before the Mercantile Library Association of Boston. He focused attention on the glory of the Union and what had been accomplished—growth, prosperity, and acquisition of power in foreign affairs. He asked how could men be "so blind to the examples of all countries, so regardless of the experience of all ages, as to believe that the happiness and peace of a family of kindred States can be promoted by the rupture of the Union that binds them together, and resolving them into rival, jealous, and hostile powers?" This was a delusion, and "it shall not be." He closed with a call to duty:

> This glorious national fabric shall not be allowed to crumble into dishonorable fragments. This seamless garment of Union, which enfolds the States like a holy Providence, shall not be permitted to be torn in tatters by traitorous hands. No, a thousand times no! Rise, loyal millions of the country! Hasten to the defense of the menaced Union! Come, old men and children! Come young men and maidens![17]

From 19 October to the close of the year Everett delivered the address twenty-six times throughout New England and New York state. After hearing his speech in Brooklyn, Henry Ward Beecher came to Everett and said excitedly that the address made him feel like enlisting.[18] On 2 January, Everett resumed his speech making, and he delivered his address sixteen times in the next three months going as far west as Buffalo and Pittsburgh. On 23 April, he set out again and spoke throughout the Middle West, including St. Paul, Minnesota, and Davenport, Iowa. The trip refreshed his enthusiasm for the pleasant and prosperous farms of the fertile Mississippi Valley. The new colleges where he so often spoke won his admiration; after visiting some public schools he declared they were easily as fine as those in Boston.

The military reverses of the Union armies and the occasional blunders of northern generals disturbed him, but he never doubted that the North would be victorious. It was the danger of foreign intervention or recognition of the Confederacy by a European power that gave him the greatest concern. Everett failed to foresee that the British were to come dangerously close to pursuing a course that could have led to diplomatic recognition of the Confederacy or even to war. The strong antislavery feelings of the public in England in the past did not suddenly disappear, but until the struggle had gone on for almost two years Britishers chose to believe that slavery was not the issue, that it was a futile struggle over which section should dominate, that the Confederacy could not be subdued, and that the bloody struggle was an exercise of futility on the part of the north. An eminent British historian, the biographer of William Gladstone, John Morley, summed up the British approach. "We applied ordinary political maxims to what was not merely a political contest, but a social revolution," he wrote. Ignoring "the cardinal realities beneath we discussed it like some superficial conflict in our old world about boundaries, successions, territorial partitions, dynastic rivalries." What was missed was that the war was tied to slavery and to a social order that was already an anachronism.[19]

When the war began Everett expected that the British, who had so long been hostile to slavery, would be partial to the North because they would see that the central issue was its abolition. All this changed during the first months of hostilities. After Lincoln declared a blockade of the Confederate states, the British promptly recognized the Confederacy as a belligerent. The British held that a blockage was only legal as a war measure and that therefore their action was sanctioned by the law of nations. Everett did not question its legal correctness, but the haste in which the British acted and their failure to wait until the new minister of the United States, Charles Francis Adams, arrived distressed him. The hostility to the North in the British press also filled him with dismay. It appeared to Everett that the British did not understand the war, and he determined to enlighten them with a campaign of letter writing to his many British friends.

The appointment of his brother-in-law, Charles Francis Adams, gave him assurance that the Union side would be well represented. In earlier years they had not found each other congenial, but this had changed. Everett wrote letters of introduction to British friends and informed them that they would find Adams an able man. He told his son Willie that his uncle "has solid talents equal to his father or grandfather, and better literary tastes and sounder judgment than either."[20]

The letters Charles Francis Adams and Everett exchanged throughout the war provide a rich source of the history of the relations between the two countries during the war years. Everett, however, expected too much of traditional friendships, and his longtime admiration of the British now led to almost bitter disillusion. Fortunately, Adams was more patient, and he recognized at once that the British would act in accordance with their conception of their best interests and that the most he could do was to avoid "an open quarrel." He found the British cabinet well disposed. Six of the members invited him to dine.[21]

Everett wrote to British Foreign Secretary John Russell, when the news that the British had granted belligerent status to the Confederacy arrived. He confided to Adams later that he had expressed himself "pretty freely on the want of sympathy evinced by him [Russell] with the government of the United States."[22]

Russell denied this. He said he respected the feelings of the North and particularly "the resolution not to permit the extension of slavery," but added, "what do you expect of us—to declare war on the South?"

A letter from Joshua Bates, the American who was a senior partner in the Barings Bank, gave Everett cause for alarm. Bates warned that under the pressure of manufacturing interests for a supply of cotton, the British government "will soon get the relations with the United States into a state, that may give them some pretense for making war, in case the blockade is strictly enforced until the cotton crop is wanted."[23]

Everett did not hesitate to tell his British friends that he was disappointed by the attitude of the British government. He wrote to Speaker Denison that he regretted that the government, given the fact that slavery was the issue, did not go "to the limits of the law of nations, in showing your sympathies with us."[24] In a second letter to British Foreign Secretary Russell, he implored him to prevent violation of the blockade of southern ports, held that the blockade was efficient—more so than the British blockade during the Napoleonic Wars, and urged him not to pay too much respect to ex parte opinions of the law officers of the Crown who had blundered in the past.[25] He explained that though "the war is not, and could not, due to the limits of federal power set forth in the Constitution be waged for the abolition of slavery, it does grow out of slavery." Southern leaders were fighting to defend slavery and would seek to restore the slave trade if successful. Instead of making slavery a subject of reprobation in the manner the British government had with the slave trade "your government has adopted what we regard as a tone of cold neutrality, while the most influential portion of the British press is decidedly—some of the journals vehemently—in the interests of the Confederates."

The British were saying that the North was not fighting to abolish slavery, and some believed that the South should be permitted to go in peace. They, Everett held, had either been misled or simply sought a pretext to break the blockade, or they were driven by fear of a strong Union. He refused to believe that the British leaders did not know that if the North won, slavery would be abolished. In the meantime they were friendly to the South who would extend slavery. "The plain truth is," he wrote, "that there are in Europe those who are ashamed to confess that they care for nothing on earth but cotton and tobacco, pretend hypocritically that they would sympathize with the North if the war was waged against slavery; but as it is only a tariff war, or a war for empire, or a war between classes, they are indifferent which side prevails."[26]

In the fall of 1861 he gave way to bitterness and impatience. While in Washington he had been told by Baron Stoeckel, the Russian minister, and Henri Mercier, the French minister, that if the blockade threatened injury to England and France and if it was not lifted those two nations would have to go to war with the North. When Everett told Mercier that France had an interest in seeing the United States strong as a counterpoise to England, the French minister asserted that France had an interest in close ties with England because of the Italian situation. Everett then raised the moral question—to which Mercier responded that self-interest ruled.[27]

In London, Adams, early in his stay, concluded that barring some unforeseen eruption, the British would adhere to neutrality unless it became clear that the North faced defeat. This conjecture rested on his faith in the cabinet. Public opinion swayed from favoring neutrality and, at times when the South was winning, shifted toward granting the Confederacy diplomatic recognition.

There was one constant, the fear of the privileged classes of a powerful United States sometime in the future. In 1861 this fear appeared to permeate all classes. "The anxiety to see us divided," wrote Adams, "is remarkable." He conversed with leaders in both the government and in the opposition, and he "always found them harping upon the enormous magnitude of the country upon the impossibility of subduing the opposition, and the expediency of a division."[28] Dislike of Americans had not surprised him so much as the fear of them. The cause of the fear was "that the continuance of our system of Government in its career of prosperity will ultimately prove the destruction of theirs."[29]

Everett was distressed by Adams's reports. Every American who called at the legation, wrote Adams, "expresses his astonishment at the general concurrence of sentiment he has met with in all public places, and in all ranks of society." The only friends were the liberal or radical party, and that party was under pressure because the Tories were exploiting anti-American feelings. Every party, thought Adams, "is reading our quarrel through the spectacles furnished by its own position at home, and hence is disqualified from all fair judgment of its merits."[30]

The *Trent* affair in November 1861 caused an immediate crisis in relations. Captain Wilkes of the Navy ship *San Jacinto* learned that two Confederate emissaries were aboard the British mail ship, the

Trent, and headed for England. He stopped the *Trent* and under the threat of force took Mason and Slidell aboard his own ship for transferral to the United States. The act was a violation of international law, but Wilkes promptly became a hero. The response of Lord Palmerston was at first ambivalent, but when the law officers of the Crown ruled that the seizure was a violation of the law of nations and released their findings to the press, the British public was indignant. Adams in London thought Wilkes had made a great mistake.

Everett defended Wilkes, holding that any enemy official carrying messages was legitimate contraband. He immediately sent off an article to the *Ledger* defending Wilkes. Failing to see that Wilkes had blundered, he wrote in his diary, "If England avails herself of this moment of weakness to make such a demand it will be an act of National Cowardice, bullying, and meanness not often paralleled."[31]

Lincoln and Secretary of State Seward showed better judgment. Secretary of the Treasury Chase also took this stand. To drive England into hostility over an act that was of minor importance would have been foolish. Mason and Slidell were released and permitted to continue their voyage to England. Everett recovered and saw things in their true light, and he read Seward's dispatch on the case and pronounced it "an extremely able article."[32]

At first, the firm British response sparked the traditional Anglophobia, but realities dictated the contrary. The shock of confronting a second war sent the stock market into a downward spin. In the inner circles in Washington, a second factor sobered demeanor. There was a desperate shortage of saltpeter, an essential element in gunpowder. Seward had sent a representative of the Dupont Company to England to purchase the supplies coming from India. These were now in London. The seizure of Mason and Slidell caused the British to place an embargo on the shipment of the saltpeter. This issue also had a part in Lincoln's decision to release Mason and Slidell and send them off to England.[33]

For a brief interlude it appeared that Everett was to have a direct part in counteracting hostility in Europe. On 8 September 1862, a telegram arrived from Seward with the message, "The sooner you come the better." Illness in Everett's family delayed his going for a month. On his meeting with Seward he found that a project that had been broached a year before was now again alive. The administration wished him to go to Europe to help present the Union side. Everett, however, saw difficulties and was cool to the proposal. The resident ministers would feel that their positions were being undermined. He cited his own experience when Tyler sent Duff Green to London as his special emissary. Lincoln saw the difficulty and offered to draft a letter that would solve the problem. The next day Lincoln showed Everett his draft. It read that no gentlemen "is better able to correct misunderstandings in the minds of foreigners in regard to American affairs" and it closed with the salutation, "While I commend him to the consideration of those whom he may meet, I am quite conscious that he could better introduce me than I him in Europe."[34] Everett noted that the letter "was everything I could wish and more than I deserve in the way of pleasant compliments, but instead of giving me any kind of representative character, it would appear to have been written mainly for the purpose of negating any such character."[35] Lincoln invited him to revise the letter in any manner he pleased, but Everett saw that this would go contrary to the heart of what the president had decided. He had three interviews with Lincoln, who was more than amiable. He read to Everett several letters he had written to American ministers abroad and assured him that he was viewed as one of the cabinet council.[36] Everett, however, concluded that he would have no more status than a traveler, that he would not have access to high officials, and that he would not be able to perform any useful service, and he declined the offer. He explained his decision to Charles Francis Adams who thought he did right in refusing to go.

By the fall of 1862 Everett was in good standing with the Lincoln administration. Both Chase and Seward had thanked him for making the strongest case for the North that had been presented. In Massachusetts the Republican party invited him to be their nominee for Congress, and predicted that he would be elected by an overwhelming majority, but he explained once again that he was more likely to win support if he was not a party man.

On the home front Everett interpreted the war as originating in the slavery question, and he asserted that the war was being fought to abolish slavery. This placed him in the camp of those who saw the war as a revolutionary movement that would strengthen the central government by removing the divisive slavery question. This clashed with those who would confine war aims to putting down secession. Many Democrats by 1863 were determined to preserve state rights, set aside the slave question, and make peace.

The rivalry between radical Republicans who pushed vigorously for immediate emancipation and Democrats who opposed it placed the president in the position of being harassed by both sides. Lincoln favored emancipation, but he had to move with caution. He decided that he could not issue a proclamation until the Confederate forces were driven out of Maryland. When a church association in Chicago sent him a lengthy appeal stating the many reasons for freeing the slaves and equated it with God's will, he replied that God had not yet spoken to him, that he wished he would, for he had only heard men who were in sharp disagreement.

In August 1862, Salmon P. Chase, secretary of the treasury, who had repeatedly advocated emancipation, asked Everett for his views on the proposal that was to become the Emancipation Proclamation. The constitutional aspect gave Everett no trouble; the president had the right to terminate slavery under his war powers. The proposed measure would be resisted by conservatives in the border states, however, and the difficulty this could lead to made him hesitant. As a matter of expediency this problem could be avoided by adhering to the course "already pursued by our generals, and now openly sanctioned by the President—that is, receiving into the public service all those slaves who chose to come, employing them in any way in which they can be useful and refusing to give them up." He added that not much was to be gained by general orders terminating slavery in areas where "we have no force to carry them into effect." Negroes could render important services of a menial nature, but they should not be limited to that. They should be encouraged to join the army, and they will do so when "they are sure of protection, freedom & wages."[37] Everett's views coincided with those of Chase.[38]

The problem of timing the emancipation had given Lincoln great concern, but after the battle at Antietam, where the Confederates were driven back, he decided the time had come. At the cabinet meeting where Lincoln proposed it, two members raised objections on the grounds that it would alienate the border states and that the Democrats would make political capital out of the move. Lincoln overruled them. He had curried the favors of the border states long enough and, as for the Democrats, they would continue to make trouble no matter which course he pursued.[39] When Everett read it in the press, his only comment was that the president undoubtedly had information not known to him.

Lincoln and Everett were in complete harmony on giving first priority to saving the Union and moving toward emancipation when emancipation was consistent with winning the war. Lincoln's views were most fully elucidated in a private letter. He wrote, "And I aver to this day, I have done no official move in mere deference to my judgment and feeling on slavery. . . . Right or wrong, I assumed this ground, and now avow it. I could not feel that, to the best of my ability, I had even tried to preserve the constitution, if, to save slavery, or any minor matter, I should permit the wreck of government, country, and Constitution all together."[40]

The response to the Emancipation Proclamation in England was electric. Adams joyfully reported that it had consolidated the popular sentiment friendly to the Union and that great public meetings took place expressing strong support for the Union cause. He informed Everett "that not even in the highest agitation of the corn laws or of reform was there a more powerful manifestation of the popular will."[41]

The announcement of the Emancipation Proclamation came at a crucial time. Russell, in the late summer and early fall, was on the verge of offering mediation and if that was rejected of recognizing the Confederacy.[42] William Gladstone, chancellor of the exchequer, declared that "Jefferson Davis and other leaders of the South have made an army; they are making, it appears, a navy; and they have made what is more than either—they have made a nation." Adams did not know at the time of Russell's intentions, and he attributed Gladstone's feelings to his close ties with Liverpool, "hot bed of secession" and to his fear of a powerful Union.[43] The American minister soon concluded that Gladstone came to regret his speech and he wrote to Everett, "He has been explaining it away ever since he made it."[44]

Later historical research indicates that the turnabout of the British in favor of the Union was more limited than the reports of Charles Francis Adams stated. In Lancashire, where there was unemployment due to the shortage of cotton, sentiment in favor of the South continued strong.[45] In some instances, it appears, the feelings extended to favoring diplomatic recognition of the Confederacy. Historians have, in some instances, concluded that the rally to support of the Union was largely the work of a few intellectuals like John Bright whose orations in behalf of the Union, thanks to their idealism, attracted the attention of historians. The Emancipation Proclamation did not change the prosouthern views of operatives in the cotton industry, but British political leaders did alter their views as a result of the Southern retreat after the Battle of Antietam, and the Emancipation Proclamation did mark a change in British policy.

Charles Francis Adams consistently held that Union failures or successes on the battle fields would be the final determining factor in shaping British policy. This, too, Lincoln knew well would determine domestic political developments. In late 1863 and early 1864 the public was war wary and therefore susceptible to peace appeals by the Democrats. George B. McClellan, the able general whose overly cautious moves and failure to pursue the enemy forces when they were vulnerable led to his being relieved of his command, saw that the prevailing temper of the public furnished an opportunity to reject Lincoln's determination to abolish slavery and make peace. The final outcome would be determined by arms.

Everett acknowledged Lincoln's difficulties, but he, too, was disturbed by the failures of Lincoln's generals. He wrote to a friend in the summer of 1863:

> What the country wants and must have is not more troops, white or black, but a change in the military administration at Washington. How the President can justify it to his conscience, to continue the influences which have within the twelve month given in the costly experiments of Pope, Burnside, and Hooker I cannot conceive.[46]

Lincoln faced almost endless difficulties with his generals throughout 1862. He was finally compelled to replace McClellan in late 1862 when that general, popular with the soldiers and standing high in public opinion, failed to follow up Lee's retreat after the battle of Antietam. Early in 1863 Lincoln relieved Burnside of his command, and he replaced him with Hooker, but Hooker too proved a disappointment. Lincoln was still looking for the right general to carry on the military campaigns in the East.

Lincoln also faced difficult political problems. The Democrats attacked him as incompetent, and within his own party, especially the radicals, some were critical of his caution on the question of abolishing slavery.[47] Everett stood by the president, accepting the fact that in a free society amid the great difficulties of fighting a war, shortcomings and difficulties were inevitable. Ever patient, Everett remained loyal. A long fifteen-month illness in 1863 and 1864, however, compelled him to decline most invitations to speak. The invitations flowed in almost at the rate of one a day.

In the spring of 1863 Everett's greatest concern was that the war efforts of the Lincoln administration were becoming the sport of politicians. In a speech in Boston he said it may be asked, "How can men support the administration in the conduct of the war, if they do not approve its measures?" He turned the question around and asked, "How, . . . can any free government carry on a war, if everyone is to stand aloof who does not approve all measures?" Errors were certain to happen in all wars, for both government officials and military leaders were fallible men.[48] After reading the speech Secretary Chase wrote to Everett stating it was "the ablest exposition of our course which had appeared since the War."[49]

Charles Francis Adams complimented Everett saying that the address "moved me most profoundly. Nothing can be finer than the spirit in which the whole of it is conceived. It wanted only an official character to make it a great moral lever of our cause in Europe as well as in America."[50]

Though he on occasion had doubts about Secretary of War Stanton and worried for a time that the criticisms of General McClellan might be unfair, Everett did not share his concerns with others. Throughout the war he placed support of the Lincoln administration as his highest priority. When he received an invitation to speak in Illinois before an election, he declined stating that though he had not always agreed with the administration he could not "but think it unpatriotic to attempt for the sake of party triumph, to make political capital out of the difficulties or if you please the errors, unavoidable incident to the conduct of a war of such great dimensions."[51]

Everett deplored party rivalry during the war. In the summer of 1863 he told one of his correspondents that the administration "finds itself thwarted on all measures, however, patriotic and beneficial their tendency, by indiscriminate opposition, aiming only at electioneering triumph."[52]

The victory of General Meade at Gettysburg during the first days of July 1863 marked a dramatic turning point. The Confederacy had been turned back in its effort to invade the North and its most powerful armies defeated. In the weeks ahead it was decided to hold a consecration of the cemetery in October. A commission of Pennsylvanians organized a corporation through which eighteen northern states would share the cost of the burial ground. On 23 September, Everett received an invitation to speak at the ceremony. He accepted immediately, asking only that if possible it be postponed to 19 November so that he would have time to prepare and to take care of family obligations.

To do honor to those who had perished required that he give an account of the battle. This was no small task, and he stated that it had taken historians two years to write an accurate narrative of lesser battles. Meade's army of eighty-eight thousand and Lee's of seventy-five thousand had fought a battle with a ghastly outpouring of blood. To master the events of three days and the many complex maneuvers he promptly set to work to gain the necessary information. He received an account of the battle from Professor Jacobs of Gettysburg College, who witnessed the hostilities. On request he also received a report from General Meade's staff. Recognizing that accounts of such a large and complex operation were subject to error, he observed that "dexterous selection of details and choice of words of the very same incidents are related in a directly opposite manner by the two parties." To check he resorted to Brahelder's print shop to study maps of the battle and to discuss details with the proprietor, who had acquired minute knowledge by interviewing Confederate prisoners and spending six weeks on the scene.[53]

On 11 November, Everett finished writing his address, but the next day he received General Meade's official report and then spent the following day making revisions.[54] Before leaving Boston he sent his address to the printer and then corrected proof sheets, a precautionary measure to avoid being misquoted. He also sent a copy to Lincoln so that the president would know in advance what he would cover.

To familiarize himself with the battle scene he arranged to arrive at Gettysburg on 16 November. Professor Jacobs greeted him and guided him over the fields of battle. He saw the grim wake of the tragedy, the corpses of horses; holes in trees, graves of men where they had fallen, and between Round Top and Little Round Top, "because no dirt was available, Confederate dead were covered with rocks." That evening he wrote a synopsis of his address so as to help him commit it to memory.[55]

Lincoln arrived late in the afternoon of the 18 November and was greeted by a huge crowd. The following day the saddened assembly heard Everett and the president, the former for two hours and Lincoln for a few minutes. Lincoln, burdened with responsibilities, had sketched out his memorable speech the night before. It was as simple in phrasing and tone as it was grand in concept.

We are gathered here, he said, not to consecrate or dedicate this hallowed ground for "The brave men, living and dead, who struggled here, have consecrated it far above our poor power, to add or detract." We are here, he said, to resolve "that these dead shall not have died in vain; that this nation, under God, shall have a new birth of freedom; and that government of the people, by the people, for the people, shall not perish from the earth." In two minutes Lincoln had written some of the finest lines ever to grace the pages of American literature. On 19 November, as one historian has said, Lincoln by word and deed interred states' rights.

Everett that day was obligated to review the battle scenes and to pay tribute to the men and women who made the bloody victory possible, but he did more than that. He placed the war guilt on the South where a small minority of "ambitious fire eaters" were intent on setting up a state they could dominate. The leaders of the South, he said, were charging that theirs was a rebellion against tyranny; in fact it was a rebellion for establishing, extending, and perpetuating injustice.

In a few words—which Lincoln was to thank him for—Everett dismissed the right of secession. The Constitution denied states the right to make treaties and declare war. How then could the same Constitution grant the right to secede, Everett asked, leaving the states free to do precisely what the Constitution denied them?

Everett then came to the concern closest to his heart: reconciliation after the war had been won. Only two weeks before he had received the invitation to speak, he had written in his diary, "Conceived the idea of a lecture on this thesis, that the exasperation induced by the belligerents in a civil war, does not prevent the restoration of harmony when the war is over." At Gettysburg he pointed out that the civil wars in ancient Greece, the Wars of the Roses, the seventeenth-century wars in England, and the internal struggles in France in the sixteenth and seventeenth centuries had ended in reunion.

The aristocrats of the South, Everett said, could not be forgiven; he thought they would be rebuked by their own people. He held there was no bitterness on the part of the masses of Southerners; there were already indications of a desire for peace and reunion. The basic forces that underlay the nation were now at work:

> The bonds that unite as one people—a substantial community of origin, language, belief, and law (the four great ties that hold the societies of men together); common national and political interests; a common history; a common pride in this great heritage of blessings; the very geographical features of the country; the mighty rivers that cross the lines of climate and thus facilitate the interchange of natural and industrial products, while the wonder-working arm of the engineer has levelled the mountain-walls which separate the East and West, compelling your own Alleghenies, my Maryland and Pennsylvania friends, to open wide their everlasting doors to chariot-wheels of traffic and travel; these bonds of union are of perennial force and energy while the causes of alienation are imaginary, factitious, and transient.[56]

This, he wrote to a correspondent, who had praised it, "was the part of the address I valued most."[57] That this should be so was natural to Everett, since his days at Göttingen he had cherished this vision of a Union bound together by forces stronger than sectional controversy.

Everett recognized at once the excellence of Lincoln's address, and the following day he wrote to him:

Permit me also to express my great admiration of the thoughts expressed by you, with such eloquent simplicity and appropriateness, at the consecration of the cemetery. I should be glad, if I could flatter myself, that I came as near to the central idea of the occasion in two hours, as you did in two minutes.[58]

Lincoln responded with an equally gracious letter thanking him for his own speech and stating "while the whole discourse was satisfactory, and will be of great value, there were passages in it which transcended my expectation." He was particularly pleased by Everett's argument in support of national supremacy.[59]

Neither man was pleased with his performance. Lincoln told a friend, "I told you, Hill, that speech fell on the audience like a wet blanket. I am distressed about it. I ought to have prepared it with more care."[60] Everett thought the audience was satisfied with his own speech, but he noted that while speaking he decided that the address was too long "so I omitted a good deal of what I had written." To this he added that parts of the address were poorly memorized, several long paragraphs condensed, several thoughts occurred at the moment as generally happens." What pleased him most was that when he sat down the president pressed his hand "with great fervor, and said, 'I am more than gratified, I am grateful to you.' "[61]

Lincoln's reelection in 1864 depended on Union success on the battlefields. Antietam and Gettysburg, in which the Confederate forces were turned back, were important turning points in the war, but a peace movement by Democrats supported by McClellan gained momentum in the spring and summer of 1864. In August, Lincoln expected to be defeated and that McClellan would be elected. War weary of the bloodshed, disheartened by the military outlook, Democrats in the North promoted the illusion that peace could be made and the Union restored if the North dropped its demand for the abolition of slavery. McClellan made this his platform.

The bloodiest campaigns of the entire war occurred in the summer of 1864. There was hand to hand fighting. Soldiers dug trenches and sought cover behind ridges. In the battles in Virginia in May and June it was reported that sixty-five thousand Union soldiers were killed, wounded, or missing. That summer General Sherman drove his forces toward Atlanta and captured this hub of the Confederate transportation system the first days of September. The victory did not end the war, but it was a decisive factor in the final defeat of the Confederates. It was likewise decisive in the reelection of Lincoln in November, when public opinion demanded that the approaching victory fought at such great costs should be fought to completion.

In the summer and fall of 1864 Everett devoted himself full-time to promoting a fund for victims of the war in eastern Tennessee where there were thousands of refugee slaves. The effort was sponsored by the Knoxville Relief Association. There were difficulties in arranging for the transportation of food and clothing to the thousands of refugees who were in desperate need. Everett encountered an embarrassing situation when the man responsible for purchases of supplies mismanaged the arrangements. For months Everett spent his days keeping in touch with the local committee in Tennessee, establishing accounts with banks in Tennessee that the committee on the scene could use. Most of the contributions were in small amounts, and it fell on Everett to acknowledge each donation by letter. The donations totaled $102,000.

The presidential election of 1864 posed the question of whether Lincoln was to be permitted to carry on the long, wearisome struggle. Late in 1863, General McClellan made known his availability as a Democratic candidate. At the Democratic convention in Chicago in August 1864 he was named on a platform calling for peace. In his acceptance speech McClellan stated, "The Union is the one condition of peace—we ask no more." The Chicago platform did not call for the abolition of slavery.[62]

Everett concluded that "a change in administration would paralyze military operations and compel a cessation of hostilities on such conditions as Mr. Davis might dictate with the inevitable result of the disintegration of the Union."[63]

Everett was concerned because many of the supporters of the Union party in 1860, including former Whigs, Robert Winthrop and Hilliard, supported McClellan. He broke with his stand of not becoming identified with either party in September when he agreed to serve as a Republican elector. When Everett was invited by Governor Andrew of Massachusetts to give an address in Fanuiel Hall on 19 October, he immediately accepted.

Everett spoke directly to the immediate issues confronting the public. Again he defended the administration. The Democratic party, he said, could not be entrusted with responsibility to carry the war to a successful conclusion. Appealing to the old-line Whigs, he reminded them of how the Democrats had repeatedly sacrificed national interests to southern sectional interests. Now the Democratic party, in the platform adopted at its convention in Chicago, was ready to set aside the slavery question and compromise with the Confederates. The same Democrats attacked Lincoln for his Emancipation Proclamation. That proclamation was necessary and just. It was slavery that was the cause of the war. By issuing it Lincoln had also greatly strengthened the Union position in Europe. Southern emissaries in Europe had promoted the falsehood that the North was not fighting to abolish slavery. The Emancipation Proclamation destroyed that effort, and the Europeans were now sympathetic to the Union.

A change in administration by election in November would be followed by three months before the new administration would take office. In the interim, clouded with uncertainty, Robert Lee would strengthen his forces, the Confederates would be encouraged by the prospect of a compromise peace, and the administration that had been defeated but which would hold office, would be unable to lead:

> Why then revolutionize our own Government for the avowed purpose of arresting a policy, by which Providence is so manifestly educing good from evil? Why seek, by unsolicited guarantees and humiliating compromises, to deprive the country, the civilized world, and humanity itself, of the great compensation for all the sacrifices and sufferings of the war into which slavery plunged us?[64]

Why, given this and the barbaric nature of slavery, "should we overturn the administration of our own Government in crisis of the struggle, in order to bring in successors who will offer to those leaders new guarantees on the subject of slavery, with the assurance beforehand that the offer will be rejected?" To change administration in the midst of the crisis would be, said Everett, to "paralyze the only arm which, by a constitutional necessity, can wield the power of the State."[65]

Everett recorded that he received the greatest number of letters praising the speech that he had ever received. That he expressed the views and feelings of the great majority in the North was verified by Lincoln's overwhelming victory in the election of 1864. Everett had now become a very popular figure. On 9 November, when he entered Faneuil Hall, the crowd stood up and cheered. "I was quite overcome," he wrote.[66]

His stand on Reconstruction was already portended in his Gettysburg Address. It was reaffirmed in the last address he was to give. On 9 January 1865, at a public meeting in Boston held on behalf of the victims of war in Savannah, he pointed out that reports from that city offered proof that the people were ready to support the Union. Everett had long believed that there was a strong Union sentiment throughout the South. "Savannah," he said, "wants our pork and beef and flour; and I say, in Heaven's name, let us send it to them without money and without price."[67]

The day of the speech he caught a cold and was confined to his home. George Ticknor called on him on 14 January. Everett could not speak above a whisper, but he was in his library and, Ticknor wrote, "moved about the room freely, giving directions and making arrangements for a person who was copying something for him." He died of stroke the next morning. Ticknor, a close friend for many years, called again after hearing of Everett's death. As it came to him what had happened he wrote, "I think I felt worse than I have at any time. It is a terrible shock."[68]

When the report of Everett's death arrived in Washington, Lincoln ordered salutes to be fired and the department buildings, the Capitol, and the White House to be draped in mourning. He had lost a loyal friend.

* * * * *

Everett's life spanned the years 1794 to 1865. The dramatic social and economic life began roughly when he entered politics in 1824. In that year John Quincy Adams was elected president thanks to minority groups dividing his opposition. He was the last of the great founding fathers to achieve that office. The men who played the leading role in establishing the republic looked on the achievement of Union and representative government as a noble and daring experiment worthy of their deepest loyalties and as enlightenment that embraced their fondest ideals, an elective franchise, a government by law, a guarantor of public order, the union of disparate sections, and the assurance of an independent court system free from interference, capable of meeting change in a quiet and orderly way. Everett belonged to their age.

Everett's admiration of the Union went far beyond patriotic admiration for the existing order. It was rooted in his private beliefs in order, in law, his distrust of mass emotions, and the assurance that the check-and-balance system would create slow and thoughtful growth. He was never able to accept real politick, the ascendancy Andrew Jackson who held himself above the Supreme Court, and the politicians who placed party interests above national interests. He deplored the rising spirit of democracy giving way to mass meetings and slogans, adventurous expansionism, and politics based not on principles but on expedient bargaining between sections.

He achieved moderate success as a useful member of Congress and distinction in diplomacy, but his doctrinaire adherence stood in the way of his becoming a leader. As Henry Adams was to say, Everett did not lack political astuteness; however, he was to a degree paralyzed by his dislike of the contemporary politics that seemed to set aside his principles. He tied the question of slavery to how to prevent the dissolution of the Union. He had made clear his opposition to slavery, but his inability to join in a passionate crusade made this suspect. Not until the outbreak of the Civil War when the abolition of slavery and the saving of the Union became one cause could he square his contradictions and stand forth for both causes in a resolute manner. Then he deserted his old Whig friends in Boston, much to their happiness, to support Lincoln and stand as elector for the Republic party.

Notes

Chapter 1. Early Years

1. The facts of Everett's childhood and early education are based on his autobiography in the Everett Papers at the Massachusetts Historical Society. The author has used the microfilm edition of the papers in the Michigan State University Library, Reel 42.
2. Perry Miller, *The Transcendentalists: An Anthology* (Cambridge: Harvard University Press, 1960), pp. 18–19.
3. Paul Revere Frothingham, *Edward Everett: Orator and Statesman* (Boston: Houghton Mifflin, 1925), p. 25.
4. Sermon delivered by Everett, 21 May 1814, Microfilm Edition of Everett Papers, Reel 34.
5. Edward Everett to Alexander Everett, 5 January 1815, Reel I, Box 2, Folder 2.
6. Ibid.
7. Edward Everett to R. Walsh, 28 December 1817, Microfilm Edition of Everett Papers, Reel I, Folder 3.
8. Edward Everett to Alexander Everett, 5 January 1815, Reel I, Box 2, Folder 2.
9. Ibid.
10. Ibid.
11. Everett's Journal on his trip to England, Everett Papers, Reel XXXIV, Folder 124.
12. Edward Everett to Alexander Everett, 2 October 1815, Reel I, Folder 2.
13. Edward Everett to Robert Walsh, 28 December 1817, Reel I, Folder 3.
14. Ibid.
15. Paul R. Sweet, "Impression of Wilhelm von Humboldt and Some Contemporaries (1816–18) (New York: Georg Olms Verlage, 1988),: From the Papers of Edward Everett," *Humanitat und Bildung Festschift fur Clements Menze zum 60. Geburstag,* pp. 36–37.
16. Edward Everett to R. Walsh, 28 December 1817, Everett Papers, Reel I, Folder (sic).
17. Edward Everett to Robert Walsh, 25 December 1817.
18. Ibid.
19. Journal of his trip to England, Everett Papers, Reel XXX, Folder 132.
20. Edward Everett to Robert Walsh, December 28, 1817, Reel 1, Box 1, Folder 3.
21. Ibid.
22. Henry Adams, *The Education of Henry Adams: An Autobiography* (Boston: Houghton Mifflin, 1878), pp. 11–12.
23. For a full account of the Boston Associates and the changes accompanying the growth of the textile industry, see Robert F. Dalzell, Jr., *Enterprising Elite: The*

Boston Associates and the World They Made (Cambridge: Harvard University Press, 1987).

24. While at Göttingen, Everett wrote a scathing letter to President Kirkland of Harvard stating that at Harvard the students were too young, driven like poor chicks from their mother hen, before they pick up their own crumbs—put in possession of almost all their time, and money to burn in their pockets—seduced from the first, by bold corruption of the advanced classes, and initiated into clubs, whose sole object is to systemize drunkenness and gluttony—and told that they must show themselves men and the way of showing themselves men is to be vicious boys. Edward Everett to President J. T. Kirkland, 19 April 1817, Everett Papers, Reel II, Folder 106.

25. Edward Everett, "The History of Grecian Art," *North American Review* January 1821: pp. 179–88.

26. Ibid.

27. Ibid. 3 January 1823, vol. 2, pp. 127–29.

28. Ibid. 28 February 1823, vol. 2, pp. 130–32.

29. Edward Everett, "Debates in Congress on the Bill to amend the several Acts for Imposing Duties on Imports," *North American Review* (July 1824): vol. 19, pp. 223–53. "The Proposed New Tariff," *North American Review* (January 1821): vol. 12, pp. 63–64, 81.

30. *The Letters of Ralph Waldo Emerson,* ed. Ralph L. Rusk, vol. 1, (New York: Columbia University Press, 1939); Ralph Waldo Emerson to John Boynton Hill, 3 January 1823 and 28 February 1823, pp. 131–132, 142.

31. Harry Hayden Clark, "Literary Criticism in the *North American Review,*" *Wisconsin Academy of Sciences, Arts and Letters* 31 (1939): pp. 299–300.

32. Edward Everett, *Orations and Speeches on Various Occasions* (Boston: Little, Brown, 1878), vol. 1, pp. 11–12.

33. Ibid., p. 13.

34. Ibid., p. 24.

35. Ibid., pp. 29–33.

36. Ibid., p. 39.

37. Ibid., p. 44.

38. John Ware, *Memoir of the Life of Henry Ware, Jr.* (Boston: American Unitarian Association, 1868), p. 181.

39. Thomas Jefferson to Edward Everett, 15 October 1824, Reel II, Folder 119.

40. Everett, *Orations and Speeches on Various Occasions,* (Boston, Little, Brown 1878), vol. 1.

41. Edward Everett to Joseph Story, 13 April 1821.

42. Edward Everett, "Sciotie and Affairs of Greece," *North American Review* (October 1823): vol. 17, p. 413.

43. Ibid. pp. 398–405.

44. Ibid., p. 416.

45. Charles M. Wiltse and Harold Moser, eds. *The Papers of Daniel Webster Correspondence* (Hanover: Published for Dartmouth College by the University Press of New England, 1944), vol. 1, pp. 327–28; Daniel Webster to Joseph Story, 12 May 1823.

46. Ibid.

47. Ibid., pp. 335–336; Daniel Webster to Edward Everett, 28 November 1823.

48. Ibid.

49. Edward Everett to John Quincy Adams, 30 October 1823.

50. Daniel Webster to Jeremiah Mason, 15 February 1824, vol. 1, pp. 351–355.

Notes

51. On 8 December Daniel Webster submitted the following resolution: That provision ought to be made, by law, for defraying by law the expense incident to the appointment of an agent, or commissioner, to Greece, whenever the president shall deem it expedient to make such an appointment. Webster later gave a speech arguing for the resolution. He gave as his reasons that the country had diverse interests in the Mediterranean and the United States should show the world that it disapproved of Turkey's despotism. He placed the question in the broad context of the contest between "the Holy Alliance and the people who were struggling to be free." He denied that he favored intervention and held that he asked no more than the American people express an opinion showing that they were on the side of liberty.

Webster put to use the material Everett had provided on the history of the Greek resolution, and he also heeded Everett's warning that it would probably be charged that the move was dictated by classicists who loved ancient Greece. Webster was careful to deny that this was so. *Annals of Congress,* 18th Cong., 1st Sess., pp. 806, 1084–90, 1190–1200.

52. Jeremiah Mason to Daniel Webster, 1 February 1824, *Papers of Daniel Webster Correspondence,* vol. 1, p. 351.

53. Ibid., p. 344; Joel Poinsett to Daniel Webster, 1824 (sic).

54. Maurce Bates, *One and Inseparable: Daniel Webster and the Union* (Cambridge: The Belknap Press of Harvard University Press, 1984), pp. 102–3.

55. Daniel Webster to Edward Everett, 5 August 1824.

56. Ibid., 15 August 1824.

57. While still at Göttingen Everett accepted the fact that he could not compete with German scholars. He wrote to his brother, Alexander: "I find I have begun too late to go into the thing as they do here, but I can get what they call the aesthetical view of the subject, which is more adapted to the American market, though I own I should have been glad to have put myself upon a footing with the critics here." Edward Everett to Alexander Everett, 1 December 1816, Reel I, Box 2, Folder 3.

Chapter 2. Everett's Role in Politics

1. Students of the first half of the nineteenth century are deeply indebted to the work of Ronald P. Formisano. His is a broad study of social and political life. He is concerned with popular beliefs and expectations that transformed political culture. His writing is distinguished by patient attention to detail, and avoidance of clichés and easy generalization. Ronald P. Formisano, *The Transformation of Political Culture: Massachusetts Parties, 1790s–1840s* (New York: Oxford University Press, 1983). For an excellent historiographical account of the development of social history see Richard L. McCormick, *The Party Period and Public Policy* (New York: Oxford University Press, 1986).

2. Frederic Cople Jaher, "The Politics of the Boston Brahmins," in *Boston 1700–1980: The Evolution of Urban Politics,* eds. Ronald P. Formisano and Constance K. Burns (Westport, Conn.: Greenwood Press, 1984), p. 77.

3. As Formisano explains, although the two lines cannot be directly applied in the study of American political history, they can be adapted to discern rough lines of alignment. It is not intended that all of the political history during this period can be explained in these terms. Formisano, *Transformation of Political Culture,* p. 6.

4. Glyndon G. Van Deusen, "Some Aspects of Whig Thought and Theory in the Jacksonian Period," *American Historical Review* (January 1958): vol. 63, pp. 305–22.

5. Ibid., p. 321.

6. *Register of Debates in Congress,* 19th Cong., 1st Sess., pp. 1570–98.

7. Journal of His Visit to Washington, Everett Papers, Reel XXXIV, Folder 123, pp. 28–30.

8. *The Statesman,* 1 June 1826, Published McDuffic's and Everett's speeches, and sharply criticized Everett. The editor held that Everett's view on slavery were peculiarly unfortunate and revolting to "the feelings and opinions of his constituents."

9. P. C. Brooks to Edward Everett, 1 April, 1826, Reel II, Folder 135.

10. *The Statesman,* 10 January 1828.

11. Lewis Cass, "Removal of the Indian," *The North American Review* (January 1830): pp. 62–121.

12. Ibid.

13. When Georgia enacted the law for taking over the Cherokee land and for a survey of those lands, John Quincy Adams notified the Senate and the House of Representatives that he had ordered the arrest of the surveyors. *American State Papers: Indian Affairs, Documents, Legislative and Executive, of the Congress of the United States, From the First Session of the First to the Third Session of the Thirteenth Congress, Inclusive: Commencing March 3, 1789, and Ending March 3, 1815. Selected and Edited, Under the Authority of Congress,* by Walter Lowries, Secretary of the Senate, and Matthew St. Clair Clarke, Clerk of the House of Representatives (Washington: Gales and Seaton, 1832), pp. 862–63.

14. The significance of Webster's speech is best summed up by the editors of the Webster Papers: "The reaction was immediate and so overwhelming as to surpass Webster's fondest hopes. The first reply restored New England's pride and renewed her sense of accomplishment; but out of the second emerged a nation, transcending any federation of local sovereignties and standing as a potential equal in the nineteenth century world of national states." *Papers of Daniel Webster,* vol. 3, p. 16.

15. *Register of Debates in Congress,* 21st Cong., 1st Sess., p. 1979.

16. Edward Everett, "Speeches on the Indian Bill," *The North American Review,* (October 1830): vol. 31, p. 397.

17. Ibid., pp. 401–2.

18. Ibid., p. 419.

19. Edward Everett to Timothy Flint, 20 October 1830, Everett Papers, Reel XXV, Folder 293.

20. Grant Foreman, *Indian Removal: The Emigration of the Five Civilized Tribes of Indians* (Norman: University of Oklahoma Press, 1953), p. 233.

21. Ibid.

22. Angie Debo, *A History of the Indians of the United States* (Norman: University of Oklahoma Press, 1970), pp. 105–6.

23. Edward Everett to Thomas Hodgkins, ? May 1832, Reel XXV, Folder 293.

24. The Cherokees, although under great pressure and suffering from thievery of their possessions, resisted removal for several years. Every possible form of harassment failed to subdue their spirits. When they did enroll with federal authorities to depart, they were loaded on flatboats but some chose to flee by foot. The valley through which they passed came to be known as the vale of tears. For accounts of their travels see Harold E. Driver, *Indians of North America* (Chi-

Notes

cago: University of Chicago Press, 1961); Angie Debo, *A History of the Indians of the United States,* and Grant Foreman, *Indian Removal.*

25. Edward Everett to Alexander Everett, Everett Papers, 4 March 1830, Reel V.

26. Edward Everett to S. D. Ingham, Everett Papers, 25 November 1831, Reel XXV, Folder 293.

27. Ibid.

28. Edward Everett to C. A. Davis, 22 October 1831, Reel XXV, Folder 293.

29. Edward Everett to S. D. Ingham, 25 November 1831, Reel XXV, Folder 293.

30. Everett wrote at length to John Sergeant of Philadelphia in April presenting his proposal. He observed that "character of times requires unusual remedies for the strange evils that afflict the body politics." He presented a lengthy list of instances in which Jackson had violated the Constitution. That was not the most formidable obstacle to success, however. The question was whether sufficient support could be mustered to impeach the president. Everett argued that there would be no difficulty in gaining the support of Clay's supporters in the House of Representatives. Now, he wrote, given the falling out of Jackson and Vice President Calhoun, support could be counted on from that direction. "The vote with those friends of Mr. Calhoun from whose eyes the scales have dropped would carry the vote to impeach the President." Calhoun, Everett pointed out, thinks himself a much injured man. Edward Everett to John Sergeant, 18 April, 1831, Everett Papers, Reel 25, Folder 293.

Everett did not send this letter to Clay until the dissolution of Jackson's cabinet in May.

31. Edward Everett to Henry Clay, 25 April 1831, Everett Papers, Reel 25, Folder 293.

32. Daniel Webster to Henry Clay, 29 May 1830, *The Papers of Daniel Webster Correspondence,* vol. 3 pp. 78–80.

33. Edward Everett to Henry Clay, 25 April 1831, Everett Papers, Reel 25, Folder 293.

34. Ibid., 5 August 1831.

35. Henry C. S. Dearborn to Henry Clay, 20 October 1832, *Papers of Henry Clay,* ed. Robert Seager (Lexington: University od Kentucky Press, 1964), vol. 28, p. 592.

36. Edward Everett and Alexander Everett to Henry Clay, 29 October 1832, Clay Papers, National Archives, Microcopy no. 212, Roll no. 5.

37. Abbott Lawrence to Henry Clay, 30 October 1832, *Papers of Henry Clay,* vol. 8, p. 594.

38. *Register of Debates in Congress,* 22d. Cong., 1st Sess., pp. 963–64.

39. John C. Calhoun to Virgol Marcy, 11 September 1830, Galloway, Marcy-Markoe Papers, quoted by William H. Freehling, *Prelude to Civil War* (New York: Harper and Row, 1966), p. 257.

40. *Register of Debates in Congress,* 21st Cong., 1st Sess., pp. 963–64.

41. Ibid.

42. Kenneth Stamp, *The Imperial Union: Essays on the Background of the Civil War* (New York: Oxford University Press, 1980), p. 33.

43. Edward Everett to Alexander Everett, 11 December 1832, Everett Papers, Reel 25.

44. Maurice Baxter, *One and Inseparable Daniel Webster and the Union* (Cambridge: The Belknap Press of the Harvard University Press, 1984), p. 21.

45. Merrill D. Peterson, *Olive Branch and the Sword—Compromise of 1833* (Baton Rouge: Louisiana State University Press, 1982), pp. 67–69.

46. *Memoirs of John Quincy Adams,* pp. 533–34.

47. Harrison Gray Otis to Daniel Webster, 18 February 1833, *Papers of Daniel Webster,* vol. 3, p. 217.

48. Robert C. Winthrop, "Memoir of Hon. Nathan Appleton," *Massachusetts Historical Society Proceedings,* vol. 5, p. 274.

49. Robert V. Remini, *Andrew Jackson and the Course of American Democracy 1833–45* (New York: Harper and Row, 1984), vol. 3, p. 121.

50. Edward Everett, "Address on the Conduct of the Administration," Everett Papers, Reel LIII, Folder 537.

51. Robert Remini, *Andrew Jackson and the Course of American Democracy,* p. 108.

52. Thomas Payne Govan, *Nicholas Biddle, Nationalist and Public Banker, 1786–1844* (Chicago: University of Chicago Press), p. 196.

53. Ibid.

54. *Register of Debates in Congress,* 33d Cong., 2 Sess., Appendix 12, pp. 1167–70.

55. *Memoirs of John Quincy Adams,* vol. 9, p. 143.

56. Edward Everett, "Spoilations of the French Prior to 1800, *The North American Review* (July 1827): pp. 153–169.

57. Henry Blumenthal, *A Reappraisal of Franco-American Relations 1830–1871* (Chapel Hill: The University of North Carolina Press, 1959), p. 207.

58. John Tyler of Virginia said: "A great part of these claims would go to the ensurers." If the government shared the losses of these companies, then the government should also share their profits. Isaac Hill of New Hampshire, the Democratic boss in that state, stated that the claims of all sorts were presented again and again. He recalled: "The value of perseverance is demonstrated in more successful cases in that of Amy Darden's horse, which, after having been brought upon the journals year after year, for at least forty years, was finally paid in the generous year of 1832, when there was quite a desire to get rid of as much money as possible from the treasury in order that high taxes might be continued for the benefit of protecting American manufacturers." *Register of Debates in Congress,* 23 Cong., 2d Sess., pp. 18 and 47.

59. *Register of Debates in Congress,* 23 Cong., 2d Sess., Appendix 12, p. 1552 Samuel Flagg Bemis, *John Quincy Adams and the Union* (New York: Alfred A. Knopf, 1965), pp. 316–17.

60. *Register of Debates in Congress,* 23d Cong., 2d Sess., appendix 12, p. 1576.

61. Ibid.

62. Everett, *Diary,* 7 July, 1834, Reel XXXVI, Folder 144.

63. Lilian Handlin, *George Bancroft The Intellectual as Democrat* (New York: Harper and Row, 1984), pp. 116–21.

64. Edward Everett to Alexander Everett, 22 April 1833, Everett Papers, Reel XXXV, Folder 293.

65. Lilian Handlin, *George Bancroft,* p. 144.

66. Ibid.

67. Friedlander and Butterfield, eds., *Diary of Charles Francis Adams,* vol. 6, p. 67; 1 March 1835.

68. Ibid., vol. 5, p. 56; 26 March 1833.

69. Ibid., p. 380; 6 September 1834.

Notes 225

70. Papers of Daniel Webster, vol. 4, p. 24; 1 February 1835.
71. P. C. Brooks to Edward Everett, 18 February, 1835, Everett Papers, Reel VI, Folder 129.
72. Friedlander and Butterfield, eds. *Diary of Charles Francis Adams,* vol. 6, p. 79; 18 February 1835.

Chapter 3. Governor of Massachusetts

1. Ronald P. Formisano, *The Transformation of Political Culture Massachusetts Parties, 1790's–1840's,* p. 254.
2. Edward Everett to Alexander Everett, 2 November 1835, Everett Papers, Reel XXV, Folder 293.
3. Friedlander and Butterfield, eds., *Diary of Charles Francis Adams,* vol. 5, p. 56.
4. Everett Papers, Reel LIII, Folder 511.
5. Inaugural Address, Reel LIII, Folder 689.
6. Boston *Daily Advertiser,* 7 January 1836.
7. Boston *The Advocate,* 29 December 1835.
8. Ibid., 18 January 1836.
9. Everett, *Diary,* 21 August, 1836, Reel XXVI, Folder 179.
10. Daniel Webster to Edward Everett, 6 June 1836, Everett Papers, Reel VI, Folder 172.
11. Edward Everett to Alexander Everett, 10 June, 1836, Everett Papers, ibid.
12. Edward Everett to John Davis, 30 January 1836, Everett Papers, Reel XXV, Folder 293.
13. Edward Everett to H. Denny, 20 October 1835, Everett Papers, Reel XXV, Folder 293.
14. Edward Everett to B. F. Hallett, 11 December 1835, Everett Papers, Reel XXV, Folder 293.
15. Extract of a letter to John Reed, 21 April 1836, Everett Papers, Reel XXV, Folder 293.
16. Edward Everett to John Reed, 2 April 1836, Everett Papers, Reel XXV, Folder 257.
17. For a description of the schools see Jonathon Messerli, *Horace Mann A Biography* (New York: Alfred E. Knopf, 1972), p. 252. Each town filed a report. The author describes the shabby schoolhouses and the crowding of fifteen or more students into rooms often no larger fourteen by eighteen feet. Furnishings in the way of books and maps were usually absent. One town proudly reported that its schools were provided with stoves, tables, pails, and dippers. Another answered "none." Some even lacked outhouses.
18. Edward Everett, "Superior and Public Education," in *Orations and Speeches,* vol. 2, p. 224.
19. Edward Everett, "Normal Schools," in *Orations and Speeches* (Boston: Little: Brown Co., 1878.) vol. 2, p. 34.
20. Ibid., p. 227.
21. Ibid, p. 229.
22. Ibid., pp. 211, 228.
23. Ibid., 344–46.
24. Ibid., vol. 2, p. 350.
25. Ibid., p. 347.

26. Ibid., p. 351.
27. William E. Nelson, *Americanization of the Common Law: The Impact of Legal Change on Massachusetts Society, 1870–1830* (Cambridge: Harvard University Press, 1975), pp. 150–53.
28. Gerard W. Gewalt, *The Promise of Power: The Legal Profession in Massachusetts 1760–1840* (Westport, Conn.: Greenwood Press, 1979), p. 181.
29. *Memoirs, Speeches, and Writings of Robert Rantoul, Jr.*, ed. Luther Hamilton (Boston: John P. Jewett & Co., 1854), pp. 279–82.
30. Edward Everett to P. O. Thatcher, 20 January 1836, Everett Papers, Reel XXV, Folder 257.
31. James McClellan, *Joseph Story and the American Constitution: A Study in Political and Legal Thought* (Normal: University of Oklahoma Press, 1972), p. 94.
32. William W. Story, eds., *Life and Letters of Joseph Story* (London: John Chapman, 1851), vol. 2, pp. 241–42.
33. Ibid., pp. 246–47.
34. William E. Nelson, *Americanization of the Common Law: The Impact of Change on Massachusetts Society* (Cambridge: Harvard University Press, 1976), pp. 150–53.
35. Frank T. Carlton, "Abolition of Imprisonment for Debt in the United States," *Yale Review* (November 1908): p. 340.
36. Ibid., p. 344.
37. Ibid.
38. Boston *Daily Advertiser,* 24 February 1836.
39. Ibid., 22 March 1836.
40. Ibid., 4 April 1836.
41. Frank T. Carlton, "Abolition of Imprisonment for Debt in the United States," *Yale Review* (November 1908): vol. 8, p. 340.
42. Ibid., p. 344.
43. John Jay Knox, *A History of Banking in the United States* (reprint, New York: August W. Kelley, 1969), pp. 362–365.
44. *Columbian Centinel,* 19 and 26 January, 1936.
45. Everett, *Diary,* 3 March, 17 April and 18 April 1836.
46. Boston *Daily Advertiser and Patriot,* 10 January 1838.
47. *Memoirs, Speeches and Writings of Robert Rantoul, Jr.*, pp. 604–11.
48. Ibid., p. 727.
49. Ibid., p. 727.
50. Edward Everett to William Jackson, 31 October 1837, Everett Papers, Reel XXVI, Folder 416.
51. Ibid.
52. For a history of the financial problems of the railroad, see Stephen Salsbury, *The State, the Investor, and the Railroad: The Boston and Albany* (Cambridge: Harvard University Press, 1967).
53. Everett, "The Western Railroad," *Oration and Speeches,* vol. 2, p. 150.
54. Salsbury, *State, Investor, and Railroad,* p. 148.
55. Everett, "An Address Delivered before the Mercantile Library Association at the Odeon, in Boston, 13th September, 1838," in *Orations and Speeches,* vol. 2, p. 294.
56. Ibid., p. 297.
57. Ibid., pp. 303–4.
58. Everett, "Opening the Railroad to Springfield," in *Orations and Speeches,* vol. 2, p. 365.
59. Ibid.

Notes

60. Boston *Daily Advertiser,* 3 August 1838.
61. Ibid., 2 November 1838.
62. Letter circulated by "The Liberal Whig Members of the Legislature," Everett Papers.
63. Robert L. Hampel, *Temperance and Prohibition in Massachusetts 1813–1852* (Ann Arbor: University of Michigan Research Press, 1982), pp. 68–69.
64. Ibid., p. 82.
65. Ibid., p. 85.
66. Ibid., p. 86.
67. Boston *Daily Advertiser,* 11 January 1839.
68. Edward Everett to Robert C. Winthrop, 24 June 1839, Everett Papers, Reel XXVI, Folder 416.
69. One member of the legislature, Mr. Buckingham, alluded to improper influence. He told the *Daily Advertiser,* "Many members of the committee were browbeaten by the prejudices of others who approved the old law. The committee was surrounded the whole time by a body of men chosen out of the temperance societies, who could have had no other object than to press their opinion of the law. And since the question had been before the House, had stood in knots in the aisles talking on it, in direct contravention of the rules of the House." Boston *Daily Advertiser,* 25 March 1839.
70. Lilian Handlin, *George Bancroft The Intellectual as Democrat* (New York: Harper and Row, 1984), p. 171.
71. Edward Everett to Daniel Webster 14 April 1839, Everett Papers. Reel XXVIII, Folder 416.
72. Russell Nye, *George Bancroft Brahmin Rebel* (New York: Alfred A. Knopf, 1945), p. 122.
73. Story, ed., *Life and Letters of Joseph Story,* vol. 2, pp. 333–34.
74. Everett, 6 February 1840, Reel XXXVII, Folder 123.
75. Ibid., 14 November 1938, Reel XXXVII, Folder 160.
76. Ibid., 10 November 1938, Reel XXXVII, Folder 160.
77. Ibid., 12 August 1838, Reel XXVI, Folder 163.
78. Ibid., September 1838, Reel XXVI, Folder 163.
79. Handlin, *George Bancroft,* p. 171.
80. Edward Everett to W. B. Banister, 23 October 1837, Reel XXV, Folder 257.

Chapter 4. Everett's Debut in Diplomacy

1. Story, ed., *Life and Letters of Joseph Story,* pp. 287–289; Joseph Story to Edward Everett, 17 April 1838.
2. Edward Everett to the Marquis of Lansdowne, 19 April 1839, Everett Papers, Reel XXVI, Folder 416.
3. In an address to the legislature in January, Everett placed the blame on the failure of the Van Buren administration to take proper measures. Boston *Daily Advertiser,* 11 January 1839.
4. Edward Everett to Secretary of War J. R. Poinsett, 18 April 1839, Everett Papers, Reel XXVI, Folder 416.
5. Ibid., ? May 1839.
6. Ibid.
7. Everett to President Martin Van Buren, 22 March 1839, Everett Papers, Reel XXVI, Folder 416.
8. Ibid.

9. Ibid., 29 March 1839.
10. Everett, *Diary,* 2 March 1839, Everett Papers, Reel XXXVII, Folder 160.
11. Ibid., 29 March 1839.
12. Charles M. Wiltse and Harold Moser, eds., *The Papers of Daniel Webster Correspondence,* vol. 4, "Memorandum on the Northeastern Boundary Negotiation," pp. 346–49.
13. Edward Everett to R. Walsh, 20 May 1839, Everett Papers, Reel XXVI, Folder 416.
14. Ibid.
15. Everett wrote to his friend Robert Walsh: "Our boundary troubles for the present are over. Lord Palmerston has sent a draft of a convention, the provisions of which have not been leaked out. The plan appears to be to institute a new survey; but this cannot possibly lead to any settlement of the controversy which all grows out of the pretention of Great Britain that the St. Johns is not one of the rivers that empty themselves into the Atlantic." Everett to Robert Walsh, 20 May, 1839, Reel XXVI, Folder 416.
16. Boston *Daily Advertiser and Patriot,* 31 March 1840.
17. Ibid.
18. Edward Everett to Robert C. Winthrop, 27 July 1841, Everett Papers, Reel XXVI, Folder 186.
19. Robert C. Winthrop to John Henry Clifford, 7 August 1841, Winthrop Papers, Massachusetts Historical Society.
20. *Perley's Reminiscences* (Philadelphia: Hubbard Brothers, 1866), vol. pp. 274–75.
21. Edward Everett to J. M. Clayton, 6 April 1849, Everett Papers, Reel XXIX, Folder 286.
22. Edward Everett to Daniel Webster, 30 November 1842, Everett Papers, Reel XXVI, Folder 268. Webster on receiving this dispatch, said it was luckily timed "for representatives from Hawaii were now in Washington and it had been decided to take the lead in acknowledging their independence." Webster to Everett, 29 December 1842, Everett Papers, Reel XII, Folder 132.
23. Edward Everett to Daniel Webster, 28 July 1842, Everett Papers, Reel VIII, Folder 147.
24. Edward Everett to Lord Ashley, 12 July 1844, Everett Papers, Reel XXVII, Folder 338.
25. Edward Everett to Abbot Lawrence, 30 April 1845, Everett Papers, Reel XXVII, Folder 333.
26. Edward Everett to Nathan Hale, 30 July 1842, Everett Papers, Reel XXVI, Folder 332.
27. Ibid.
28. Ibid., 3 September 1842.
29. Edward Everett to George Bancroft, 1 February 1843, Everett Papers, Reel XXVI, Folder 338.
30. Edward Everett to Hiram Powers, 12 June 1844, Everett Papers, Reel XXVI, Folder 338.
31. Edward Everett to W. H. Prescott, 31 October 1843, Everett Papers, Reel XXVII, Folder 285.
32. Stevenson and Palmerston both stubbornly adhered to positions ruling out give-and-take, and Stevenson, after Aberdeen became foreign secretary, unwisely pushed every issue before Lord Aberdeen had time to familiarize themselves with the issues. Everett, at the request of Webster, explained the tactics of his predecessor. Everett to Webster, 31 January 1842, Reel XXVI, Folder 260.

Notes 229

33. Everett wrote to Webster that the war in China had caused grave concern. "There was well grounded fear, that the progress of the war would teach the Chinese how to fight, as it had shown that they did not lack courage." Everett to Webster, 29 November 1842, Everett Papers, Reel VIII, Folder 198.

34. Edward Everett to Daniel Webster, 19 May 1842, Everett Papers, Reel XXXI, Folder 333.

35. Ibid., 16 June 1842.

36. Daniel Webster to Everett, 14 June 1842, Everett Papers, Reel XXVI, Folder 332.

37. Lord Aberdeen to Lord Ashburton, 2 July 1842, quoted in Wilson Devereux Jones, *Lord Aberdeen and the Americas* (Athens: University of Georgia Press, 1958), p. 13.

38. Daniel Webster to Lord Ashburton, 8 July 1842, *The Papers of Daniel Webster: Diplomatic Papers,* vol. 1, pp. 605–13.

39. The heat of summer in Washington and the fatiguing effect of the long negotiations led to frustration, but the delay caused by Webster having to wait for approval from the dissident parties caused Lord Ashburton to consider returning to England. On 1 July he protested: "I do not see why I should be kept waiting while Maine and Massachusetts settle their accounts with the General Government. I am rather apprehensive that there is an inclination *somewhere* to keep this negotiation in suspense on grounds unconnected with the mere difficulties of the case itself. Pray save me from these profound politicians, for my nerves will not stand so much more cunning wisdom." Lord Ashburton to Daniel Webster, ibid., p. 604.

40. Ibid., 26 April 1842, pp. 544–47.

41. Howard Jones, *To the Webster-Ashburton Treaty: A Study in Anglo-American Relations, 1783–1843* (Chapel Hill: University of North Carolina Press, 1977), pp. 134–36.

42. In the aftermath of the negotiation a controversy broke out over maps that had come into play. British critics protested that Webster had withheld the Sparks map used by Webster to convince the Maine commissioners and members of Congress. American critics protested when they learned of the Oswald map that British supporters of the treaty cited to defend the treaty. Robert Peel and Webster both held that the importance of maps had been exaggerated, and that none of the maps were authoritative.

43. Daniel Webster to Edward Everett, 10 March 1843. *Diplomatic Instructions of the Department of State to Minister in Great Britain,* National Archives.

44. Edward Everett to Daniel Webster, 27 April 1842. *Diplomatic Instructions of the Department of State to Ministers in Great Britain,* National Archives.

45. Howard Jones, *To the Webster-Ashburton Treaty: A Study in Anglo-American Relations, 1783–1843* (Chapel Hill: University of North Carolina Press, 1973), p. 142.

46. Hugh Legaré to Edward Everett, 25 May 1843. *Diplomatic Instructions of the Department of State to Ministers in Great Britain,* National Archives.

47. Ibid.

48. Ibid.

49. Lord Ashburton to Lord Aberdeen, 26 April 1842. *Papers of Daniel Webster Diplomatic Papers,* ed. Kenneth E. Shewmaker (Hanover, N.H.: University Press of New England, 1983), vol. 1, pp. 544–47.

50. Joseph Story to Daniel Webster, 26 March 1842, *Papers of Daniel Webster Diplomatic Papers,* vol. 1, pp. 525–27.

51. Daniel Webster to Lord Ashburton, 8 August 1848, ibid., pp. 672–73.

52. John Tyler to Daniel Webster, 7 August 1842, ibid., pp. 672–81.
53. Lord Ashburton to Lord Aberdeen, 9 August 1842, ibid., pp. 680–81.
54. Edward Everett to Lord Aberdeen, 1 March 1842; *Dispatches from the United States Minister to Great Britain,* National Archives.
55. Lord Aberdeen to Edward Everett, 2 May 1842, ibid.
56. Daniel Webster to Edward Everett, 18 May 1842, ibid., pp. 560–61.
57. Hugh Legaré to Daniel Webster, 29 July 1842, ibid., p. 657.
58. Daniel Webster to Lord Ashburton, 1 August 1842, ibid., pp. 655–58.
59. Lord Ashburton to Daniel Webster, 6 August 1842, ibid., pp. 666–69.
60. Baxter, *One and Inseparable,* pp. 350–51.
61. Edward Everett to Daniel Webster, 17 October 1842, Everett Papers, Reel XXVI, Folder 338.
62. Editor's Introduction to "Oregon Question," *Papers of Daniel Webster Diplomatic Papers,* vol. 1, pp. 826–31.
63. Edward Everett to Daniel Webster, 18 November 1842; *Dispatches from the United States Minister to Great Britain.* National Archives. *Papers of Daniel Webster,* vol. 1, p. 830.
64. Edward Everett to Daniel Webster, 1 February 1843, Everett Papers, Reel XXVI, Folder 338.
65. Edward Everett to Daniel Webster, 27 February 1843, Everett Papers, Reel XXII, Folder 514.
66. *Papers of Daniel Webster Diplomatic Papers,* vol. 1, p. 831.
67. Daniel Webster to Edward Everett, 28 November 1842, Everett Papers, Reel VIII, Folder 132.
68. Robert E. Winthrop to Edward Everett, 15 October 1843, Everett Papers, Reel IX, Folder 144.
69. Daniel Webster to Edward Everett, 29 January 1843, Everett Papers, Reel VIII, Folder 133.
70. Edward Everett to Daniel Webster, 17 October 1843, Everett Papers, Reel XXXVII, Folder 338.
71. Edward Everett to Robert C. Winthrop, 25 December 1845, Everett Papers, Reel XI, Folder 164.
72. Fletcher M. Green, "Duff Green, Militant Journalist of the Old School," *American Historical Review* (January 1947): vol. 52, pp. 247–64.
73. Edward Everett to President Tyler, 17 May 1843; Edward Everett to Daniel Webster, 18 May 1843, Everett Papers, Reel XXII, Folder 514.
74. Hugh Legaré to Edward Everett, 13 June 1843, *Diplomatic Instructions of the Department of State to Ministers in England,* National Archives.
75. Edward Everett to Robert C. Winthrop, 17 November 1842, Everett Papers, Reel XXII, Folder 516.
76. Edward Everett to Daniel Webster, 2 January 1843, Everett Papers, Reel XXVI, Folder 332.
77. Edward Everett to Caleb Cushing, 10 October 1842, Everett Papers, Reel XXVI, Folder 332.
78. Edward Everett to P. C. Brooks, 2 November 1842, Everett Papers, Reel XXVI, Folder 392.
79. Daniel Webster to Edward Everett, 10 March 1843, Everett Papers, Reel VIII, Folder 84.
80. Edward Everett to Christopher Hughes, 7 April 1843, Everett Papers, Reel XXVI, Page 338.
81. Edward Everett to Sydney Brooks, 17 April 1843, Everett Papers, Reel XXVI, Folder 338.

Notes

82. Edward Everett to Daniel Webster, 3 April 1843, Everett Papers, Reel XXVI, Folder 338.
83. Robert Seager, *and Tyler too: A Biography of John & Julie Gardiner Tyler* (New York: McGraw-Hill Book Company, 1963), p. 217.
84. Ibid., pp. 215–16.
85. Edward Everett to Robert C. Winthrop, 28 January 1843, Everett Papers, Reel XXVI, Folder 338.
86. Edward Everett to President Tyler, 17 May 1843, Everett Papers, Reel IX, Folder 178.
87. W. D. Jones, *Lord Aberdeen and the Americas,* pp. 32–35. Jones concludes that Aberdeen was moved by consideration of diplomacy and "not the value of an independent Texas." He emphasizes the fact that France was of greater importance to Aberdeen than the United States.
88. Abel P. Upshur to Edward Everett, 28 September 1843, *Diplomatic Instructions of the Department of State,* National Archives.
89. Edward Everett to Abel P. Upshur, 3 November 1843, Everett Papers, Reel XXVI, Folder 338.
90. Ibid.
91. Edward Everett to Robert C. Winthrop, 18 June 1844, Everett Papers, Reel XXVI, Folder 338.
92. Ibid.
93. Edward Everett to Thomas Sewall, 3 January 1845, Everett Papers, Reel XXVI, Folder 338.
94. Edward Everett to Secretary of State Abel Upshur, 17 August 1843, *Dispatches from the United States Minister to Great Britain,* National Archives.
95. Abel Upshur to Edward Everett, 9 October 1843, *Department of State Instructions to the Minister of Great Britain,* National Archives.
96. Ibid., 2 November 1843.
97. Ibid., 14 November 1843.
98. Ibid., 2 December 1843.
99. Ibid.
100. Ibid.
101. Ibid.
102. Ibid.
103. Ibid.
104. Everett, *Diary,* 6 November 1843, Everett Papers, XXXVII, Folder 250.
105. Ibid., 11 February 1842, Everett Papers, Reel XXVII, Folder 253.
106. Edward Everett to John Nelson, secretary of state *ad interim, Dispatches from the United States Minister to Great Britain,* National Archives.
107. Ibid.
108. Edward Everett to Secretary of State John C. Calhoun, 2 August, 1844, *Dispatches from the United States Minister to Great Britain,* National Archives.
109. Ibid., 2 August 1844.
110. Ibid., 28 February 1845; William Sturgis to George Bancroft, 6 August 1845, Papers of Massachusetts Historical Society.
111. Everett, *Diary,* 29 March to 18 April 1845. In February 1852 Everett wrote a letter to Francis Bowen relating his meeting with Mr. Senior and the writing of the article. Everett at this time claimed a bit more for the influence of the Senior article in preparing the public mind for the final settlement than it deserved, although it was of some importance.
112. David Pletcher, *The Diplomacy of Annexation: Texas, Oregon and The Mexican War* (Columbia: University of Missouri Press, 1975), pp. 247–48.

113. For a clear and factual discussion on these happenings see Pletcher, *The Diplomacy of Annexation,* pp. 291–96.
114. Ibid., p. 316.
115. Ibid.
116. Edward Everett to Lord Aberdeen, 14 November 1845, Everett Papers, Reel XXVII, Folder 285.
117. Ibid., 10 December 1845.
118. Edward Everett to Robert Walsh, 13 December 1845, ibid.
119. Edward Everett to George Bancroft, 5 February 1846, Everett Papers, ibid., Folder 271.
120. Albert Gallatin, "Letters on the Oregon Question," no. 3, Gallatin Papers.

Chapter 5. Harvard Presidency

1. Everett, *Diary,* 13 November 1845, Everett Papers, Reel XXXVIII, Folder 253.
2. Letter from Harvard faculty, 9 March 1846, Everett Papers, Reel XXVII, Folder 271.
3. Daniel Webster to Edward Everett, 28 January 1846, Everett Papers, Reel XII, Folder 159.
4. Edward Everett, "Inaugural Address," Everett Papers, Reel LIII, Folder 689.
5. Everett Papers, Reel XXVII, Folder 271.
6. Ibid.
7. Ibid.
8. Ibid.
9. Ibid.
10. *The Journals and Miscellaneous Notebooks of Ralph Waldo Emerson,* eds. William H. Gilman, George P. Clark, Alfred R. Ferguson, and Merrill R. Davis (Cambridge: Harvard University Press, 1960), p. 388.
11. Samuel A. Eliot, *Sketch of History of Harvard and Its Present State* (Boston: Charles C. Little and James Brown, 1848), p. 117.
12. Ibid., p. 127. A total of six hundred students in all of the schools made up the university.
13. Edward Everett to P. C. Brooks, 4 April 1846, Everett Papers, Reel XXVII, Folder 271.
14. Edward Everett to Louis Agassiz, 23 October 1848, Everett Papers, Reel XXVII, Folder 296.
15. Edward Everett to George Bancroft, 25 December 1847, Reel XXVIII, Folder 320.
16. For an informative account of the struggle to establish graduate schools at various universities, see Richard J. Storr, "In the Age of the Colleges," in *The Beginnings of the Future: A Historical Approach to Graduate Education in the Arts and Sciences* (New York: McGraw-Hill Book Company, 1973).
17. Edward Everett to the Rev. Dr. Allen, 20 September and 22 September 1848, Everett Papers, Reel XXVIII, folder 288.
18. Edward Everett to Dr. Holland, 30 July 1847; Edward Everett to Alexander Everett, 9 August 1847, Everett Papers, Reel XXVIII, Folder 292.
19. Edward Everett to Dr. Holland, 30 July 1847, ibid.
20. Storr, *Beginning of the Future,* p. 27.

21. Ibid.
22. Edward Everett to F. I. Child, 11 February 1848, Everett Papers, Reel XXVIII, Folder 286.
23. Edward Everett to Dr. Holland, 11 December 1848, Everett Papers, Reel XXVIII, Folder 286.
24. Everett, *Diary,* 20 September 1846, Everett Papers, Reel XXXVIII, Folder 251.
25. After one faculty meeting Everett wrote in his diary that there was "no heartiness in the work, each is his own little crotchet, there is no master will." Diary, 28 December 1846, Reel XXXVIII, Folder 253.
26. Edward Everett to Charles G. Loring, 13 December 1847, Everett Papers, Reel XXVII, Folder 320.
27. Edward Everett to Charles Sumner, 22 August 1846, Everett Papers, Reel XXVII, Folder 320.
28. Edward Everett to Charles Loring, 13 December 1847.
29. John Langdon Sibley's private journal, Harvard University Archives, Cambridge.
30. Edward Everett to Robert C. Winthrop, 30 December 1848, Everett Papers, Reel XXVIII, Folder 286.
31. Edward Everett to Dr. Holland, 13 November 1847 and 31 March 1848, Everett Papers, Reel XXVIII, Folders 320 and 290.
32. Edward Everett to Charles G. Loring, 13 December 1847, Everett Papers, Reel XXVIII, Folder 320.

Chapter 6. Voice of Moderation amid Reckless Adventurism

1. Edward Everett to Robert C. Winthrop, ? February 1848, Everett Papers, Reel XXXIII, Folder 271.
2. Daniel Webster to Edward Everett, 20 October 1850, Everett Papers, Reel XXIII, Folder 112.
3. Ibid.
4. Ibid.
5. Edward Everett to Daniel Webster, 24 October 1850, Everett Papers, Reel XXX, Folder 282.
6. Daniel Webster to Edward Everett, 21 December 1850, Everett Papers, Reel XIII, folder 112.
7. Everett, 2 January 1851, Everett Papers, Reel XXXVIII, Folder 245.
8. Ibid.
9. Edward Everett to Robert C. Winthrop, 4 January 1851, Everett Papers, Reel XXX, Folder 283.
10. Edward Everett to Mrs. Everett, 24 February 1851, Everett Papers, Reel XXX, Folder 282.
11. Ibid., 7 March 1851.
12. Everett, *Diary,* ? March 1851, Everett Papers, Reel XXXVIII, Folder 245.
13. Ibid., 25 May 1851.
14. Secretary of Navy William Alexander Graham to Secretary of State Daniel Webster, 8 June 1852, U.S. Serial Set no. 621, Senate Executive Document 106.
15. Secretary of State Daniel Webster to J. Randolph Clay, U.S. minister to Peru, 30 August 1842, ibid.
16. Ibid.

17. Secretary of State Edward Everett to J. E. Osma, Peru's minister to the United States, ibid.

18. J. Randolph Clay, U.S. minister to Peru, to Secretary of State Edward Everett, 21 December 1852, ibid.

19. For an elaboration on the Young America movement within the Democratic party and the role of George Law and Romulus Saunders see Basil Rauch, *American Interest in Cuba: 1848–1855* (New York: Columbia University Press, 1948), pp. 222–44.

20. *Congressional Globe,* appendix, 32d Cong., 2d Sess., p. 575.

21. Ibid., 1st Sess., p. 895.

22. *Congressional Globe,* 33d Cong. 1st Sess., appendix, p. 913.

23. Kenneth E. Shewmaker, " 'Hook and line, bob and sinker': Daniel Webster and the Fisheries Dispute of 1852," *Diplomatic History,* 9, no. 2 (Spring 1985): pp. 113–29.

24. Edward Everett to the editor of the London *Times,* 11 September 1852.

25. Ibid.

26. Shewmaker, " 'Hook and line, bob and sinker,' " p. 125.

27. Edward Everett to W. H. Trescott, 2 November 1852, Everett Papers, Reel XXX, Folder 281.

28. Rausch, *American Interest in Cuba,* p. 192.

29. New Orleans *Daily Picayune,* 12 October 1852.

30. Basil Rausch in his book *American Interest in Cuba* presents the factual details of the negotiations with the Captain General. The facts themselves and the reports of the communications are located in the Department of State Archives, *Notes from Legations: Spain,* XIV.

31. Charles Conrad, acting secretary of state to George Law, 25 October 1852, quoted Basil Rausch, *American Interest in Cuba,* p. 234.

32. Edward Everett to Comte de Sartiges, 2 December 1852, U.S. Serial Set., no. 660, 32d Cong., 2d Sess.

33. Ibid.

34. The speech was published in pamphlet form, and it is in the Everett Papers. See also the *Congressional Globe,* 32d Cong., 2d Sess., appendix, pp. 284–90.

35. Ibid.
36. Ibid.
37. Ibid.
38. Ibid.
39. Ibid.

Chapter 7. To the Point of No Return: The Kansas-Nebraska Act

1. Robert F. Dalzell, Jr. *Enterprising Elite: The Boston Associates and the World They Made* (Cambridge: Harvard University Press, 1987), pp. 33, 46.

2. *The Many Voices of Boston: A Historical Anthology,* eds. Howard Mumford Jones and Bessie Zeban Jones (Boston: Little, Brown, 1975) from Francis Ferenez Aurel and Theresa Pulozky, *White, Red, Black: Sketches of American Society in The United States,* (Redfield, N.Y.), vol. 2, pp. 177–80.

3. Dalzell, *Enterprising Elite,* p. 3.

4. Ibid.

5. *Massachusetts Spy,* 15 January 1845.

Notes

6. *Letters and Journal of Samuel Gridley Howe,* ed. Laura E. Richards (Boston: Dana, Estaes and Co., 1909), vol. 2, p. 265.

7. *The Journal of Richard Henry Dana.*

8. Everett, *Diary,* 7 November 1848, Everett Papers, Reel XXXVIII, Folder 252.

9. David Potter wrote: "If a compromise is an agreement between adversaries, by which each consents to terms desired by the other, and if the majority vote of a section is necessary to register the consent of that section, then it must be said that North and South did not consent to each other's terms, and that there really was no compromise—a trace perhaps, an armistice, certainly a settlement, but not a true compromise." David Potter, *The Impending Crisis* (New York: Harper and Row, 1979), p. 154.

10. Ibid., p. 118.

11. Ibid., p. 116.

12. Ibid., p. 128.

13. Friedlander and Butterfield, eds., *Diary of Charles Francis Adams,* vol. 8, p. 50.

14. "When the gods fail, the faithful turn upon them with greater scorn and fury than that directed against moral enemies because of the loss of their own identity. Emerson grieved over Webster's fall because he believed that the man who once promised to represent the American people just as they are, with their very material interests, materialized intellect and low morals. Heretofore their great men . . . have been better than they, as Washington, Hamilton, and Madison. But Webster's absence of moral faculty is degrading to the country." Irving Bartlett, *Daniel Webster* (New York: W. W. Norton, 1978), p. 268.

15. Edward Everett to Robert C. Winthrop, 1 February 1850, Everett Papers, Reel XXX, Folder 282.

16. Ibid.

17. Everett, *Diary,*

18. Edward Everett to Dr. Henry Holland, 9 December 1850, Everett Papers, Reel XXX, Folder 282.

19. For a very useful account of the committee working for Webster's nomination see Maurice Baxter, *One and Inseparable: Daniel Webster and the Union* (Cambridge: The Belknap Press of the Harvard University Press, 1984), pp. 485–86.

20. Edward Everett to Daniel Webster, 2 September 1851, Everett Papers, Reel XXX, Folder 59.

21. Edward Everett to George Morey, 2 September 1851, ibid.

22. Edward Everett to Daniel Webster, 3 September 1851, ibid.

23. Edward Everett to Joseph E. Sprague, 4 September 1851, ibid.

24. For a full account of the differences that arose among the Fusionists, the Free Soilers, and Charles Francis Adams see Martin D. Duberman, *Charles Francis Adams 1807–1886* (Boston: Houghton Mifflin, 1960), pp. 176–86.

25. David Herbert Donald, *Charles Sumner and the Coming of the Civil War* (Chicago: University of Chicago Press, 1960), pp. 178–89. Diary of Edward Everett, 3 April 1851, Everett Papers, Reel XXXVI, Folder 245.

26. At the close of January 1851 Everett wrote an article for the Boston *Advertiser* entitled "Bribery and Corruption." In it he discussed "the profligate bargaining" between the Free Soilers and Democrats. Diary, 31 January 31, 1851, Everett Papers, Reel XXXVIII, Folder 245.

27. Ibid., 26 October 1851.

28. Ibid., 30 July 1851.
29. Ibid., 26 October 1851.
30. Duberman, *Charles Francis Adams,* p. 183. *Journal of Richard Henry Dana,* vol. 2, p. 599.
31. Duberman, *Charles Francis Adams,* p. 186.
32. Lucid, ed., *Journal of Richard Henry Dana,* vol. 2, 11 February 1854.
33. Michael Holt, *The Political Crisis of the 1850's* (New York: John Wiley, 1978), p. 13.
34. Robert W. Johannsen, *Stephen A. Douglas* (New York: Oxford University Press, 1973), p. 22.
35. The movement to organize Nebraska and open the way for the construction of a railroad began in 1844. It had strong public support, but became involved in sectional rivalry. A railroad bill came before Congress in December 1852 and dominated discussion in the Senate throughout the early winter of 1853. There now arose organized support for the organization of the entire territory. Douglas was the enthusiastic leader. In the course of the debates Joshua Giddings, of Ohio, ardent opponent of slavery and a Free Soiler, was asked if the bill would have any effect on the Missouri Compromise. When he answered that it would not, Southern representatives, critics of the Missouri Compromise, raised questions. They saw in a prospective free state prohibiting slavery a strengthening of the North that would reduce them to a subcolonial status. Ibid., pp. 390–97.
36. Johannsen, *Stephen Douglas,* p. 398.
37. Douglas assumed responsibility for the bill, stating that he had written it while in the privacy of his own room. He had been under pressure from Atchison of Missouri, however, and from three of the most powerful members of the Senate—Mason and Hunter of Virginia and Butler of South Carolina. Johannsen, in his biography of Douglas, challenges this view. He thinks their influence has been exaggerated. "Their importance lay principally in developing a strategy for the measures passage. Its provisions conformed to Douglas' well-known convictions, and it was a logical extension of his western program." Johannsen, *Stephen Douglas,* pp. 407–8.
38. Johannsen writes that southern party leaders saw it as a test of party loyalty and that it was intended to rebuke Pierce who had not excluded Free Soil Democrats from patronage. It was so interpreted not only by southern Democrats but also by the press. The *New York Tribune* noted that it was intended "to try the potentiality of Government power and patronage. Johannsen, *Stephen Douglas,* p. 409.

Eric Foner elaborates further. The Free Soilers in the Democratic party were embittered by a new test of party loyalty. Gideon Welles complained: "The administration has identified itself with this new test and, wielding the powers and the patronage of the government, it assumes an attitude of open hostility to any democrat who does not conform to its views." The revolt in the party of Free Soil Democrats who had been loyal for years marked the beginning of the breakdown of the party and also opened the way for the organization of the Republican party. Foner states: "Just as the administration had wielded the patronage to force wavering Congressmen into line, so in state after northern state the party hierarchy demanded obedience to the Douglas measure." Foner, *Free Soil, Free Labor, Free Men,* pp. 155–59.

39. Everett at this point joined the Free Soilers, men like Sumner, Chase and Wade, in attacking the Kansas-Nebraska Bill. Given that he had stood apart from the radicals, his attack on the bill is revealing in understanding his position. He was

Notes 237

as strongly opposed to the bill as Chase and Sumner, but he differed from them in not believing that slavery would make its way into Kansas.

40. Everett was correct in stating that slavery would not move into Kansas. By 1860 there were only two slaves in Kansas. However, Southerners too recognized that it was unlikely that slavery would establish itself in Kansas, and this raises the question as to why they took the position they did.

They looked on the repeal of the Missouri Compromise from a political rather than an economic view. Just as they saw in the Wilmot Proviso a denial of their rights, they saw in closing Kansas to slavery an insulting denial of their rights. Southerners rallied to support of the bill because the northern attacks on the bill were loaded with vindictive indictments of the "slave power" and slavery. Consequently, as Michael Holt states, "passage of the bill became a symbol of southern honor." Holt, *The Political Crisis of the 1850s,* p. 148.

41. Donald, *Charles Sumner,* p. 223.
42. *Congressional Globe, Appendix,* 33rd Cong., 1st Sess., pp. 262–270.
43. Ibid.
44. Everett, *Diary,* 21 February 1854, Everett Papers, Reel XXXIV, Folder 263. *Congressional Globe, Appendix,* 33rd Cong., 1st Sess., pp. 152–163.
45. Allan Nevins, *Ordeal of the Union* (New York: Charles Scribner's Sons, 1947), vol. 2, p. 139.
46. Eric Foner, *Free Soil, Free Labor, and Free Men: The Ideology of the Republican Party Before the Civil War* (New York: Oxford University Press, 1970), p. 95.
47. Everett, *Diary,* 31 March 1854, Reel XXXIX, Folder 173.
48. Nevins, *Ordeal of the Union,* vol. 2, p. 337.
49. Everett, *Diary,* 20 March 1854, Reel XXXIX, Folder 173.
50. *The Journal of Richard Henry Dana, Jr.,* ed. Robert F. Lucid (Cambridge: The Belknap Press of Harvard University Press, 1968), p. 637.

Chapter 8. Everett the Orator

1. Everett, "The Battles of Lexington," *Orations and Speeches.* (Boston: Little, Brown and Company, 1878) vol. 1, pp. 526–60.
2. Ibid., p. 555.
3. Ibid., p. 547.
4. Ibid., p. 560.
5. Edward Everett, "Eulogy on Lafayette," ibid., p. 509.
6. Ibid., p. 524.
7. Edward Everett, "Eulogy on Adams and Jefferson," ibid., p. 133.
8. Ibid., pp. 132–33.
9. Edward Everett, "The Education of Mankind," ibid., p. 406
10. Ibid., pp. 409–11.
11. Ibid., pp. 413–14.
12. Edward Everett, "Education Favorable to Liberty, Morals, and Knowledge," ibid., p. 609.
13. Ibid., p. 610.
14. Ibid., p. 575.
15. Diary of Edward Everett. Everett Papers, 26 January 1856. Reel XXXIX, Folder 340.

16. Friedlander and Butterfield, eds., *Diary of Charles Francis Adams,* vol. 5, 6 September 1834.
17. Everett, "The Character of Washington," *Oration and Speeches,* vol. 4, p. 23.
18. Ibid., p. 28.
19. Ibid., p. 27.
20. Edward Everett to Peter Cooper, 21 March 1860, Everett Papers, Reel XXXI, Folder 290.
21. For his experiences while traveling across the country to deliver his lecture on Washington see Everett Papers, Reel 39, Folder 2.
22. *Mount Vernon Papers,* D. Appleton and Company 1860.
23. Everett, "Charitable Institutions and Charity," *Orations and Speeches,* vol. 3, p. 569.
24. Ibid., p. 571.
25. Ibid., p. 573.
26. Ibid., p. 575.

Chapter 9. Everett Confronts the New Age

1. William E. Gienappe, *The Origins of the Republican Party 1852–1856* (New York: Oxford University Press, 1987), pp. 22–31.
2. Ibid., pp. 61–64.
3. Ibid., p. 7.
4. Ibid., p. 444.
Concerning the importance of the Kansas issue, Gienapp writes: "Yet as Michael Holt points out, if prevention of the extension of slavery, particularly into Kansas, was the issue Republicans used to publicize their persuasion, it was not their primary motivation. Kansas offered only a convenient issue with which to wage a much larger, more basic struggle. Close inspection of what Republicans said suggest that they were concerned less about slavery than the Slave Power, that it was the white slave holders—not black slaves—whom they hated, and that it was the growing threat to white liberties, not black that they feared most. For all his hatred of slavery, Charles Sumner contended that the Kansas crisis was incidental to a more fundamental conflict. Writing to Henry J. Raymond to congratulate him on his address issue by the Pittsburgh convention, which focused almost exclusively on the aggression of the slave power, Sumner declared: "For a long time my desire has been to make an issue with the Slave Oligarchy; and provided that this can be had, I am indifferent to the special point selected. Of course, at this moment Kansas is the inevitable point. In protecting this territory against tyranny we are driven to battle with the tyrants, who are the Oligarchs of Slavery." Gienapp, *Origins of the Republican Party,* p. 357.
5. Potter, *Impending Crisis,* p. 174.
6. Eric Foner focuses his attention on the development of conflicting ideologies. He wrote: ". . . resentment of southern political power, devotion to the Union, anti-slavery based upon the free labor argument, moral revulsion to the peculiar institution, racial prejudice, a commitment to the northern social order and its development and expansion—all these elements were intertwined in the Republican world view. What they added up to was the conviction that the North and South represented two social systems whose values, interests, and prospects were in sharp, perhaps mortal conflict with one another. The sense of difference, of

Notes 239

estrangement, and of growing hostility with which the Republicans viewed the South, cannot be overemphasized." Foner, *Free Soil, Free Labor, Free Men,* p. 310.

    7. Nevins, *Ordeal of the Union,* p. 282.

    8. Everett, *Diary,* 7 February 1855, Everett Papers, Reel XXXIX, Folder 246.

    9. Ibid., 1 November 1854, Everett Papers, Reel XXXIX, Folder 263.

    10. Ibid., 9 January 1855, ibid., Folder 246.

    11. Congressional Globe, 34th Cong., 3d Sess., p. 92.

    12. Everett, *Diary,* 5 November 1856, Reel XXXIX, Folder 240.

    13. Edward Everett to Thomas Macauley, 5 November 1855, Reel XXXI, Folder 290.

    14. David Donald speculates as to Sumner's motives for attacking the individual senator. He cautiously concludes that Sumner sought to vindicate himself and Massachusetts from past slurs. David Donald, *Charles Sumner,* p. 281.

    15. Everett, *Diary,* 25 May 1856, Everett Papers, Reel XXXIX, Folder 340.

    16. Newspaper clipping in diary for 27 May 1856, ibid.

    17. Everett, *Diary,* 25 May 1856, ibid.

    18. Edward Everett to Charles Sumner, 16 June 1856, Everett Papers, Reel XXXI, Folder 280.

    19. Edward Everett to Mr. Harrison, 20 June 1856, ibid.

    20. Edward Everett to Millard Fillmore, 16 July 1856, ibid.

    21. Edward Everett to C. A. Davis, ? September 1856, ibid.

    22. Everett, *Diary,* 5 November 1856, Everett Papers, Reel XXXIX, Folder 340.

    23. *The Atlas and Daily Bee,* 9 December 1859.

    24. Ibid., 5 December 1856.

    25. Ibid., 10 December 1856.

    26. Frank Otto Gatell, *John Gorham Palfrey and the New England Conscience* (Cambridge: Harvard University Press, 1963), pp. 187–88.

    27. Edward Everett to Robert Bonner, 31 May 1860, Everett Papers, Reel XXXI, Folder 295.

    28. Edward Everett to W. W. Corcoran, 6 June 1860, ibid.

    29. Edward Everett to A. H. H. Dawson, 25 October 1860, Everett Papers, Reel XXXI, Folder 282.

    30. *Massachusetts Spy,* 14 November 1860.

    31. Ibid., 14 November 1860.

    32. *Daily Atlas & Bee,* 6 February 1861.

    33. Edward Everett to J. J. Crittenden, 23 December 1860, Everett Papers, Reel XXXI, Folder 295.

    34. *Daily Atlas & Bee,* 6 February 1861.

    35. Quoted in *Daily Atlas & Bee,* 6 February 1861.

    36. Everett, *Diary,* 25 January 1861, Reel XXXI, Folder 292.

    37. Edward Everett to C. A. Davis, 27 November 1860, Everett Papers, Reel XXXI, Folder 292.

    38. William Barbey, *The Road to Secession: A New Prospective on the Old South* (New York: Praeger Publishers, 1972), p. 160.

    39. George B. Forgie, *Patricide in the House Divided: A Psychological Interpretation of Lincoln and His Age* (New York: W. W. Norton & Co., 1979), pp. 161–72.

    40. Richard Henry Dana, Jr., "An Address upon the Life and Services of Edward Everett delivered before the Municipal Authorities and Citizens of Cambridge," 22 February 1865, Everett Papers, Reel LII, Folder 250.

Chapter 10. Role of the Orator in the Civil War

1. James M. McPherson, *Battle Cry of Freedom: The Civil War Era* (New York: Oxford University Press, 1988), p. 213.

Bruce Catton places the same emphasis on the tensions that cut off throughtful deliberation. Catton wrote: "But there was still deep confusion and bewilderment, and in such times men of intense singleness of purpose can often drive through to their chosen goal and compel their fellows to trail along after them. The Southern men, who, in November of 1860, proposed secession and the creation of a new nation had the advantage of knowing precisely what they wanted and of standing for immediate, emotion-releasing action. Those who counseled delay and full exploration of the possibilities of compromise were using the kind of talk that should have been (but was not) voiced in the presidential campaign; now it came too late, it had no force in it, and state and regionalism patriotism were generating a pressure that made it sound empty." Bruce Catton, *The Coming Fury* (New York: Doubleday and Co., 1961), p. 112.

2. McPherson, *Battle Cry of Freedom,* p. 230.

3. As secession got underway many of the radical abolitionists took this position. Garrison and Wendell Philips had long been ready to bid farewell to the Union. Now there were others, including Horace Greeley, and he wrote a series of editorials urging peace immediately after the election. No one dreaded war more than Edward Everett. He had long feared that it would not only be a war between the North and South but war between the opposing factions within the states. In the first days after Fort Sumter fighting did take place in Maryland, Missouri, and Kentucky between those favoring secession and those opposing it.

4. McPherson, *Battle Cry of Freedom,* pp. 244, 254–57, 284, emphasizes that the alleged Union feelings in the South were practically nonexistent. The unionism that was manifested, he states, was "highly conditional" and dependent on the North not taking any steps toward coercion. The first opposing secession "simply preferred to wait for unity of action." Once secession took place then loyalty to the state took precedence over loyalty to the Union.

This is not to say that all Southerners were ready to fight to defend slavery. They were ready to fight to prevent equality of the races, however. Catton, *Coming Fury,* p. 203.

Slavery was so much an integral part of Southern culture that it was difficult to delineate between the two.

It was the attack on southern culture that gave rise to southern regionalism and state loyalty. McPherson stresses that the South decided on secession and possible war out of their conviction that what they saw as the revolution that Republicans were intent on launching must be stopped before it began. It was pre-emptive war. McPherson, *Battle Cry of Freedom,* p. 245.

5. Everett, *Diary,* 25 January 1861, Everett Papers, Reel XL, February 7, 1861.

6. Ibid., 2 February 1861.

7. McPherson, *Battle Cry of Freedom,* p. 271.

8. Ibid., p. 274.

9. Bruce Catton, *Coming Fury,* p. 286.

10. Everett, *Diary,* Reel XI, Folder 180.

11. Edward Everett to Robert Bonner, 13 May 1861. Everett Papers, Reel XXXI, Folder 115.

12. William H. Seward to Edward Everett, 23 May 1861, Everett Papers, Reel XVIII, Folder 1.

Notes

13. Charles Francis Adams to Edward Everett, 5 October 1861, Everett Papers, Reel XVIII, Folder 2.
14. Everett, "The Questions of the Day," in *Orations and Speeches,* vol. 4, pp. 245–411.
15. Edward Everett to George Lunt, 21 April 1863, Reel XXXII, Folder 119.
16. Edward Everett to Thomas Gardener, 30 September 1861, Everett Papers, Reel XXXII, Folder 115.
17. Everett, "The Causes and Conduct of the Civil War," in *Orations and Speeches,* vol. 4, pp. 464–89.
18. Edward Everett to Sidney Everett, 29 October 1861, Everett Papers, Reel XXXII, Folder 115.
19. John Morley, *The Life of William Ewart Gladstone* (New York: The Macmillan Company, 1903), vol. 4, p. 70.
20. Edward Everett to his son William, 31 March 1861, Everett Papers, Reel XXXII, Folder 114.
21. Charles Francis Adams to Edward Everett, 14 June 1861, Everett Papers, Reel XXXI, Folder 109.
22. Edward Everett to Charles Francis Adams, 28 May 1861, Everett Papers, Reel XXXII, Folder 114.
23. Ibid., 29 May 1861.
24. Edward Everett to Speaker Denison, 22 July 1861, Everett Papers, Reel XXXII, Folder 114.
25. Edward Everett to Lord John Russell, 19 August 1861, Everett Papers, Reel XXXII, Folder 115.
26. Edward Everett to Joshua Bates, 11 November 1861, Everett Papers, Reel XXXII, Folder 115.
Everett had not forgotten the Logan Act forbidding a private citizen from negotiating with a foreign power, and he was careful to forward his own letters and those he received as well as copies of his speeches to Secretary of State Seward who expressed appreciation. William H. Seward to Edward Everett, Reel XXXII, Folder 287, 5 August 1861.
27. Everett, *Diary,* 1 November 1861; Edward Everett to Charles Francis Adams, 29 October 1861, Everett Papers, Reel XXXII, Folder 115.
28. Charles Francis Adams to Edward Everett, 12 July 1861; ibid., 2 May 1862, Everett Papers, Reel XXXII, folder 115.
29. Ibid., 27 December 1862.
30. Ibid., 25 October 1861.
31. Everett, *Diary,* 30 December 1861, Everett Papers, Reel LX, Folder 188.
32. Ibid., 30 December 1861.
33. McPherson, *Battle Cry of Freedom,* p. 390.
34. Abraham Lincoln to Whom It May Concern, 24 September 1862, *The Collected Works of Abraham Lincoln,* ed. Roy P. Basler (New Brunswick, New Jersey, 1953), vol. 5, pp. 437–48.
35. Edward Everett to F. P. Blair, 3 October 1862, Everett Papers, Reel XXXII, Folder 117.
36. Everett, *Diary,* 24 August 1862, Everett Papers, Reel XL, Folder 181.
37. Edward Everett to Salmon P. Chase, 14 August 1862, Everett Papers, Reel XXXII, Folder 117.
38. Salmon P. Chase, *Inside Lincoln's Cabinet: The Civil War Diaries of Salmon P. Chase,* ed. David Donald (New York: Longmans, Green and Co., 1954), pp. 20, 99.
Everett's cautious reply was in contrast with forthrightness of George Bancroft

who had written to Chase and urged him that the war could never be successful unless it was given a moral impetus by freeing the slaves everywhere.

39. McPherson, *Battle Cry for Freedom,* p. 557.

For a graphic report of the cabinet meeting and Lincoln's decisiveness see *Diary and Correspondence of Salmon P. Chase: Annual Report of the American Historical Association, 1902,* vol. 2., pp. 49, 87–89.

40. *Works of Abraham Lincoln,* vol. 7, pp. 281–82.

41. Charles Francis Adams to Edward Everett, 13 February 1863, Everett Papers, Reel XXXII, Folder 188.

42. Ibid., 17 October 1862, Reel XXXII, Folder 117.

43. E. D. Adams in his book *Great Britain and the American Civil War,* vol. 2, p. 73, states: "For America Russell's mediation plan constitutes the most dangerous crisis in the war for the Restoration of the Union." Adams's account of the crisis is useful. Adams was kept in the dark at the time and when he became distrustful and questioned Russell directly if there was to be a change in policy, Russell denied it. At the moment what Russell said was correct, but a change in policy was still under consideration. Two other valuable accounts are those of Martin Duberman in *Charles Francis Adams 1807–1886* (Boston: Houghton Mifflin, 1961) and John Morley, *The Life of William Ewart Gladstone* (New York: Macmillan, 1903). Everett was, of course, wholly uninformed of the crisis.

44. Everett Papers, 24 October 1862, Reel XXXII, Folder 292.

45. Mary Ellson, *Support for Secession: Lancashire and the American Civil War* (Chicago: University of Chicago Press, 1972).

46. Edward Everett to S. G. Ward, 5 August 1863, Everett Papers, Reel XXXIII, Folder 119.

47. By 1863 a large minority of the Democrats were calling for peace and denouncing Republicans who called for the abolition of slavery. A mass meeting of New York Democrats resolved the war was unconstitutional, and the Democratic candidate for governor, Horatio Seymour, denounced emancipation as "bloody, barbarous, revolutionary." Quoted by McPherson in Wood Gray, *Hidden Civil War,* p. 147.

48. Everett, "Inauguration of the Union Club," in *Orations and Speeches,* vol. 4, p. 579.

49. Edward Everett to Robert Bonner, 14 May 1863, Everett Papers, Reel XXXIII, Folder 119.

50. Charles Francis Adams to Edward Everett, 29 April 1863, Everett Papers, ibid.

51. Edward Everett to James C. Conkling, 24 August 1863, Everett Papers, Reel XXXIII, Folder 289.

52. Edward Everett to James C. Conkling, 24 August 1863. Everett Papers, Reel XXXIII, Folder 119.

53. Everett, *Diary,* 6 November 1863.

54. Ibid., 16 November 1863.

55. Ibid., 18 November 1861.

56. Everett, "National Cemetery at Gettysburg" *Orations and Speeches,* vol. 4, pp. 627–59.

57. Edward Everett to Mr. Cramer, 14 December 1863, Everett Papers, Reel XXXIII, Folder 286.

58. Edward Everett to Abraham Lincoln, 20 November 1863, Everett Papers, Reel XXXIII, Folder 286.

59. Abraham Lincoln to Edward Everett, 20 November 1863, *The Collected Works of Abraham Lincoln,* vol. 7, p. 24.

Notes

60. Svend Petersen, *The Gettysburg Addresses: The Story of Two Orations* (New York: Frederick Ungar Publishing Company, 1963), p. 25.
61. Everett, *Diary,* 19 November 1863.
62. Quoted from S. L. Barlow Papers by James M. McPherson, *Ordeal by Fire The Civil War and Reconstruction* (New York: Alfred A. Knopf, 1982), p. 441.
63. Edward Everett to A. Burwell, 19 September 1864, Everett Papers, Reel XXXIII, Folder 201.
64. Edward Everett, "The Duty of Supporting the Government," in *Orations and Speeches,* vol. 4, pp. 698–726.
65. Ibid.
66. Everett, *Diary,* 9 November 1864.
67. Edward Everett, "The Relief of Savannah," in *Orations and Speeches,* vol. 4, pp. 753–59.
68. *Life, Letters and Journals of George Ticknor* (London: Sampson Low, Marston, Searle, & Rivington, 1876), vol. 2, 469–70.

Bibliography

Unpublished Private Papers
Edward Everett Papers. Massachusetts Historical Society, Boston.
John Langdon Sibley Journal. Harvard University Archives, Cambridge.
George Ticknor Papers. Dartmouth College Library, Hanover, N.H.
Daniel Webster Papers. Dartmouth College Library, Hanover, N.H.
Robert C. Winthrop Papers. Massachusetts Historical Society, Boston.

Unpublished Papers
Harvard College Papers. Harvard University Archives.
President's Letters. Harvard University Archives.

Published Private Letters
Cabot, J. E., ed. *Lectures and Biographical Sketches by Ralph Waldo Emerson.* Boston: Houghton Mifflin Co., 1911.
Friedlander, Marc and Butterfield, L. H., eds. *Diary of Charles Francis Adams.* Cambridge: Belknap Press of Harvard University, 1974.
Gilman, William H.; Ferguson, Alfred R.; Davis, Merrill R.; Sealts, Jr., Merton; Hayford Harrison; eds. *The Journals and Miscellaneous Note Books of Ralph Waldo Emerson.* Cambridge: Belknap Press of Harvard University, 1965.
Hilliard, George S., ed. *Life, Letters, and Journals of George Ticknor.* London: Sampson, Law, Marston, Searle, and Rivington, 1876.
Lucid, Robert F., ed. *The Journal of Richard Henry Dana, Jr.* Cambridge: The Belknap Press of Harvard University Press, 1968.
Richards, Laura E., ed. *Letters and Journals of Samuel Gridley Howe.* Richards. Boston: Dana, Estaes and Co., 1909.
Shewmaker, Kenneth D., ed. *The Papers of Daniel Webster Diplomatic Papers.* Hanover, N.H.: University Press of New England, 1983.
Story, William W., ed. *Life and Letters of Joseph Story.* London: John Chapman, 1851.
Wiltse, Charles N. and Mower, Harold D., eds. *The Papers of Daniel Webster Correspondence.* 5 vols. Hanover, N.H.: University Press of New England, 1974–1980.
The Diary of William Bentley. 4 vols. Salem, Mass.: Newcombe and Gauss Printers, 1914.

Books
Adams, Charles Francis, ed., *Memoirs of John Quincy Adams.* Philadelphia: J. B. Lippincott & Co., 1974–1877.

Bibliography

Adams, E. D., *Great Britain and the American Civil War*. New York: Russell and Russell, 1924.
Adams, Henry, *The Education of Henry Adams An Autobiography*. Boston: Houghton Mifflin Co., 1918.
Barnum, P. T., *Barnum's Own Story The Autobiography of P. T. Barnum*. New York: Dover Publications, Inc., 1961.
Bartlett, Irving E., *Daniel Webster*. New York: Norton, 1978.
Baxter, Maurice G., *One and Inseparable Daniel Webster and the Union*. Cambridge: The Belknap Press of Harvard University, 1984.
Bemis, Samuel Flagg, *John Quincy Adams and the Foundations of American Foreign Policy*. New York: Alfred Knopf, 1950.
———, *John Quincy Adams and the Union*. New York: Alfred Knopf, 1950.
Blumenthal, Henry, *A Reappraisal of Franco-American Relations 1830–1871*. Chapel Hill: The University of North Carolina Press, 1959.
Brauer, Kinley, *Cotton versus Conscience: Massachusetts Whig Politics and Southwestern Expansion, 1843–1848*. Lexington: University of Kentucky Press, 1967.
Cameron, Kenneth Walter, *Research keys to the American Renaissance; scare indexes to the Christian Examiner, the North American Review, and the New Jerusalem magazine for students of American literature, culture, history, and New England Transcendentalism*. Hartford: Transcendental Books, 1967.
Chase, Salmon P., *Inside Lincoln's Cabinet The Civil War Diaries of Salmon P. Chase*, ed. David Donald. New York: Longmans, Green and Co., 1954.
Dangerfield, George, *The Awakening of American Nationalism*. New York: Harper & Rowe, Publishers, 1965.
Dalzell, Robert F., *Daniel Webster and the Trial of American Nationalism, 1843–1852*. Boston: Houghton Mifflin Co., 1973.
Dalzell, Jr., Robert F., *Enterprising Elite The Boston Associates and the World They Made*. Cambridge: Harvard University Press, 1987.
Darling, Arthur B., *Political Changes in Massachusetts 1824–1848 A Study of Liberal Movements in Politics*. Cos Cob, Conn.: John E. Edwards, 1968.
Donald, David, *Charles Sumner and the Coming of the Civil War*. New York: Alfred A. Knopf, 1960.
Duberman, Martin, *Charles Francis Adams 1807–1886*. Boston: Houghton Mifflin, 1961.
———, "Behind the Scenes as the Massachusetts 'Coalition' of 1851 Divides the Spoils," *Essex Institute Historical Collections,* April, 1963, pp. 152–160.
Dubofskym, Melvin, "Daniel Webster and the Whig Theory of Economic Growth: 1828–1848," *New England Quarterly,* December 1969, pp. 551–572.
Epstein, David, *The Man who Spoke at Gettysburg: The National Political Career of Edward Everett*. Unpublished honors thesis at Harvard University.
Everett, Edward, *Orations and Speeches on Various Occasions,* 4 vols. Boston: Little and Brown and Co.
———, *The Mount Vernon Papers*. New York: D. Appleton and Co., 1860.
Forgie, George B., *Patricide in the House Divided A Psychological Interpretation of Lincoln and His Age*. New York: Norton & Co., 1979.

Foner, Eric, *Free Soil, Free Labor, Free Men The Ideology of the Republican Party Before the Civil War*. New York: Oxford University Press, 1970.

Formisano, Ronald, *The Birth of Mass Political Parties Michigan*. Princeton: Princeton University Press, 1971.

Frothingham, Paul Revere, *Edward Everett Orator and Statesman*. Boston: Houghton Mifflin Co., 1923.

Gatell, Frank Otto, *John Gorham Palfrey and the New England Conscience*. Cambridge: Harvard University Press, 1963.

Gienapp, William E., *The Origins of the Republican Party 1852–1856*. New York: Oxford University Press, 1987.

Hammond, Bray, *Banks and Politics in America from the Revolution to the Civil War*. Princeton: Princeton University Press, 1957.

Handlin, Lilian, *George Bancroft The Intellectual as Democrat*. New York: Harper and Row Publishers, 1984.

Harrington, Fred Harvey, *Fighting Politician Major General N. P. Banks*. Philadelphia: University of Pennsylvania Press, 1948.

Holt, Michael, *The Political Crisis of the 1850's*. New York: John Wiley & Sons, 1978.

Howe, Daniel Walker, *The Political Culture of American Whigs*. Chicago: University of Chicago Press, 1979.

Johannsen, Robert W., *Stephen A. Douglas*. New York: Oxford University Press, 1973.

Jones, Howard, *To the Webster-Ashburton Treaty*. Chapel Hill: University of North Carolina Press, 1977.

Jones, William Devereux, *Lord Aberdeen and the Americas*. Athens: University of Georgia Press, 1958.

Katz, Michael B., *The Irony of Early School Reform Educational Innovation in Mid-Nineteenth Century School Reform*. Boston: Beacon Press, 1968.

Many Penney, George W., *Our Indian Wards*. New York: De Capo Press, 1972.

McCaughey, Robert A., *Josiah Quincy 1772–1864 The Last Federalist*. Cambridge: Harvard University Press, 1974.

McClellan, James, *Joseph Story and the American Revolution A Study in Political and Legal Thought*. Norman, Oklahoma: University of Oklahoma Press, 1971.

McPherson, James M., *Ordeal by Fire The Civil War and Reconstruction*. New York: Alfred A. Knopf, 1982.

———, *Battle Cry of Freedom: The Civil War Era*. New York: Oxford University Press, 1988.

Merk, Frederick with the collaboration of Lois Bannister Merk, *Fruits of Propaganda in the Tyler Administration*. Cambridge: Harvard University Press, 1971.

Messerli, Jonathon, *Horace Mann A Biography*. New York: Alfred A. Knopf, 1972.

Morison, Samuel Eliot, *Three Centuries of Harvard 1636–1936*. Cambridge: Harvard University Press, 1936.

Nelson, William E., *Americanization of the Common Law The Impact of Legal Change on Massachusetts Society, 1760–1830*. Cambridge: Harvard University Press, 1976.

Bibliography

Nichols, Roy Franklin, *The Disruption of American Democracy.* New York: The Free Press, 1948.

Nye, Russell, *George Bancroft Brahmin Rebel.* New York: Alfred A. Knopf, 1945.

Peabody, Andrew P., *Harvard Reminiscenes.* Boston: Ticknor and Co., 1883.

Peterson, Svend, *The Gettysburg Addresses The Story of Two Orations.* New York: Frederick Ungar Publishing Co., 1963.

Pletcher, David, *The Diplomacy of Annexation: Texas, Oregon, and the Mexican War.* Columbia: University of Missouri Press, 1973.

Poore, Ben Perley, *Reminiscences of Sixty Years in the National Metropolis.* Philadelphia: Hubbard Brothers, Publishers, 1886.

Potter, David, *The Impending Crisis.* New York: Harper and Row Publishers, 1979.

Remini, Robert, *Andrew Jackson and the Course of American Freedom,* New York: Harper & Row Publishers, 1981.

———, ed., *Age of Jackson.* Columbia, S.C.: University of South Carolina Press, 1972.

Salisbury, Stephen, *The State, the Investor, and the Railroad The Boston and Albany.* Cambridge: Harvard University Press, 1967.

Seager, Robert, *and Tyler too A Biography of John and Julia Gardener Tyler.* New York: McGraw Hill Book Co., 1963.

Sherwin, Oscar, *Prophet of Liberty The Life and Times of Wendell Phillips.* New York: Bookman Associates, 1958.

Stanwood, Edward, *American Tariff Controversies in the Nineteenth Century.* New York: Russell and Russell, 1903.

Tyack, David, *George Ticknor and the Boston Brahmins.* Cambridge: Harvard University Press, 1967.

Ware, John, *Memoir of the Life of Henry Ware, Jr.* Boston: American Unitarian Association, 1868.

Journals

Carlton, Frank J., "Abolition of Imprisonment for Debt," *Yale Review* (November 1908); vol. 8, p. 340.

Cass, Lewis, "Removal of the Indian," *North American Review* (January 1830); vol. 31, pp. 66–121.

Clark, Henry Hayden, "Literary Criticism in the North American Review." Wisconsin Academy of Sciences, Arts and Letters (31).

Davis, David Brion, "The Movement to Abolish Capital Punishment," *American Historical Review;* vol. 63, p. 35.

Everett, Edward, "The History of Grecian Art," *North American Review* (January 1821); vol. 25, pp. 179–188.

"Sciotic and Affairs of Greece," *North American Review* (October 1823); vol. 17, p. 413.

"Speeches on the Indian Bill," *North American Review* (October 1830); vol. 31, p. 397.

Green, Fletcher M., "Duff Green, Militant Journalist of the Old School," *American Historical Review* (January 1947); vol. 52, pp. 247–264.

McKay, Ernest A., "Henry Wilson and the Coalition of 1851," *New England Quarterly* (September 1963): 338–357.

Phelps, Reginald H., "The Idea of the Modern University Gottengen and America," *The Germanic Review* (October 1954).

Shewmaker, Kenneth, "Hook and time, bob and sinker Daniel Webster and the Fisheries Dispute of 1852," *Diplomatic History* (Spring 1985); vol. 9, pp. 113–129.

Siousaat, St. George, "Duff Green's England the United States' with an Introductory Study of American Opposition to the Quintuple Treaty of 1841," *Proceedings of the American Antiquarian Society* (October 1930).

VanDeusen, Glynden, "Some Aspects of Whig Thought and Theory on the Jacksonian Period," *American Historical Review;* vol. 63, pp. 305–332.

Winthrop, Robert C., "Memoir of Hon. Nathan Appleton," *Massachusetts Historical Society Proceedings,* vol. 5, p. 274.

Index

Adams, Charles Francis: criticism of Whigs and his criticism of Everett, 63–64; criticisms of Whig party, 157; role in the founding of the Free Soil Party, 150; holds that slavery accounts for the lack of moral principle in politics, 159; splits with Free Soilers, 164, 199, 200, 205, 209

Adams, John Quincy: the Monroe Doctrine, 32–33; stands on Indian removal, 43; his furious war speech, 59, 64, 112

Agassiz, Louis: professor at Harvard, 131

Ashburton, Lord, 99–102, 115–21, 124–26

Bancroft, George: the Bank question, 62

Bank of the United States, 54–57

Bay of Fundy and question of fishing rights, 146–49

Bentley, William, 17

Boston: rise of the elite, 37–38; economic, social, and political changes in Boston and New England, 155–56

Brooks, P. C., 23, 93

Brown, John: raid at Harper's Ferry, 188

Buchanan, James, 123

Buckminster, Joseph, 17

Byron, Lord, 17, 20

Calhoun, John C., 52, 115

Caroline affair, 87

Carter, James, 72

Cass, Lewis: favors removal of Indians, 44, 107, 113, 146

Channing, William Ellery, 78

Chase, Salmon P.: speech "Appeal of the Independent Democrats," 169–70

Clay, Henry, 49, 50–51; compromise tariff, 53–54, 92, 122

Compromise of 1850: provisions, 158; Everett's views on, 162

Constitutional Union Party, 189–92

Creole, 102–7

Cuba and the new imperialists, 145–46; *Crescent City* affair, 149–50

Cushing, Caleb, 111; the New England expansionist, 122

Dana, Richard Henry, 157, 164, 172, 194

Davis, John, 59

Diplomacy and policy of annexation, 87–126; factors contributing to settlement of Oregon question, 126

Douglas, Steven, 146, 153; Douglas and the Kansas-Nebraska Bill, 166, 171

Eichhorn, John Gottfried, 20, 22

Election of 1860 in Massachusetts, 191

Emerson, Ralph Waldo, 18, 26, 129–30

Everett, Alexander, 16, 18, 19, 50–51, 83

Everett, Edward: family background, 15–16; ministry, 18–19; changes in religious beliefs, 19; student at University of Göttingen, 21–23; interest in philology, 21; marriage to Charlotte Brooks, 23–24; editor of *North American Review,* 25–27; orations, 27–28; supports revolution in Greece, 30–33; decision to enter politics, 34; his nationalism, 36; becomes an ardent Whig, 39–41; opposes removal of Indians, 42–47; opposes Jackson's program, 47–49; seeks a compromise on tariff, 48–49; Everett and the Anti-Masonic Party, 50–51; support of U.S. Bank, 54–57; claims against France, 57–59; plays part of

Webster's handyman, 65; elected governor of Massachusetts, 65; reforms recommended, 66–67; difficulties with Benjamin Hallett, 68–69; calls for reform of education, 69–72; opposes imprisonment for debts and capital and capital punishment, 74–75; stand on slavery, 77–78; promotes railroads, 79–80; Temperance question, 80–83; minister to England and the Webster-Ashburton Treaty, 98–107; the Oregon negotiations, 117–26; difficulties with Webster, 111–13; northeast boundary dispute, 87–92; views of economic and social conditions in England, 95–97; relations with Lord Aberdeen, 99–126; distrust of Webster, 111–13; Harvard presidency, 127–39; revolutions of 1848 in Europe, 140–48; secretary of state under Fillmore, 143–51; defends fishing rights in the Bay of Fundy, 147–49; elected to Senate and defends British position on Bulwer Treaty, 152; repudiates Steven Douglas, 152–53; denunciation of Mexican War as a war of conquest, 157; opposition to the Kansas-Nebraska Bill, 167–71; Everett the orator, 27–30, 173–80, 201–2, 212–13, 215–16; denounces Know Nothingism, 184–85; criticisms of Everett, 186, 187–89; candidate of the Union Party, 189–90; opposes trying to hold secessionist states in the Union by force, 198; supports Union after firing on Fort Sumter, 198, 201; sees slavery as the cause of the war, 207; speech at Gettysburg, 213–14; supports Lincoln in election of 1864, 215; Everett's views on slavery question, 41, 77–78, 154, 157–64, 172, 185–88, 190, 199, 204, 207, 215–16

Fillmore, Millard, 141, 146, 149–50
Free Soil party: founding, 157; fears of Everett, 158; success in promoting its views, 159; possible fusion with the Democrats splits the party, 163–64
Fugitive Slave law: rejected by Everett, 161–62

Gallatin, Albert, 126
Green, Duff, 110–11

Hale, Nathan, 91, 111–12
Harvard College: Everett's evaluation as a former student, 23, 33, 34; situation at Harvard when Everett became president, 130–31; faculty, 131; inaugural address, 127–29; Everett's interest in science, 132–34; discipline problems, 135; Everett's unhappiness with his position, 136–39

Indian removal, 42–47

Jefferson, Thomas, 29

Kansas-Nebraska Bill, 166–72
Know Nothing party, 182–85

Legaré, Hugh Swinton, 103–4
Lobos Islands, 143–45

McDuffie, George, 40, 45, 52, 113
McLane, Louis, 123
Maine and the northeast boundary dispute, 87–88, 99–103
Mann, Horace, 70
Mitchell, Marie: astronomer, 133–34
Mitchell, William: astronomer, 133

Oratory of Everett, 27–30, 173–80, 201–2, 212–13, 215–16
Oregon question, 107, 117–26

Pakenham, Richard: rejects Buchanan's boundary proposal on Oregon, 123–24
Pierce, Franklin: nominated for President by Democrats, 165, 166
Polk, James K., 121–22, 126
Protectionism, 41, 51–54

Rantoul, Robert, 70, 77
Republican party, 182, 185, 188, 190–92, 193, 196; election of 1864, 214–16
Rise of political parties, 36–37; party differences, 60–61; failures of the Whigs, 61–62, 85

Scott, Winfield: arranges truce in Maine, 90, 165

Index

Stevenson, Andrew, 95
Story, Joseph, 73, 83–84
Stuart, Moses, 17
Sumner, Charles: nominated for Senate, 163; elected after four-month fight in state Senate, 163; Everett's estimate of Sumner, 164; speech in Senate attacking the South, 168–69; Everett's response to Sumner's speech, 169; response of southerners and party regulars, 169, 182, 186–87, 192

Temperance movement, 80–83
Texas, 113–16
Tyler, John, 92, 103–4, 105, 108, 114

Upshur, Abel Parker, 113, 117, 119

Van Buren, Martin, 89

Webster, Daniel: the question of Greece, 31–32; opposed to election of John Quincy Adams to the Senate, 63, 64–65; secretary of state and negotiates Webster Ashburton Treaty, 98–107; fails to authorize Everett to negotiate on Oregon question, 108–9, 111; names Everett to special mission to China, 111–13; the letter to Hülseman, 141–42; supports Compromise of 1850 including Fugitive Slave Law, 158; seeks nomination for president, 161–62
Welcker, F. G., 21
Whig party: weakness of, 60–61
Whigs and Jacksonians, and how they viewed each other: a Whig view of Jacksonians, 61; a Jacksonian's view of the Whigs, 52; one historian minimizes the difference, 40
Whig views of the role of the Union, 35–36, 38, 55, 160, 217
Wilmot Proviso, 158
Winthrop, Robert C., 93, 94, 142, 162–63

Young America, 146

DATE DUE